HANDBOOK FOR ALUMNI ADMINISTRATION

Edited by
Charles H. Webb

D0068916

Sponsored by
The Council for Advancement
and Support of Education

AMERICAN COUNCIL ON EDUCATION ★
ORYX PRESS ★
Series on Higher Education
1995

The rare Arabian Oryx is believed to have inspired the myth of the unicorn. This desert antelope became virtually extinct in the early 1960s. At that time several groups of international conservationists arranged to have 9 animals sent to the Phoenix Zoo to be the nucleus of a captive breeding herd. Today the Oryx population is over 1,000, and over 500 have been returned to the Middle East.

© 1995 by American Council on Education and The Oryx Press
Published by the Oryx Press
4041 North Central at Indian School Road
Phoenix, Arizona 85012-3397

Published simultaneously in Canada
Printed and Bound in the United States of America

∞ The paper used in this publication meets the minimum requirements of American National Standard for Information Science—Permanence of Paper for Printed Library Materials, ANSI Z39.48, 1984.

Library of Congress Cataloging-in-Publication Data

Handbook for alumni administration / edited by Charles H. Webb.
p. cm.—(American Council on Education/Oryx Press series on higher education)
Originally published: New York : American Council on Education : Macmillan Pub. Co., ©1989, in series: American Council on Education/Macmillan series in higher education.
Includes bibliographical references and index.
ISBN 0-89774-984-7 (alk. paper)
1. Universities and colleges—Alumni and alumnae—United States. 2. Universities and colleges—Alumni and alumnae—United States—Societies, etc.—Administration. I. Webb, Charles H. II. Series.
[LB2411.H36 1995]   94-42259
378.73—dc20   CIP

Contents

PART SIX: COMMUNICATIONS

PART SEVEN: ALUMNI EDUCATION PROGRAMS AND SERVICES

PART EIGHT: TYPE OF INSTITUTION

PART NINE: MANAGING THE FUTURE

    The Planning Starts Now   297
    Dan L. Heinlen and Linda S. Crossley

34. *Future Prospects for Alumni Administration*   306
    Paul B. Chewning

    Bibliography   309

    Contributors   315

    Index   321

Foreword

New alumni directors who have endured free advice from me at CASE summer institutes and elsewhere know of my occasional admiration for the late nineteenth-century American philosopher and psychologist William James. Perhaps best known for having a famous younger brother who was a prolific novelist, the elder James was widely respected as a pragmatist. He regularly offered advice on educational issues, and much of it makes eminent good sense today. Among said observations was his important suggestion, probably an admonition to a group of deans or vice presidents, that "Organization and method mean much, but contagious human characters mean more in a university."[1]

People—enthusiastic, caring individuals—are, I suggest, what make our trade such a rich one today. Consider, as examples, the extraordinary talents and energies of our professional colleagues, the spiritedness and seemingly unshakable loyalty of our principal volunteers, the generosity of our faculties and students, or the knowledge that counterparts at other institutions actually welcome all manner of calls for assistance and invitations to share experiences and advice. All of these colleagues—be they our friends, mentors, commiserators, or kibitzers—combine to constitute a remarkable array of resources for our work and a rich addition to our lives.

It is obviously a plus to enjoy what one does for a living. What makes literally hundreds of alumni directors regard our work as quite a bit more than a mere livelihood is simply finding ourselves, time after time, day after day, issue after issue, crisis after crisis, squarely amidst all those contagious human characters that James correctly identified as the real stuff of educational institutions.

This book is, in a sense, Exhibit A for my point. It was (obviously) not undertaken for personal gain. The editors didn't simply recycle a bunch of old articles from the CASE magazine. Better yet, our work and in some cases our spirits will be strengthened by having it. It is a prime example of the kind of people resources on which we can call for authoritative counsel on a broad array of issues. It is additionally a reminder of the generosity and collegial professional regard that seem to be available for the asking—whenever and wherever needed in support of the alumni relations effort.

For all that, we each owe Chuck Webb and the contributors to the handbook our profound thanks.

Incidentally, James also wrote that "the art of being wise is the art of
knowing what to overlook."[2] I hope you'll turn to this volume as you would
a favorite dictionary or a well-thumbed directory. It is likely to be most
useful if you don't try to digest or make sense of it all in one sitting but
instead keep it handy for reference and for that occasional (but important)
orientation or refresher course. There is already a place for it behind my
desk—next to all those quotation books.

William E. Stone
Executive Director
Stanford Alumni Association

Notes

1. Quoted in John W. Gardner and Francesca Gardner Reese, comps., *Quotations of Wit and Wisdom* (New York: W.W. Norton, 1975), 83.
2. Quoted in Laurence J. Peter, comp., *Peter's Quotations: Ideas for Our Times*
(New York: Morrow, 1977), 495.

Preface

In February 1913 in Columbus, Ohio, 23 alumni secretaries met to discuss their mutual experiences and shared concerns. A result of this gathering was the formation of the Association of Alumni Secretaries (AAS). In 1927 this organization became the American Alumni Council, one of the predecessors of the Council for Advancement and Support of Education (CASE). It is not too much to say that from the efforts of those early alumni people and their successors sprang all the various activities that today we call institutional advancement.

In February 1988, to celebrate the founding of the AAS, alumni professionals convened in Columbus, Ohio, at the Columbus II Colloquium, to discuss the future of alumni administration. One of the major findings of these senior professionals was that alumni relations has always relied on "the oral tradition"—anecdote, mentoring, and the informal sharing of information—rather than on written sources. As a result, there is no solid foundation of published work, no "bible" of alumni relations, no compendium to set forth the basic principles of the profession.

We believe that the publication of the *Handbook for Alumni Administration,* as part of the American Council on Education/Oryx Press Series on Higher Education, will be an important step toward remedying this situation. This book represents an important step in creating a lasting collection of the best of alumni administration practice and theory. CASE is grateful to Charles H. Webb and the chapter authors for making it possible.

Strengthening alumni administration is critical because, today more than ever, we need our alumni and their support—and not just their financial support. During my first year as president of CASE, I learned that there was a serious and growing polarization of views between on-campus and off-campus constituencies concerning the role and performance of higher education. We need to understand what our citizens and institutions want and expect of higher education and what our colleges and universities can do, and are doing, to help meet the new challenges of today's world. Moreover, the public needs to understand that the many different kinds of institutions of higher education serve as individual paths to achieving the educational missions of teaching, research, and service.

And who better to keep us informed *and* to spread the word among our many publics than our alumni? As Jack Miller says in his chapter on the alumni role in governance, alumni are "major stockholders in the well-being of their own institutions as well as that of higher education in general. . . . They are the advocates of higher education; they represent higher education in the halls of leadership in this country and, indeed, in the higher offices of our government."

Unlike students, faculty, and even administrators, alumni do not "move on." They may become inactive, uninvolved, or even (unfortunately) "lost alumni," but they are still out there representing their alma mater in one way or another. They are our only lifelong constituency.

How, then, should we deal with them? What should we do for them, and why? And what can they do for us? In this handbook, 34 professionals give their various answers to these questions. And yet, I think you will find that the answers are basically the same. We must deal with our alumni sensitively, enthusiastically, wisely, and above all lovingly. And we must do it not only for the sake of our many institutions of higher education but for society in general. Educated, committed, and caring alumni provide the core of leadership needed to face the problems of today and the needs of the future.

Gary H. Quehl
President
Council for Advancement
and Support of Education

Acknowledgments

The *Handbook for Alumni Administration* has been a collaborative effort on the part of the Council for Advancement and Support of Education (CASE), the general editor, and the publisher. Chapter authors were chosen for their extensive leadership, experience, and effectiveness in the field. The authors represent a diverse group of institutions and geographic locations. They represent the current thinking and practices in alumni administration throughout the country.

In summary, the authors are professionals with varying perspectives but a common understanding of the ingredients necessary for a successful alumni program. They have been my inspiration and guidance throughout the months of writing and editing.

This book has been made possible through CASE's cooperation and support. CASE President Gary Quehl, Vice President for Alumni Administration Paul Chewning, and Immediate-past Vice President for Alumni Administration John Hall have been a source of guidance and encouragement throughout this project. We are deeply indebted to CASE's Director of Marketing and Publications, Julie Landes, for her numerous professional contributions which were essential to the success of this book. A special thanks to the book editor, Susan Hunt, who so capably worked with the draft manuscripts. Also, a special thanks to my administrative assistant, Juanita Grinage, who handled much of the organization for this project, and to gifted editor Bob Bao.

Appreciation from alumni association professionals throughout the country goes to the publisher of the American Council on Education/Oryx Press Series on Higher Education for recognizing the importance of this book to education.

Introduction

CHARLES H. WEBB

One of my favorite cartoons was created by syndicated cartoonist Phil Frank. It shows a couple of archaeologists studying an ancient tablet inscribed with hieroglyphic symbols. Both sport puzzled looks. One finally ventures to say, "It appears to be one of the first alumni newsletters!"

The humor, of course, turns on juxtaposing the modern concept of "alumni" in ancient Egypt. What makes it work is our sudden, perhaps shocking, realization that the pharaohs survived very well with nary a trace of what seems so woven into the fabric of modern society—namely, alumni organization.

That higher education occupies a paramount role in our society today can hardly be debated. Nor can the fact that alumni form one of the most valued resources in fulfilling that role. The subject of alumni administration, however, has received less than total attention. This book intends to fill that void.

Alumni constitute perhaps the greatest single resource on which an institution can depend. They offer the richest potential as resources for advice, advocacy, student recruitment, and financial support. As the products of the institutional effort, alumni are in a better position to understand the educational mission, needs, and goals of their academic institutions than any other single constituency. As students they were the receivers of a quality education and as graduates they become the givers.

There is a consensus today that an institution of higher education cannot reach its fullest potential without the active involvement and commitment of its alumni. Organizing the alumni into a constructive and cohesive force, therefore, is not only the key challenge of alumni administration today, but it remains a keystone for the success of the institution.

Broadly defined, alumni administration is a comprehensive and systematic approach to encourage alumni to serve their alma mater and to encourage their alma mater to serve its alumni. The purpose of this

1

Handbook for Alumni Administration is to bring together for the first time in more than 50 years a definitive look at the field. While it does not date back to King Tutankhamen, it nonetheless remains the oldest profession within institutional advancement.

The book's 34 chapters are divided into nine sections: an introductory overview, alumni as an essential resource, people management, budget and records, programming, communications, alumni education programs and services, type of institution, and managing the future.

Chapter topics cover a wide range of alumni issues and activities. Subjects include the history and philosophy of alumni administration, alumni as advocates, academe and governance, development, student recruitment, career placement, staff selection and development, alumni boards, volunteers, budget and funding sources, management information systems, alumni research, clubs and chapters, professional schools and constituent associations, reunions, student programs, publications and periodicals, attitude surveys and image building, telecommunications, alumni lifelong education programs, merchandise and member services, travel programs, minority alumni programs, athletic events, strategic and long-range planning, and alumni programming at various types of institutions.

I am confident that professionals within institutional advancement and educators representing every size and type of institution will find this *Handbook for Alumni Administration* useful.

An Overview of Alumni Administration

CHAPTER
1

Alumni Relations— A Perspective

Robert Forman

A UNIQUE SYSTEM

What is a university? Over the years many people have answered this question in many different ways. The poet John Masefield had this to say:

> There are few earthly things more beautiful than a University.
> It is a place where those who hate ignorance
> > may strive to know, where those who perceive truth
> > may strive to make others see. . . .
>
> > ("The University")

Masefield describes the purpose of a university as romantic and "lofty." And, indeed, this lofty purpose—to enrich the lives of individuals and to promote the good of society—is one shared by all educational institutions: independent schools, two-year colleges, four-year liberal arts colleges, and research universities alike. And those of us who choose to make our livings in the field of alumni relations play a major role in the fulfillment of this purpose.

We can't define a university, college, or school without using the words "knowledge" and "learning." An educational institution is a place to teach, to learn, and to investigate. What is learned, how it is learned, and who is permitted to learn are integral components of the various philosophies and missions of individual institutions.

The chancellor of a major German university recently stated that there was no difference between his university and other German universities— a statement all the more remarkable inasmuch as his university had

5

several Nobel Prize winners on its faculty. But the chancellor was referring to the fact that most educational institutions are state-supported in Germany. Students are assigned by computer to an institution, and faculty are regarded as employees of the state.

Unlike the German chancellor, no American university president would suggest that any other educational institution could meet the specific mission or goals of his or her university. Each institution has its own mission, and although that mission may be neglected or even changed, it still remains specific to that particular institution.

What is unique and wonderful about American education is that no two institutions are alike. Harvard graduates will quickly tell you they are different from Yale men and women. Michigan boosters will enthusiastically defend their alma mater when it is compared with the University of California, Berkeley. Even though the rest of the world may categorize institutions as large or small, public or private, research- or liberal arts-oriented, and so on, each American college, university, and independent school possesses those one or two features that make it unique.

THE ROLE OF ALUMNI
IN THEIR UNIVERSITY

If you ask the various members of a university community who is responsible for the development of the institution's mission, the most frequent answer is "the governing board." Yet no self-respecting faculty member would admit that he or she does not have a hand in shaping the institution's mission. Administrators credit governing boards with this responsibility even while they continue to invent policy themselves, and students have not infrequently brought an institution to its knees by insisting on their right to help determine goals and destiny.

Few people within the university community would suggest that alumni should play a *major* role in determining institutional goals and mission. Yet even a cursory examination of a university reveals that alumni are the only nontransient segment of that community. On the average, the university president stays at an institution less than seven years. Faculty and administrators have fallen victim to—or become the beneficiaries of—highly competitive bidding for their services. Students, try as they may, cannot avoid graduating or at least moving on to other pursuits.

Who, then, provides the constant overview of a university? Alumni. They have a lifelong commitment to their alma mater, although possibly a self-serving one in that the value of their degrees depends on the current assessment of the institution's quality. Yet alumni are also motivated by that which the academic community frequently dismisses as emotional and irrational—love. This love for alma mater and for college days is an intangible not generally included in definitions of a university. But, in fact, alumni live and breathe a genuine concern for the well-being of "their" university.

In order to develop a sound philosophy of alumni relations, you need to understand the peculiar relationship between alumni and their university. Like a family, alumni quarrel among themselves, fighting bitterly over certain issues; but also, like a family, they stand together in times of need and adversity.

Just as no other single group should run educational institutions, neither should alumni. Yet they should have considerable input. Thus, if you hope to develop a sound alumni relations program, you must first educate your alumni. If alumni are to contribute meaningfully to institutional governance, they need to be informed.

Second, you must provide them with opportunities for service. Winston Churchill is said to have commented, when he was told that a telephone cable to Africa had been installed, "Now that we can speak to Africa, what is it we wish to say?" Once your alumni are informed and motivated, what is it that you wish them to do and what are the avenues for doing it? If alumni have certain rights and responsibilities, the alumni organization must be designed to ensure those rights and enable them to fulfill those responsibilities.

LOOKING BACK

Emblazoned on the wall of the William L. Clements Library of Americana at the University of Michigan is the expression, "In darkness dwells the people which knows its annals not."[1] For those of us working in the field of alumni relations, it is important to understand where we came from.

In 1792 Yale alumni designed an organization based on class structure and appointed class secretaries to gather information that would be published in a series of newsletters to alumni. It was only a matter of time until similar organizations took root in the other private institutions of the East. And these class activities quickly led to two outgrowths: (1) the solicitation of alumni for donations and gifts, and (2) the creation of local clubs and chapters in principal cities around the country.

At its 1821 commencement, Williams College organized a society of alumni in order that "the influence and patronage of those it has educated may be united for its support, protection and improvement." The University of Virginia organized its alumni society in 1838. Subsequently, similar organizations took shape in many eastern colleges. Bowdoin had an alumni organization in 1840, Amherst in 1842, Princeton as early as 1826.

The Princeton organization was unique in its ambitions; in 1832 it tried to raise $100,000 but ultimately had to settle for half that amount. The money was used to build a new telescope and to add three professors to the faculty.

State universities also developed alumni organizations. The University of Michigan founded its alumni association in 1897 and was the first to have a full-time alumni secretary whose salary was paid entirely by the alumni body.

The formation of these early alumni organizations throughout the country recognized the importance of alumni in the governance of educational institutions. Many of the private institutions of the East saw the need to include alumni on their boards of trustees and governors.

Evident from the outset of alumni activities was a direct correlation between an institution's dependence on alumni financial support and its willingness to share governance with the alumni body. Those institutions whose financial viability is predicated on substantial alumni giving have always acknowledged the role of alumni in providing advice, counsel, and direction in the establishment of the policies governing the institution.

The public institutions of the Midwest and the West, on the other hand, had boards of trustees and governors who were elected by the people—alumni status was not among the requirements. Only in recent years have public institutions recognized the necessity of alumni financial support and, consequently, begun to allow alumni involvement in institutional governance.

It is clear that much of institutional advancement today is based on the accomplishments of our early predecessors in alumni administration. During my early years in alumni relations, I benefited greatly from observing and learning from some of the elder statesmen in the field. Although the particular lessons had to do with large alumni associations of major research universities, they also had a universality and relevance to the work of professionals in the field today.

The Big Ten alumni directors have met regularly since the early twentieth century. In recent years, they have expanded their meetings to include alumni directors from institutions of similar size and mission from across the country. My first meetings were nearly a quarter of a century ago, and they were attended by some of the elder statesmen whose national reputations were considerable and even, in some instances, notorious. Among their many outstanding qualities was a sense of humor. Their pranks and horseplay were legendary.

The deliberations of this group provided an opportunity for a newcomer to learn firsthand about the role of an alumni administrator. They would argue endlessly that, of all the university's constituencies, it is alumni who provide a constant, ongoing role; that alumni alone maintain a constant vigil, watching in the manner of a proud parent or loving child. They believed that it made no sense to educate people through the university system and then not provide opportunities for them to have feedback into that system.

They would stay up all hours of the night debating such questions as: Should the principal mission of an alumni association be service to alumni or service to a university? Some claimed that it is only by providing services and benefits addressing the needs of alumni that we can cultivate and educate alumni to become dedicated persons who will serve the university. Others argued that programs should be directed at providing alumni with opportunities to serve their alma mater through scholarship programs, student recruitment, and public information programs.

The majority of the Big Ten alumni associations then, as today, were independent—that is, their policies were developed by an elected board of directors, not by the university's administration. Both then and today, however, at some of the Big Ten institutions, the alumni program is administered as a department of the university. Many hours were spent discussing the relative merits of these two approaches: should an alumni organization be an association of alumni brought together to serve the university or a department of the university created to serve alumni and interpret the interests of the university? Arguments would wax hot and heavy, and the only agreement ever reached was to go on arguing about it the next day.

Despite the endless debates, a consensus did emerge from these meetings, and that was the following summary of the nature of alumni work: to develop motivated and committed alumni, properly informed so that they might be called upon to respond to the various needs of the university, whether this be in the form of financial support, counsel, or simply interpreting the university to various constituencies. Cultivation of alumni, as well as their continuing education, is the principal objective of an alumni program. The alumni directors all agreed that alumni must be treated as full partners in the educational enterprise, along with other segments of the university community.

How an alumni organization develops specific programs to meet these objectives can, and indeed does, vary from institution to institution. It has been my own observation over the years—and one with which I am sure my Big Ten predecessors and contemporaries would agree—that those alumni programs that best serve both alumni and the university are the ones in which the alumni are given an opportunity to develop their own policies and program objectives. Such an approach can be incorporated into any form of alumni organization, be it independent, interdependent, or totally dependent upon the university.

Those past giants of the Big Ten had models and idols of their own. Their "alumni secretaries," as they were called until the late 1960s, were men and women of considerable accomplishment. They frequently held two positions, serving as secretary of the university (or its board of trustees) as well as alumni leader. Many moved on to become institutional officers and, not infrequently, presidents. They were often called upon to be the principal historian and biographer of the institution. They shaped the early programs that today have become the functions of institutional advancement.

ALUMNI RELATIONS TODAY

As you can see, the profession of alumni relations has a rich tradition, yet present-day perceptions tend to ignore the past. Alumni relations is often seen as subordinate to development and fund-raising departments, with alumni directors just people who dress in the school colors, present awards and plaques, and remember names and football scores. They are often paid less than their development counterparts and are left out of institutional decision making.

Those responsible for perpetuating this false stereotype are largely within our own profession. In many ways, we have come to look at ourselves as others see us; we have been content to play this lesser role that others prescribe. For many in our profession, alumni administration is only an interim step to other areas of institutional advancement, principally educational fund raising. Others are "rejects" or lame ducks from other administrative posts. Ex-coaches are often named alumni directors; they're good at golf, are fine storytellers, know lots of people, and can help raise funds—what else do you need?

Recently, however, meeting under the auspices of the current Big Ten directors, alumni directors who share a common philosophy have been reexamining the role of alumni administration and developing more substantial roles for alumni in support of the ongoing needs of higher education. Most of the institutions represented at these meetings are similar in that their governing policies are shaped by alumni and they are supported financially, at least in part, by alumni dues and contributions.

The group also includes universities—both public and private, large and small—that have other organizational approaches. The meetings place a heavy emphasis on the recognition of institutional needs and the role of effective alumni programs in meeting these needs.

The Council for Advancement and Support of Education (CASE) has also worked to enhance the self-image of those in the field of alumni relations. Above all, CASE has contributed dramatically to the understanding by institutional chief executives of the importance of alumni administration. CASE's special conferences and institutes on alumni relations, which place a heavy emphasis on professionalism, have done much to demonstrate to other institutional advancement professionals the importance of alumni contributions.

In recent years, there has also been a rekindling of the statemanship and professionalism of the alumni relations field. A gradual shift has taken place. While the university community once assumed that any reasonably intelligent person who had some knowledge of higher education could handle alumni relations, it is now becoming recognized as a highly skilled and demanding field of work, professional in its character and requiring training and experience.

THE CHALLENGE

The career of alumni relations offers opportunities for extraordinary challenge. Although compensation may not be competitive with that of other areas of institutional advancement, the work is rewarding and fulfilling. If you choose to make it your life's work, you will find it a combination of many professions: teacher, manager, market analyst, researcher, public speaker, business administrator, public relations specialist, and educational statesperson. Each day will present a new challenge. Most important, the work relates to two fundamental aspects of the world in which we live: the advancement of society and the improvement of the quality of life.

Alumni are, by definition, educated people. The advantages obtained through their educational opportunities enable them to assume responsibility in attempting to resolve the challenges of our world. For those of us who have chosen a career in alumni relations, the work is important, the rewards gratifying, and we have the satisfaction of knowing that we have made a difference in the world we live in.

Note

1. Written in 1923 by Professor Ulrich B. Phillips, noted historian on the University of Michigan faculty.

CHAPTER
2

Alumni Administration as an Integral Part of Higher Education

John A. DiBiaggio

One fundamental premise I have learned in my years in higher education administration is that no group is more critical to a university than its alumni. I believe it is very difficult to run a university successfully without the support and commitment of alumni. The converse may not necessarily be true, but there is little doubt that a supportive alumni corps can dramatically enhance the success of an institution's programs.

It follows, therefore, that alumni administration today must play an integral role in higher education. The good old days of the "good old boys" clearly no longer suffice to meet today's needs.

Let me first explain in some detail why I think alumni are so critical to the college or university. First of all, alumni are the one group whose self-interest is furthered by their support of the institution. If alumni are not committed to their alma mater, then how can we expect anyone else to have that commitment?

Many institutions, public as well as private, are currently in the midst of, or about to begin, a capital campaign. When development officers visit corporate leaders and ask them to make a major contribution, the response tends to be, "How many of your alumni contribute?" rather than "How *much* do they contribute?"

It's a valid question. If the alumni don't care to support the institution, then why should others who are not related to it?

12

Support for a college or university extends, of course, beyond the purely financial. Indeed, there is an almost limitless spectrum of activities that alumni perform to help their alma mater—activities that alumni administrators encourage literally every day of the year. Alumni give guest lectures, argue legislative issues, recruit new students for the university, and, more broadly, help the university every time they say something positive about it to others who may, as a result, develop a new linkage with the university.

I also happen to think that alumni help the university every time they criticize it. Constructive criticism helps the university keep on its toes and improve. What better source of valid criticism could there be than a person who has gone through the system and who consequently not only knows and understands it best but also has a built-in stake in seeing it improve?

Just as important, alumni are critical to the institution because they are potential advocates for it. Most universities and colleges, whether they are public or private, depend to a significant extent on federal funds. That being the case, someone has to argue for us with our representatives, whether in the state legislature, in the governor's office, in the executive branch of the federal government, or in Congress.

When college and university officials go to those groups, they are seen as parochial and self-serving. But when our alumni go, they are seen as voting constituents. So if enough alumni speak out strongly within their own communities and to their own representatives, there is a great likelihood that federal and state support will be forthcoming or further expanded.

Finally, alumni are critical to the institution because they add to its morale. Faculty and staff are encouraged in their efforts when they know that alumni feel strongly about the education they received and that alumni are speaking out for the institution—spreading the gospel, if you will.

The role of alumni administration, in great part, is to ensure this vital linkage of alumni to their institution—by giving them opportunities for support, providing them with proper information, and eliciting significant feedback from them. As alumni are critical to the university today, alumni administration lies at the very epicenter of higher education.

We no longer think of an education as a neat, four-year package. In a world characterized by change, the educated person looks at education as a lifelong process. It is clear that the university must cater to the lifelong needs of the individual. And alumni administration is a natural place to put the responsibility for this very important role.

Although some may view the rising importance of alumni administration in higher education management as a coming of age, the phenomenon might be more accurately described as coming full circle. After the first inchoate stirrings of alumni organization in 1792, as Bob Forman recounts, the alumni secretary served essentially as the right hand of the president. That position of honor and responsibility eroded over time, and it was not long ago that alumni directors were viewed externally—and, yes, even internally—as "good old boys." They were typically *men* who wore the school colors on their pants, played golf with the coaches, and led booming renditions of the fight song. At the same time, some of these directors very willingly stayed away from issues and complexities inside the institution.

Many alumni directors openly declared their independence and intentionally held themselves aloof from issues on campus. Too often, alumni were told only what someone thought they wanted to hear, rather than what they *needed* to hear.

Also, too often, alumni associations existed outside the central administration of the college or university and decided for themselves what aspects of the institution to communicate to alumni. Presidents might have one sense of the institution's mission, and alumni directors another.

All that, happily, is history. On many campuses today, alumni directors are valued professional providers of advice and information that can be obtained from no other individuals. The contemporary alumni director is more and more an expert on organizational and political behavior, marketing, advocacy, and strategic planning.

Today's alumni directors are not only at the table when institutional decisions are made—they frequently are leading the discussions. They know all about tuition issues and the institution's role in economic development. They are as likely to be interested in a debate over undergraduate education reform as they are in next season's gridiron predictions.

In the years ahead, I predict that presidents will seek from their alumni directors more and more input. This will happen because of the critical role of alumni—a role clearly accentuated by the demographics of the rising number of living alumni—as well as the increasingly strategic role of the alumni director. Indeed, the alumni director has advanced to the point where, with all the sources, data, surveys, skills, and staff, he or she can make a real impact on the educational institution.

And this is true whether the alumni organization is "independent" or part of the college or university—an issue that occupied much of the time of the elder statesmen of an earlier era.

It does not really matter whether an alumni organization is "independent" or "dependent"—whatever that means. What matters is that the relationship between alumni and the institution be healthy. At Michigan State, where the alumni association is an integral part of the university, the relationship is effective because the director of the association is an active part of the university administration. He is every bit as important as the various vice presidents and the provost. He meets with the university's top management team regularly and has as much input into the decision-making process as any vice president.

If this kind of relationship exists, then the linkage between alumni and the administration is functional. On the other hand, if the alumni director and the alumni staff are shoved down the line so far that they don't feel they have any authority, then of course the tendency is going to be toward wanting independence.

In my administrative career, I have never been impressed with organizational charts. What the charts show is not important. It is *people* who make the difference.

Therefore, rather than judge the effectiveness of the relationship between alumni administration and the institution on the issue of independence, we should focus on the extent to which a mutual understanding of goals and objectives exists between the alumni administrator and the college or university and, furthermore, on the extent to which that mutual view is shared and advocated among the alumni at large.

During the past couple of years, I have been giving talks on leadership expectations for the 1990s. I have often lamented that the term "manager" has been glorified at the expense of the term "leader." An alumni director must be a good manager, but good management alone is not enough. Leadership carries with it much more risk than does mere management. A good manager can successfully reach a bottom line by taking safe roads. But a good alumni leader, more than ever, must be willing to take risks—inside the institution and outside as well. A good alumni leader must be able to risk debate and discussion with alumni and with vice presidents—and, yes, even with the president.

As a communicator, the alumni director must avoid giving sole attention to communicating the institution to alumni. It is just as crucial to a college or university for the director to bring the views of alumni back to campus. Often, alumni will not like what the director tells them. But to advise *and* advocate honestly is an obligation a president should expect of the alumni administrator.

Most alumni directors today would not fear such an expectation because they represent institutions where 99 percent of the information is positive. Yet blind loyalty can get in the way of credibility. Alumni directors must be open to criticism because often what they hear can help not only the association but, more important, the institution.

Sometimes, of course, alumni have a view of the institution based largely on "the way we were." Frequently, "the way we are" challenges that long-held picture. Decisions made by the administration and/or the governing board very often threaten cherished memories or perceptions.

The college or university today exists in a vastly different world, however, from that which many alumni remember. If we are honest with ourselves, we have to admit that some alumni recall institutions that were not as equitable, open, sensitive, and compassionate as we hope we are today. Institutional change has been traumatic for many of our alumni who have criticized us for allegedly abandoning some traditions they held dear.

It is the mission of alumni directors and university administration to demonstrate how change has not tampered with the core values and traditions of our institutions. We must show at Michigan State, for example, that the land-grant mission is as sacred, honored, and *relevant* as ever. But we must also show how affirmative action, the abolition of discriminatory practices and organizations, and renewed commitments to *all* the people build upon—and do not threaten—the Spartan tradition.

Many presidents are not graduates of the institutions they lead. And some alumni believe the myth that unless the president is an alumnus of the institution, he or she cannot understand, appreciate, and hold dear its traditions. But many a president accepted leadership of a college or university *because* he or she appreciated its traditions, albeit from a non-alumni vantage point.

Alumni directors need to be challenged. They need to be as well-versed as possible on issues that affect higher education in general and their institutions in particular—issues that may appear to have little bearing on alumni association matters today.

How attuned is an alumni director to the criticisms of higher education that seem to abound as never before? How conversant are alumni directors with the views expressed in the best seller *The Closing of the American Mind* by Allan Bloom?[1]

The alumni director, through visits with alumni, through publications, and through lifelong education programs offered to graduates, must be ever aware of the issues in American higher education. He or she must be able to respond to alumni with answers about how the institution fits into this alleged closing of the American mind.

The alumni director must have access to the president and to fellow administrators—and they, in turn, must have access to the alumni director. Formal networks with faculty and students need to be established as well. Faculty and students—our raison d'être—often get placed in subsidiary positions by those who need them the most. That's a lamentable irony. The more distant we get from students and faculty, the more distant we get from our obligations. The true vitality of a college or university is created by the students and the faculty, who collectively provide a great institutional and personal energy source.

There are five areas in which alumni directors can provide leadership through their enhanced relationship with the administration, students, and faculty, and their special position of communication vis-à-vis the alumni:

- explaining the commitment higher education must have to both access and quality;
- explaining the difference between science and technology (we hear a lot about technology—the applied use of science—but advances in technology are typically preceded by advances in basic science);
- explaining the cost of education in light of its value, which, of course, has little to do with the starting salaries of graduates;
- explaining the difference between efficiency and effectiveness (critics of higher education often charge that it is not efficient, but, as Peter Drucker tells his management audiences across the country, "Efficiency is concerned with doing things right; effectiveness is concerned with doing the right things"); and
- explaining that higher education must not only reflect changes in society, but it must *lead* in societal reforms.

Alumni administration today is not only a more integral part of higher education administration, but it has evolved into a function that goes far beyond its traditional role as designated cheerleader for the institution. This evolution, as they all do, presents a great challenge but one that is well worth meeting.

Note

1. Allan D. Bloom, *The Closing of the American Mind* (New York: Simon & Schuster, 1987).

CHAPTER
3

Alumni Relations: A Perspective for Presidents

JAMES L. FISHER

Alumni are the constituency a president[1] is most likely to take for granted. Yet, without a strong and positive base of alumni support, a president is bound to fail in virtually any effort to enhance his or her charismatic power. Whether alumni are of modest achievement and means or rich and powerful, they must not be overlooked in favor of other external groups. Without their interest and involvement, a president can neither gain lasting friends among nonalumni, generate a broad base of public support, raise money from nonalumni benefactors, nor significantly influence trustees, politicians, or the media.

Alumni are "grown-up" students, and whatever else they become, remain students until the day they die. Indeed, it often seems as if a cycle were at work. Many undergraduates become intensely committed to their institutions, leave after graduation or for other reasons, apparently with only passing interest in their former schools. As the years go by, however, they return to their alma mater fired with appreciation and interest. It is this spirit that a president should ethically exploit to the fullest.

A wise president communicates honestly and completely with alumni, even if the news isn't always popular. That is why the first steps with alumni are so important. It is only logical that most alumni remember their alma mater as it was, and want it to stay as they remember it. The president's plans must be presented as ways to make the alma mater even more excellent while preserving and respecting many of the old traditions. There is a tendency among alumni to resent dramatic changes—even new presidents—that may develop if warm and convivial relationships with

18

the alumni leadership are not immediately established by a new president.

ALUMNI ASSOCIATIONS

Most colleges and universities cultivate their alumni communities through the creation of alumni associations. These are staffed by professional officers charged with representing either the alumni or the institution or both. This is an easy relationship until there is conflict, an inevitable circumstance between alumni and a changing institution. For this reason, the alumni officer at a dynamic institution has perhaps the most schizophrenic position of anyone on the institution staff. Regardless of the nature of the alumni association, for a president to constrain the officer to the same absolute conditions of staff loyalty expected of other staff is to render the alumni officer finally ineffective in working with this key constituency.

Whatever your experience with and attitudes toward alumni associations, do not rush off pell-mell upon appointment and abruptly change its nature. Any changes in this area should come only after strong relationships are firmly established with key alumni leaders. Presidents who encounter difficulties with alumni aren't saved by the support of the governing trustees. To seek their assistance may actually cause greater harm. Alumni do not fear trustees, staff, faculty, big givers, politicians, or a president. It is their hearts that are vested in the institution. Presidents who have offended alumni have literally been driven from office. A president has legitimate, reward, and expert power with alumni only so long as they agree with him or her. Coercive power is virtually nonexistent. A president must rely almost exclusively on his or her ability to develop charismatic power. Initially, trustees grant the new president a certain grudging respect, but their affection and support must be won. Perhaps more than anyone else, alumni must trust and like the president before really giving their support. Without it, a short term lies ahead.

INDEPENDENT AND DEPENDENT
ALUMNI ASSOCIATIONS

Most alumni associations depend on the institution for support and staff. Others are partially independent, and a few provide for themselves completely. The prime source of support for the alumni association doesn't matter. What counts is to have alumni involved in a serious and constructive manner in the affairs of the institution.

With independent associations, the risk is run of less efficiency and of an association's developing so much autonomy that it becomes an unrestrained adversary. The staff officers of independent alumni associations do not report to the president but to their alumni boards. However, although this can produce anxious moments, in reality it may prove to the president's advantage. If a president is willing to gamble on his or her charismatic skills, an independent alumni association can become the most effective milieu for cultivating alumni support. Alumni of public institutions will often give more under such a relationship. If the president is perceived as a more confident and open president, the alumni association, the institution, and the president will prosper.

Should the more comfortable, dependent association structure be chosen, the result need not be dramatically less productive. The imperative here is that the president realize that the paid alumni officer must honestly render to the president or a delegate the attitudes and opinions of alumni. While the alumni officer may be expected to represent the interests of the institution to alumni, he or she must also be able to represent the interests of the alumni in a way that is reassuring to them. Although alumni do not mind being influenced or persuaded, they will not accept coercion at all. Information and persuasion must be applied to convince alumni that the president's way is best. The presentation should not invite disagreement, but inform convincingly.

Alumni and especially alumni officers realize that their interests are better served if the incumbent president of the alma mater receives their support. There is no case with which I am familiar in which an alumni association took the first step towards a hostile relationship with a new president. Most alumni associations will let the president do as he or she pleases, so long as it is done with thoughtfulness and care.

CULTIVATING ALUMNI

The charisma established on campus and with other external groups will be helpful in developing good relationships with alumni. However, attention is due to the special importance of an institution's alumni, and the president must make the alumni know how important they are. This applies regardless of whether alumni are genuinely accomplished or of modest achievement and means. Of course, the president should be presidential with alumni, and distance, trappings, ceremonies, and other charismatic qualities apply as much to alumni as to other groups.

A variety of approaches to alumni—such as special letters and off-campus speeches to alumni groups—are effective, but should not be so frequent or regular as to become taken for granted. Occasionally, a president can attend part of an alumni board meeting to make a brief presentation. One-to-one sessions with important alumni leaders include visits to their homes and offices. Attending virtually all campus alumni functions, campus athletic activities, and other events where large numbers of alumni may be present will help to build support.

THE ALUMNI OFFICER

If a president inherits a chief alumni officer of senior tenure, he or she should try to keep the person aboard. Experienced alumni officers will respect a new president and are prepared to be supportive. However, perhaps more than anyone else on the staff, alumni officers have a deep and abiding affection for the institution, and a new president wisely makes serious efforts to convey the same feeling to them. They often have closer ties in the alumni community than anyone else on campus or off.

Should the inherited alumni officer be inexperienced, educate him or her as quickly as possible. What comes naturally simply doesn't effectively realize full alumni potential. Send the alumni officer to professional meetings and especially to special conferences designed to instruct alumni officers in appropriate techniques. Encourage them to read professional magazines, articles, and books. Foster the continuing education of alumni staff, and soon alumni will be contributing as never before.

Note

1. This chapter is excerpted from *Power of the Presidency*, published in 1984 by American Council on Education and Macmillan. It was written for college and university presidents, for whom alumni support is vital, and thus provides insight into an important perspective on alumni administration. The five types of power to which Fisher refers are explained in *Power of the Presidency* as follows. *Coercive power* employs threats and punishments to gain compliance. *Reward power* implies the ability of one individual to accomplish desired outcomes by favors, recognition, or rewards to group members. *Legitimate power* is based on a group's acceptance of common beliefs and practices. *Expert power*, reflecting the deference accorded a perceived authority, tends to legitimize leaders and make them more effective. *Charismatic power*, the single most effective form of influence, is based on the admiration and liking that people feel for an individual. (Adopted from a topology developed by J. R. P. French and B. Raven, "The Bases of Social Power," in *Studies in Social Power*, ed. D. Cartright [Ann Arbor: University of Michigan, Institute for Social Research, 1959].)

PART

2

Alumni as an Essential Resource

CHAPTER
4

Alumni as Advocates for Your Institution

STEPHEN L. BARRETT

THE PLACE OF ALUMNI IN INSTITUTIONS OF HIGHER EDUCATION

Over 50 years ago, President Nicholas Murray Butler of Columbia University said:

> It is fixed doctrine at Columbia University that the alumnus is permanently a member of the University. He has come to it of his own accord, has placed his name upon its books. By these several acts he has become a member of the University family, entitled to recognition as such and bearing responsibility as such. He is always and everywhere, whether willingly or not, whether consciously or not, a representative of his university's training and ideals.[1]

Alumni have been an important part of the American collegiate scene ever since the first graduates emerged from the hallowed halls of our oldest institutions of higher education. At first, alumni did not necessarily have any official function or position at the institution; they just wanted to be involved once again in the academic process at a place they had grown to love—the scene of their intellectual enlightenment and the beginning of the personal relationships that, over the years, would mean so much. This spontaneous "return to the spawning ground," so to speak, was something even the founders of the institutions had not foreseen. But since those early days, in ever-increasing numbers and in more and more innovative ways, alumni have been involved with their alma maters.

25

THE TRADITION OF
ALUMNI INVOLVEMENT

Alumni involvement is a phenomenon that was originally unique to the United States, although today it has also become entrenched in Canada. In recent years, alumni associations have been formed in South Africa and in a few other parts of the world as interest has grown in the concept.

Alumni involvement appears to have grown fastest in the presence of two factors:

- a strong tradition of private education, and
- government endorsement of the concept of individual tax relief for private support to institutions that provide educational opportunities for its citizens (this tax-relief concept long ago stopped being the exclusive venue of the private school and has now entered the public sector as well).

The founding fathers of the United States and the writers of the Constitution—faced with the huge task of building a new nation—provided that the federal government would not get directly involved with education. This left support of educational enterprises to the private sector or to the individual states.

Most early educational efforts were started by individuals, communities, or religious groups. And most were in need of outside financial support, almost from the beginning. Cash funds for tuition and other expenses were hard to come by in those early days. The histories of most institutions are replete with stories of sacrifices that were made by many, faculty and students alike, to keep the educational process operative. It was at this point that the former students, who kept returning pretty much for social reasons, and the resident administrators began to see that the institution could be aided by this group of supporters.

In 1949, Douglas D. Woodruff made this observation:

> The alumni form the most important off-campus public of most colleges and universities, and there is no limit to the good they can do for their institutions provided: 1) the experiences of their own undergraduate years can be recalled with appreciation and pleasure; 2) they are kept fully informed regarding the objectives, policies, progress, and problems of their alma mater; 3) they are given an opportunity to perform challenging tasks for their institutions.[2]

Thus, the relationship between alumni and their institution has become a long-standing one and one of mutual benefit.

EXAMPLES OF
ALUMNI INVOLVEMENT

Professional alumni administrators have all noted the phenomenon that takes place in the life of an undergraduate as he or she moves into the world of the alumni. A. I. Dickerson of Dartmouth College described it 50 years ago:

> All of us have observed the very rapid metamorphosis which comes after the recent graduate's departure from the campus. A nostalgia for the place grows up, a gratitude seems to appear for the things which were taken for granted as an undergraduate, and within two or three years the young alumnus is really receptive to a suggestion that he participate in support of the college.[3]

This receptive attitude and willingness to give support are at the heart of the profession of alumni relations.

"FORMAL" ADVOCACY BY ALUMNI

There are many formal avenues through which your alumni can be advocates for your institution.

The Board of Trustees

Many universities have a number of spaces on the board of trustees reserved for alumni. Sometimes the alumni association chooses the trustees for these seats; sometimes they are chosen by other methods, such as election or selection by the governor, for example. Like other trustees, alumni trustees hold their positions for the purpose of giving the board the benefit of their guidance, experience, and professional expertise. They are responsible, as are all the trustees, for setting policy and determining the general direction of the institution.

But in addition to these responsibilities, alumni trustees must also represent the alumni constituency in matters of interest to former students and in the best interests of the institution. For this purpose, alumni trustees must establish channels of communication with the alumni body to keep them informed and to receive feedback from them. This may well be done through a close working relationship with the alumni association.

Committee Assignments

You can also appoint alumni to advisory councils, curriculum committees, public relations groups, and so on. On these various councils and committees, alumni can use their specific expertise for the benefit of the institution. As alumni are the end result of the educational effort as well as the future users (employers) of the institution's graduates, they should assist in determining what will be taught. They can serve as a valuable asset to the entire university and especially to the individual colleges or departments that need to keep current with changes and developments.

Recently two alumni were invited back to their small western alma mater to advise a college dean on a programs and curriculum committee. First they met for several hours with the faculty; then the entire committee toured the physical facilities (in this case, the chemistry laboratories). After seeing what was there (or rather what was *not* there), the two alumni decided that the place needed more from them than simple talk, so they gave of their own funds and encouraged others to assist with equipment and expertise. Out of this attempt to get academic feedback came a much better equipped facility which, in turn, led to improved teaching and learning.

While you should not necessarily *expect* this kind of result when you invite alumni to join committees, it is just the kind of serendipitous benefit that will come along.

Alumni Association Board of Directors and Committees

Alumni associations have traditionally been major users of alumni volunteers. In the second edition of the *Handbook of Institutional Advancement*, I outlined the following basic standard for volunteer involvement: "At least one-half to one percent of the total alumni body should be involved in a volunteer capacity in alumni leadership at any given time."[4]

At a 1987 meeting of the alumni leaders of the 50 largest alumni associations in the United States and Canada, it was estimated that those institutions collectively had some 6,951,000 living alumni. If we apply my standard to this figure, it would amount to a force of many thousands of volunteer workers assisting in the advancement of their alma maters in this country and Canada—and this figure only represents 50 institutions. When you remember that the volunteers change to some degree every year, you will begin to appreciate the magnitude of this type of service as a cultivational tool. Involving alumni in the work of your institution can be one of your most productive efforts.

Serving on the alumni board of directors is perhaps the most visible form of alumni leadership. Alumni board size varies from institution to institution; it can be as small as 12 or as large as several hundred. Alumni boards also differ in responsibility and procedures—some are almost autonomous while others serve primarily as a sounding board—but all attempt to bring alumni closer to the mission and operation of the institution so that they can assist in its development.

Ad Hoc Assignments

University administrations are often in need of various types of expertise that alumni can provide. For example, an alumni association that wanted to do a major continuing education program in the publishing field brought onto campus, as a volunteer, the recently retired chief editor of one of the nation's prestigious book publishing companies. This alumnus served for several years to get the effort launched.

LEGAL LIABILITY FOR ALUMNI VOLUNTEERS

In these days when the dominant mood seems to be "When in doubt, sue," alumni are not invulnerable to the fear of liability and, in fact, it may be dampening the desire to serve on the part of some former volunteers. According to Mike McNamee, writing in the May 1987 CASE *Currents*,

> the biggest problem for alumni associations may be in the area of directors and officers—or D&O—coverage for governing boards and association employees. Increasingly, volunteers are asking alumni directors whether they'll be covered against suits charging "errors and omissions" in the decisions they make and carry out for the group.[5]

Many alumni associations are forced to provide their own board liability insurance coverage and pay premiums that have risen dramatically in the last two years. And in some cases, it is hard to find and keep insurance, particularly D&O coverage. On the other hand, some associations are covered by their universities' policies. The connection between the association and its college or university may determine whether it needs its own coverage. As McNamee says:

> The crisis [in liability insurance] is forcing many associations to examine the often-murky connections they have with their colleges and universities. When an organization's dependence or independence isn't spelled out plainly—and for many alumni groups, the arrangements are far from straightforward—its insurance protection might not be either.[6]

Each association or alumni office needs to examine its own situation and activities carefully.

INFORMAL ADVOCACY BY ALUMNI

Alumni support their institution in many informal ways. To tap into this support, you need an alumni records system that is constantly updated and an alumni communication program that works. Without these you cannot keep the alumni informed nor can you reach them quickly and effectively when you need them. The longer your records system and communication program continue to be effective, the greater the credibility and trust you will earn from your alumni.

General Support for Alma Mater

Support for an institution comes in many forms besides financial support, as important as that is. An institution of higher education needs moral and often practical support from dedicated and interested people who are committed to its mission.

A number of years ago, Brigham Young University (BYU) suddenly found itself with a very negative PR position because of a long-standing ecclesiastical doctrine of its sponsoring church, which did not, at that time, admit blacks to its governing priesthood. That situation no longer exists, and, as is usually the case, the perceived image was based mostly on erroneous information and a great deal of misunderstanding—the university itself did not discriminate in any way.

Nevertheless, some very serious and even dangerous events took place. For example, one institution refused to play BYU in future athletic competition, even though contracts were in force. In another instance, a riot ensued at a state university where a fire bomb was thrown out onto the playing floor during a league basketball game.

The problem was especially severe in one of the major metropolitan areas of the Southwest. A group of interested and concerned BYU alumni from that community took it upon themselves to invite community leaders from government, education, and religion to visit the BYU campus. At their own expense, they provided a chartered airplane, ground transportation, housing accommodations, and so on. During this 24-hour visit, these leaders listened to, among others, church officials, university and community leaders, and students, and they came away with a new and different perspective. In turn, they assisted in diffusing the feelings of many and in improving the feelings in their own community.

This event was the key to solving a serious problem that, but for these ready-and-willing alumni, could have gotten much worse. We couldn't have purchased this kind of support—even if we could have afforded it—nor could we have arranged an event that would have been nearly as effective as this spontaneous local response to our needs.

Support through Recruitment

Most institutions benefit from alumni efforts to recruit students. Alumni are particularly effective when they serve as the eyes and ears of particular departments or schools within the university and attempt to bring the very best students to campus.

Support in Fund Raising

Even when alumni are not able to give major gifts themselves, they can often act as "finders" of those who can. They can cultivate those individuals by bringing them to the campus, introducing them to the administrators, faculty, and others who can assist in interesting the potential donor in the needs of the institution.

HOW TO BUILD ADVOCACY

How much advocacy your alumni give to your institution depends on several factors:

- the degree of trust built up over the years,
- the degree of commitment alumni feel for the institution,
- how much information an institution is willing to share with its alumni, and
- how well the institution articulates its needs to this constituency.

The process of building trust and commitment must begin while the future alumni are still students. Faculty members have much to do with how students feel about the institution; they determine the quality of the teaching students receive as well as the quality and quantity of more informal interactions between student and professor. The administration also plays a vital role in determining the nature of the campus experience.

Years ago an alumni director was trying to get the faculty of his institution to participate in a particular alumni program that he felt was important. His most compelling argument was that the alumni would give more support to the faculty if they could see individual faculty members involved in programs outside the classroom. A starchy older faculty member responded, "If you were half the alumni director you say you are, we wouldn't need to do this thing you are asking of us. And furthermore," he continued, warming to the task, "if those alumni of yours were any good at all, they would give us what we are really worthy of without us having to tramp out into the hinterlands!"

To this the alumni director's rejoinder was, "I may be only half an alumni director, but I am given only those students that you have spent the past four years influencing and if they are no good, then I don't see how you can blame me—look to yourself!"

After the students graduate, the ball passes to the alumni relations office and the alumni association. They must build upon the past (or overcome it, as the case may be) and work to communicate, involve, and motivate alumni to keep their connection with the institution alive and well.

CONCLUSION

As President Butler said, speaking of the alumnus of Columbia College, "He has become a member of the University family. . . ." Those alumni who are treated as members of such a family are those you can count on to craft and protect the reputation of the institution—it is in their best interests to do so. They are, in fact, the university!

The administrators, the president, the faculty, and the buildings come and go; the curriculum changes with the times; but the alumni and what they have accomplished with their education are the real makers and shapers of what the institution has been and will yet become. It is the alumni who must, on the one hand, build the stature of the institution and, on the other hand, bear the brunt of the mistakes of the current itinerant inhabitants of the campus. The alumni, after all, have the ultimate stake in the institution's future.

The place of the alumni in any institution of higher education, then, is inextricably linked, welded, and sealed with the past, present, and future of the institution—who better to be involved as advocates for your institution?

Notes

1. Nicholas Murray Butler, quoted by Clarence Lovejoy in *Report of the Twenty-third Annual Conference* (Washington, D.C.: American Alumni Council, 1937), 26.

2. Douglas D. Woodruff, "The Opportunity of the Challenging Task," in *Report of the Thirty-fourth Annual Conference* (Washington, D.C.: American Alumni Council, 1949), 36.

3. A. I. Dickerson, "Responsibilities of a Fund Executive," in *Report of the Twenty-third Annual Conference* (Washington, D.C.: American Alumni Council, 1937), 103.

4. Stephen L. Barrett, "Basic Alumni Programming," in *Handbook of Institutional Advancement*, 2d ed., ed. A. Westley Rowland (San Francisco: Jossey-Bass, 1986), 418.

5. Mike McNamee, "The Liability Loophole," CASE *Currents*, May 1987:44.

6. Ibid.

The Role
of Alumni
in Academe
and Governance

JACK MILLER

Some institutions are accused of believing that alumni exist only to give money—that the ideal alumnus is mute and holds out a well-filled sack of cash into which the university administrators are encouraged to dip. However, in the modern world of accountability, alumni are becoming significant players in academia—and they should be. The best colleges and universities have discovered in the last 10 years that there is much to be gained from alumni who are involved in both the academic progress of the institution and its governance. Too often alumni are viewed only as noisy backers at athletic events or donors to the annual fund or recruiters of students. Too rarely are they sought for their opinions and their thoughts on major issues facing America's colleges and universities.

AN ACADEMIC ROLE FOR ALUMNI

More and more universities and colleges are asking how alumni can be involved in the world of academia, a peculiar question in some respects. After all, our graduates have spent from two to as many as 12 years as residents on our campuses. But residency and the student experience don't always equip a person to deal with the inside workings of today's colleges and universities. Alumni, for example, do not normally understand the slow pace at which higher education arrives at decisions and therefore become frustrated when dealing with committees dominated by institutional officials. They can, however, contribute much more than token service on presidential search committees and on committees to increase the annual fund or raise capital funds.

Alumni as Role Models

Alumni can serve as role models for all types of students, and a variety of special programs on college and university campuses around the country make extensive use of alumni experience. Programs range from informal sharing of experience through campus dialogues to formal distinguished alumni lecture series, but most important is the fact that alumni spend time encouraging students to succeed in their goal of being educated. Institutions can creatively involve alumni as role models through careful thought and planning.

This is particularly valuable for minority students, first-generation college students, and students from lower social and economic backgrounds.

Placement and career counseling is one of the logical avenues for this important role model function. And alumni themselves often have a personal interest in this area. If colleges and universities were to survey their own new alumni just at that point when the graduates prepare to leave the institution, they would find a number of weaknesses in the educational system they were part of. Many may find the institution's career counseling and placement services to be inadequate. Alumni should serve as volunteers in these programs, but they should also have a strong advisory role as the placement office develops these programs. Alumni are only too glad to share their expertise and their knowledge with placement personnel as well as with the students they serve.

Adjunct Faculty

Alumni can have an important role in the classroom as adjunct faculty both for credit and for noncredit courses. Several successful courses involving alumni on an ad hoc basis have evolved from the Purdue Old Masters program started over 20 years ago. In this model, alumni share their insights, aspirations, and firsthand experiences with undergraduates over a period of several days. Courses range from business to liberal arts and everything in between; only accrediting and academic policies restrict the possibilities.

A Voice in the Academic Mission

Wherever alumni go they carry the name of their alma mater almost as if it were stamped on their foreheads. Because of that identification they are, as it were, major stockholders in the well-being of their own institutions as well as that of higher education in general.

Too often, mission statements for higher education institutions are developed entirely by internal university committees. Seldom are alumni involved in the process—even though many have great expertise in formulating mission statements and have played major roles in the development of corporate goals and objectives. In the college or university setting, there seems to be some feeling that only those who are employed by the institution have the magic key that can solve its problems.

Alumni must have, and should insist upon, a role in the continued improvement of higher education. They are the advocates of higher education; they represent higher education in the halls of leadership in this country and, indeed, in the higher offices of our government. Failing to involve alumni as full-fledged partners in the future of higher education could be one of the great American tragedies. Alumni have so much to offer and are so willing to serve, but we in higher education must invite them to cross the doorstep and enter the hallowed halls.

A ROLE FOR ALUMNI
IN GOVERNANCE

The role of alumni in the governance of the institution has been slow to evolve, but gradually many institutions have taken the first steps toward acknowledging alumni as partners in the higher education enterprise.

Serving on the Board

For years, alumni at many private institutions have been members of boards, directly involved in institutional governance, while at state institutions boards were normally appointed and/or elected. In many institutions now, both public and private, a certain number of the trustees or members of the board must be alumni. This provides a balance to these boards and ensures that alumni input is available to the highest leadership of the institution.

Involvement in Committees

There are many other, less obvious ways in which alumni can participate in institutional governance. At more institutions today than ever before, through participation in alumni associations, alumni serve as full-fledged members of university senate and/or faculty committees. While it is not true that alumni should serve on *every* university committee, there are many where alumni expertise, background, and input are desirable or even necessary.

For many years, many college and university presidents have turned to informal advisers (often alumni) in time of need as they sought direction for their institutions. Alumni have nearly always been effective in this role and now, in many cases, alumni serve on formal advisory committees to the chief executive officers of America's higher education institutions. This vital role enables alumni to use the wealth of knowledge accumulated in their careers and their ability to examine issues from a variety of viewpoints.

Academic Advisory Councils

Last but not least, academic advisory councils have served important roles in colleges and universities over the years. But only recently have higher education institutions begun to involve many people on these committees, councils, and advisory groups. As the number of colleges and universities has grown significantly in the last 20 years, they have begun to reach out and broaden the sphere of volunteer opportunities available on the campus, thus involving significant numbers of people in the deliberations and, consequently, the future direction of their respective institutions.

While alumni who serve on institutional committees and are involved in the academic side of the institution cannot solve all the problems of higher education, they certainly bring to the conference table the desire to work constructively for the continued improvement of American higher education. And they help create a knowledge base that is badly needed in higher education with all the political, social, and economic pressures of today's world. Alumni bring with them the practical knowledge of the world often missing from the ivory towers of a college or university, and provide real-life expertise that cannot be duplicated on the typical campus.

THE FUTURE OF
ALUMNI INVOLVEMENT

In the future, I believe that colleges and universities will devise even more creative ways to involve alumni. Surveys and research have shown that involved alumni and friends of the institution not only provide valuable input in determining its direction, but, in times of financial need, they respond openly with their personal resources as well as influencing giving decisions at America's corporations and foundations. While many other aspects of alumni administration are crucial to the future of American higher education, there are none more important than the involvement of alumni in the very highest levels of higher education in this country.

Not all alumni are (or will ever be) in a position to endow their alma mater, but many are in a position to offer—through personal service and expertise—knowledge and insights that cannot be bought in the consulting marketplace. Alumni are truly advocates not only of individual institutions, but of higher education as a whole.

Alumni want to be involved in the future of higher education, and as the primary stockholders in the enterprise, they should be an active part of higher education's plans for the coming age.

CHAPTER 6

Alumni as an Essential Resource for Development

Stephen W. Roszell

The chapters in this section of the *Handbook for Alumni Administration* will show you that alumni are a valuable institutional resource that can be creatively and strategically utilized to advance an academic institution. If you are an alumni administrator, you know this already. It is your job to orchestrate alumni support through involvement programs for the betterment of your institution. Your work is based on the concept that the alumni constituency is a natural pool of resources and talent, that alumni know the institution and have a stake in its well-being.

What may not be as obvious, from the alumni administrator's point of view, is that alumni are also an essential resource for development. Alumni professionals often fear that the alumni resource might be exploited or even destroyed by an overly aggressive short-term approach to meeting financial needs.[1] When alumni and development professionals pursue their own separate priorities, the question of ownership arises: "Whose alumni *are* they anyway?" The answer that I would give is that they are the institution's and, in fact, they are the institution's most essential resource for advancement. Alumni are stewards of the institution and as good stewards they provide essential financial support, volunteer service, and valuable advice.

HISTORICAL BACKGROUND

Any student of history will readily admit that, to understand today, we must study yesterday. For most colleges and universities, organized groups of alumni were the first special-interest groups. And most alumni organizations have their origins in reunions of the earliest graduating classes. Former students chose to continue their relationship with the institution through organizations and programs that met their own needs.[2]

At Williams College in 1821, alumni were first organized into a society formed so "that the influence and patronage of those it has educated may be united for its support, protection and improvement."[3]

And every such alumni organization had as a goal the development of funds to support the institution. Thus, fund raising—and most programs of university support—originated in the early alumni association movement. It is only within the past 40 years that we have seen development become professionalized and segregated in its own department within the institution. Today most major institutions in this country have well-staffed development offices as well as professionally managed alumni organizations.

SHAPING THE ALUMNI RESOURCE

Alumni are the raw material of successful institutional advancement. The institution's success depends on how well alumni and development organizations systematically cultivate, nurture, and use this resource. Shaping this resource takes a great deal of effort and careful planning. First, before you can ask alumni to give or to serve, you must take four important preliminary steps of cultivation.

Basic research is the first step. You must understand the demographics and the attitudes of your alumni constituency. *Identification* is the second step. You identify certain segments of the alumni group that then become targets for the third and fourth steps—*informing* and *involving*. Once identified, informed, and involved, alumni are cultivated to the level of interest in, and commitment to, the institution necessary to respond positively to your call to action.

The process of building alumni support through these four steps should begin in the freshman year and continue throughout the lifetime of each graduate. William Pickett, President of St. John Fisher College, explains why:

> The aim of institutional advancement is to build voluntary, long-term relationships between persons and organizations. During the course of each relationship, there will be calls to action, which will be invitations for the person to take supportive action toward the organization. In educational fund-raising, these calls to action will be gift solicitations.[4]

If you treat your alumni and future alumni, at every stage of their connection with your institution, as a resource that requires cultivation and nurturing, they will respond when you ask them for financial as well as other types of assistance.

SUCCESSFUL UTILIZATION OF
THE ALUMNI RESOURCE

Several key ingredients are essential to a successful institutional development program.

The Case Statement

Before you can ask your alumni to support your institution, you must have a persuasive case statement. The case statement is the primary sales tool for development. It should be the careful and thoughtful statement that comes out of an extended planning process, and it should clearly articulate the institution's future direction. It should include a list of needs, the rationale for those needs, and the resources required to achieve those needs within an established timetable.[5]

A good case statement stirs the imagination. Most institutions put a lot of time and effort into its preparation. The elements of the proposed case statement are tested, either by consultants who do feasibility studies or by university officers who hold informal interviews with key alumni leaders and other university constituents. While the institution's president must provide the primary leadership in communicating and promoting the case statement, alumni can serve as a valuable conduit for broader distribution—if you have developed and maintained an effective communication strategy involving alumni.

Volunteers

The case statement is only a hollow document unless volunteers are able to use it to achieve development goals. For most institutions, alumni represent the best pool of voluntary support. They are an informed, interested, and involved group, willing to commit valuable time to support the institution. In the *Handbook of Institutional Advancement*, Barbara Snelling addresses the importance of volunteers:

> Volunteers provide to an institution strength that is available from no other source. The testimony of volunteers concerning their beliefs builds trust in others. Through their dedication, they visibly demonstrate their personal endorsement of the institution's mission and objectives, lending their own reputations as validation of that mission. Because they act without direct self-interest, volunteers provide a depth of credibility that no one else can offer. Their message in support of the institution carries a compelling sincerity and conviction that employees of the institution, because of their presumed self-interest, cannot manage.[6]

We all know how important our committed alumni volunteers are, whether they serve in student recruitment, mentoring programs, or other alumni relations activities. The strength of the alumni volunteer component has a direct relationship to the success of our efforts. This is most apparent in development. Major gifts by corporations, foundations, or individuals frequently are the result of peer solicitation, and often the peer relationship has its roots in a collegiate experience shared by the alumni volunteer and the donor.

You can never overestimate the importance of nurturing your alumni volunteers, both present and potential. Volunteer commitment is unique to the United States and Canada and fundamental to the success of most of our nonprofit organizations. The Center for Philanthropy estimates that in 1987 there were $93 billion of volunteered services in this country.[7]

In higher education, alumni have been and will continue to be the primary source of volunteer leadership.

Prospects

The third and often the most important component of a successful development effort is the identification of prospects. Alumni are an obvious source of prospects because they contribute themselves and have contacts with others who are able to contribute. In 1985–86, according to the Council for Aid to Education (CFAE), alumni contributed $1.82 million to higher education. At 951 core colleges and universities monitored by CFAE, alumni giving increased 26.0 percent to become the largest single source of support for these institutions. Alumni gave an average of $1.3 million per institution to the institutions reporting to CFAE in 1985–86.[8]

But although alumni give generously, their importance to development goes beyond their own financial contributions. Through memberships on corporate and foundation boards, alumni directly influence the primary sources of funding that support higher education. Thus, alumni are essential to the prospecting component of the development enterprise.

Over the years, Dartmouth College has had one of the better records of alumni involvement and support of development initiatives. As J. Michael McGean, described by Steven Calvert as "the driving force in alumni relations at Dartmouth" for nearly 30 years, pointed out some years ago, "There is no question that a strong alumni program is an invaluable contributor to successful development activities. Without a positive, well-balanced alumni effort, fund-raising would be infinitely more difficult."[9]

The Role of the President

Clark Kerr once observed, "Of the problems confronting higher education in the coming years, the greatest will be leadership." Unless the president articulates a special vision, mission, or cause for the institution, he or she will not be viewed as a true leader. Inherent in the office of president is the need to communicate with multiple constituencies, and alumni are the constituency that is most often taken for granted. But, as former CASE President James Fisher says:

> Without a strong and positive base of alumni support, a president is bound to fail in virtually any effort to enhance his or her charismatic power. . . . Without [the] interest and involvement [of alumni], a president can neither gain lasting friends among nonalumni, generate a broad base of public support, raise money from nonalumni benefactors, nor significantly influence trustees, politicians, or the media.[10]

Thus, the president must make alumni support one of his or her top priorities and make a significant time commitment to it. And it is the institutional advancement professional's job to help the president most effectively utilize his or her time. First, the president must establish a pattern of contact and communication that involves the alumni constituency in the life of the institution. While the president obviously cannot have personal contact with each member of the alumni constituency, he or she can use a thoughtful communications strategy to establish meaningful communication with alumni. An open letter to alumni in the alumni magazine and a tracking and clipping system that allows the president to congratulate or recognize alumni when they are featured in local newspapers are useful techniques.

Second, the president—with the help of institutional advancement professionals—must devote a significant amount of time to eliciting meaningful commitments from alumni, whether for important volunteer service or for substantial financial contributions. This requires the president's personal involvement at the appropriate moment in the cultivation and solicitation process.

Since time is a limited resource for every president, it is useful to understand the cultivation process for your prospects. Think of your prospects as passing through three stages: first, you attract their attention; then you establish understanding; and, last, you engage commitment. The president's involvement in the first stage (attracting attention) should be only minimal and just slightly greater in the second (establishing understanding). The president, however, should be prepared to commit a substantial amount of time to the last stage—engaging commitment.

THE ROLE OF PROFESSIONAL STAFF

Cooperation of alumni and development staff is extremely important in maximum utilization of the alumni resource. Most alumni have little comprehension of staff roles and responsibilities. When a staff member provides face-to-face linkage for alumni, the alumni then assume that that person has a broad portfolio encompassing all the activities that advance the institution. This view of the administrator as an ombudsman comes naturally for alumni, but it's a difficult role for most professional staff to assimilate.

As with many other activities in our society, alumni and development functions are performed by professionals who have become specialists. Certain activities are "development" while others are "alumni." But all staff members need to remember that what occurs in the process of cultivation and development of the alumni resource is not foreign to either department, nor the exclusive property of either.

On the other hand, resources to support higher education are too scarce to permit duplication of effort—that is, if the development office is doing prospect research, the alumni office should not be doing it too. Communication between alumni and development professional staff is essential. Each staff organization needs to know what the other is doing, and both must be ready to hand off certain responsibilities to the other at the appropriate time.

Involving alumni in achieving results can be extremely satisfying for staff and rewarding for the institution. Sometimes the results are dollars but sometimes they are less tangible yet equally important to our institutions. But the real reward for the alumni administrator is participation in the process. There is no more humbling experience than to observe dedicated alumni devoting their full energy to a cause in which they believe. Our future depends on our ability to expand this group of committed alumni to meet the significant challenges that will face our institutions in the years ahead.

Notes

1. Robert G. Forman, "A-L-U-M-N-I Doesn't Just Spell M-O-N-E-Y: Thoughts of a Professional Alumni Administrator," CASE *Currents*, September 1984:26.

2. Wilfred B. Shaw, *Hand Book of Alumni Work* (Ann Arbor, Mich.: Association of Alumni Secretaries, 1917), 10–11.

3. Ibid., 11.

4. William L. Pickett, "Fund-Raising Effectiveness and Donor Motivation," in *Handbook of Institutional Advancement*, 2d ed., ed. A. Westley Rowland (San Francisco: Jossey-Bass, 1986), 236–237.

5. Francis Pray, "The Case Statement as Development Tool," in *Handbook for Educational Fund Raising*, ed. Francis Pray (San Francisco: Jossey-Bass, 1981), 19.

6. Barbara W. Snelling, "Recruiting, Training, and Managing Volunteers," in *Handbook of Institutional Advancement*, 2d ed., ed. A. Westley Rowland (San Francisco: Jossey-Bass, 1986), 68–69.

7. Hank Rosso, "Founder of the Fund Raising School," address at the Big Ten Development Directors Conference, Ohio State University, Columbus, Ohio, June 1987.

8. *Voluntary Support of Education 1985–1986* (New York: Council for Aid to Education, 1987), 8.

9. Quoted by Gary A. Ransdell in "Understanding Professional Roles and Program Mission," in *Handbook of Institutional Advancement*, 2d ed., ed. A. Westley Rowland (San Francisco: Jossey-Bass, 1986), 381.

10. James L. Fisher, *Power of the Presidency* (New York: American Council on Education/Macmillan, 1984), 173.

CHAPTER
7

Alumni Involvement in Student Recruitment

Merilyn H. Bonney

"Alumni are a college or university's permanent trustees," says William Stone, Executive Director of the Stanford Alumni Association. It follows that alumni have a very high stake in assuring the ongoing excellence of their alma mater by becoming involved in the recruitment of maximally qualified students.

The positive impact alumni involvement can have on the quality of the student body has been well proven by institutions such as Brown, Dartmouth, and the University of Pennsylvania. The benefits of involving alumni in diverse and meaningful ways in the admissions process are so great that we at the University of Redlands regard our alumni as the key to facing the joint challenges of improving the quality of matriculants while recruiting from a declining pool of college students.

To begin a program that produces a corps of alumni recruiters who are well informed, well trained, and well motivated to help you meet your particular admissions challenge, think in terms of these three stages: planning, building, and maintaining.

PLANNING

Before you begin your program, you must have the full endorsement of the administration. Because tensions will inevitably develop between the alumni and admissions offices, broad institutional commitment is imperative.

Next, the alumni and admissions offices should clearly define the roles they will play in the program and establish regular channels of communication. Since the program at Redlands has been run out of the admissions office for the past eight years, we have drawn up a contract of understanding between the two offices so that no details will fall through the cracks.

Opinions around the country vary as to where the primary responsibility for such programs should settle. While the alumni staff knows best the talents of the alumni population and is skilled at serving and communicating with this group, the admissions staff knows more precisely what help it needs in the student recruitment effort. Until recently, the prevailing opinion favored location in the admissions office, but more and more programs are coming under the supervision of the alumni office.

You must do a needs assessment before you establish the direction of your program. Do you have a large pool of prospects inquiring about your institution? If not, your program should emphasize asking alumni to refer names of prospective students. Does an appropriate percentage of the inquiry pool actually apply? If not, use your alumni volunteers to contact prospects in the inquiry pool. Does an appropriate percentage of students who are admitted pay their deposits? If not, use alumni representatives to make phone calls or hold informal meetings in their homes. Do most of those who pay their deposits actually show up in the fall? If not, use alumni to hold midsummer send-off parties to introduce new students in the area to each other and to current students.

Once you have determined your institution's needs, you should develop a budget and have it approved. Be sure to include sufficient staffing and funding to achieve your goals. You will damage the whole alumni relations and admissions effort if you don't have the staff and the money to do what you say you're going to do.

After your budget has been approved, staffing is the next step. Hiring the right person to serve as alumni/admissions coordinator may be your most important task. And it is also the task most likely to cause conflict with your colleagues in admissions. This is because you need someone in this position whose skills and abilities resemble yours, rather than those of an admissions counselor. He or she should be a good writer, a good teacher, a good "detail person," and have a good track record of organizing events. He or she should be enthusiastic and unfailingly reliable with follow-through. But most important, the alumni/admissions coordinator needs to be an enabler, a behind-the-scenes person who facilitates the productive involvement of others. He or she should be ready and willing to give credit to the alumni volunteers when the program succeeds and to accept responsibility if it should fail.

BUILDING YOUR PROGRAM

Start to build your program by identifying the alumni volunteers you'll need. It is fairly easy to build a large corps of volunteers by a combination of selective direct mail and personal recruiting. You can prepare a direct mail piece inviting alumni to become involved in student recruiting and send it to the age and geographical groups you have selected. It's important to have volunteers who live in your primary admissions markets, so you may need to do some special recruitment to get the right volunteers in the right places. Select enthusiastic and articulate volunteers who have demonstrated reliability in follow-through in other types of service.

As your program grows in sophistication, you can establish recruitment committees in key areas so that your top volunteers are leading and involving other talented volunteers. Your volunteers will need to be trained before they can participate in the recruitment program. While all institutions benefit from and appreciate the informal involvement of alumni who refer the children of friends and relatives to their alma maters, today's admissions programs need more sophisticated help. On-campus training is ideal, but off-campus training, well-written volunteer handbooks, and training videos are possible alternatives.

MAINTAINING YOUR PROGRAM

Three elements are necessary to maintain an effective alumni/admissions program: alumni must be kept informed; they must receive prompt and reliable service from the office staffing the program; and they must be given frequent and appropriate recognition.

Information

After the initial training, alumni should receive handbook updates, current admissions materials as they come out, and a regular newsletter. Other information that they may need should be given them by telephone.

Service

Service to volunteers needs to be regular and prompt. Specific questions must be answered promptly and feedback on the status of prospective students given as appropriate.

Recognition

Key to the maintenance of a good alumni/admissions program is frequent, public, personal thank-yous to individual volunteers and regular public acknowledgment of the cumulative impact of the program on student recruitment.

OTHER WAYS TO INVOLVE ALUMNI
IN STUDENT RECRUITMENT

An early 1980s study of undergraduates showed that in most cases the final decision on attending an institution was made because of the strong recommendation of a friend, teacher, or member of the family. A 1981 study at Redlands identified alumni as the second most important influence in a student's decision to come to Redlands, the quality of the academic program being the first. And a 1987 study for Redlands by Jan Krukowski Associates showed that successful alumni are an important factor in a prospective student's choice of college.

While not all of your alumni will be able or willing to serve in the alumni/admissions program, they can still help in the recruitment effort. Through articles in our alumni publications and suggestions at alumni events, we attempt to instill a sense of pride in the past, present, and future of the University of Redlands. We suggest to alumni that they mention their alma mater in professional and social conversations, and that they display memorabilia such as Redlands car decals or wear Redlands T-shirts. We frequently publish coupons asking alumni to send us the names of prospective students, and we plan activities for alumni children during major campus events. We send letters to alumni whose relatives apply to Redlands, praising them for passing on the "Redlands tradition." Almost all alumni are pleased to be informally involved in these subtle forms of student recruitment.

Alumni who are willing to be more involved in student recruitment may participate in the following activities, for which they will need some training:

1. *Making phone calls to prospective students in inquiry, application, and admitted stages.*   Recruit alumni volunteers according to geographical patterns determined by the admissions office and assign the alumni to prospective students with the same ZIP code. This is most effective when the same alumni volunteer nurtures a student through inquiry, application, and matriculation.

2. *Hosting parties for prospective students.*   Alumni volunteers can host parties in their homes or make hotel arrangements for local student recruitment events. For example, Redlands alumni hold small gatherings in their homes for high-achieving high school juniors. In the fall or winter, they organize meetings for prospective students; in the spring they host dessert parties for admitted students; and in midsummer they co-sponsor send-off parties with current students. Other institutions have been successful with holiday parties that bring together current and prospective students in an area.

3. *Working as liaison to high school staff.* Prominent alumni "opinion leaders" sometimes carry more clout with high school administrative and teaching staffs than admissions professionals. They can obtain referrals of prospective students and do groundwork for high school visitations.

4. *Assisting at information sessions.* Alumni are valuable assistants at college nights or fairs and (with training) can even serve as primary staff when these events are held at a considerable distance from campus.

5. *Interviewing prospective students.* There is no substitute for personal contact in selling the institution and in making an accurate assessment of the applicant. With appropriate training, alumni can interview prospective students who cannot visit campus. In doing so, alumni serve as a role model for those prospective students who are your future alumni.

6. *Hosting dinners for high school counselors and other alumni in secondary education.* These dinners can give high school opinion leaders a chance to learn about the institution. High school personnel need up-to-date information if they are to direct to your institution the right students for the right reasons.

7. *Watching local newspapers for news of outstanding high school students and sending these articles to the admissions office.* The admissions office can follow up by sending recruiting materials to these students.

8. *Providing an alumni scholarship.* Many alumni clubs raise money for scholarship assistance for an outstanding local student. This not only benefits the recipient, but it increases awareness of the institution among the high school and parent populations.

9. *Offering services to admitted students.* Alumni can help a new student by providing a summer job, transportation to school, and introductions to current undergraduates in the area.

10. *Providing specialized recruiting assistance.* Some alumni are more comfortable recruiting for a particular field or school within the institution—a physician may wish to recruit pre-med students, for example.

SUMMARY

At the University of Redlands, we've developed a list of do's and don'ts that we follow in dealing with volunteers:

1. *Do* make your volunteers feel special; make them feel that they were recruited for the program because they are the elite of the alumni population.

2. *Do* give frequent and complete information so that your volunteers will feel comfortable and will give accurate information.

3. *Do* thank your volunteers regularly for the helpful things they do.

4. *Don't* create expectations for the volunteers that you can't deliver. *Do* make sure you have the staff for prompt accurate follow-through on requests for assistance or information. *Do* be compulsive about follow-up: earn a reputation for reliability, concern, and appreciation.

5. *Do* identify and then attempt to recruit the type of person you consider to be the ideal representative of your institution.

Some institutions, for example, prefer to use young alumni as recruiters. At Redlands, we consider several factors when we recruit our recruiters: activities while on campus, other involvement as alumni, articulateness, enthusiasm, and record of follow-through. We are particularly pleased when we find a married professional couple, who have glowingly bright and popular high-school-aged children and who just happen to live in a great house for meetings!

Once your alumni become active in the alumni/admissions program, you will find that the incentive for continued involvement is built in. Alumni are proud to be valued for their service; they are enthusiastic about helping to assure the continuing quality of the student population of their alma mater. They are gratified at being part of the solution to the problem of the declining pool of college-bound students.

Even a minimally staffed and budgeted but sensitively run program can improve both the quality and the quantity of matriculants, and as a result the admissions budget can often be reduced. And not only does the institution receive these obvious benefits, but as the alumni recruiters become more involved in the institution and more knowledgeable about it, they will become active financial supporters and enthusiastic volunteers in other areas of service.

CHAPTER
8

Alumni and Career Placement

JOHN B. CARTER, JR.

No one can be sure about the genesis of alumni career placement. The alumni association executive who first helped an alumnus find a job probably did so as a favor to a friend. This kind of informal networking likely occurred for years before anybody thought of formalizing the process. Such is the nature of services typically provided by an alumni association. Without the formal structure of the association, many services might be construed as acts of friendship. And what could be friendlier than helping someone find a job?

Among the dividends of helping alumni find jobs are the loyalty and commitment they feel toward the alumni association and the university as a result. This alone is reason enough to consider adding an alumni career placement program to the services already offered by an alumni association.

At its simplest level, a career placement program provides a mechanism for matching qualified alumni with openings in the job market. The more sophisticated career placement program includes several levels of advisory and referral services ranging from job bulletins to open resume files to research libraries to career conferences.

You can begin a career placement program with the simpler services and add more as staff and funding become available. You will also need a business plan for the program, allowing enough time for it to develop and achieve self-sufficiency.

But before you add an alumni career placement program to your activities, you should consider these seven key points:

1. *Funding.* The alumni association must be prepared to invest start-up funds for a three- to five-year period. How much depends upon the services to be provided.

2. *Staffing.* At bare minimum, the program should start with a full-time director and a half-time secretary. The qualifications of these individuals will depend on the specific services to be offered.

3. *Location.* It is vital that the placement program have a permanent location visible to alumni and to companies planning to use the service. An ideal location is near the student placement operation. This provides visibility among graduating students and companies coming to campus to hire graduates.

4. *Identity and cost.* There must be a clear distinction between student placement and alumni placement. Student placement comes under the scrutiny of the College Placement Council and typically operates free of charge to hiring companies. This is the main difference between student and alumni placement. Successful alumni placement programs usually charge companies for the privilege of access to alumni. By the time graduates return to the alumni association for help in finding a new job, they are experienced members of the work force. And the fee is extremely low compared to the cost of hiring experienced workers through traditional methods, that is, professional recruiters and advertising. The alumni themselves should not pay for the placement service, although you will probably charge a fee if you offer seminars or workshops on career planning or career transitions.

5. *Supply and demand.* If you are evaluating the feasibility of an alumni placement program, look at the student placement program at your institution. If private industry is actively supporting this operation, it will probably support an alumni program as well. For example, private industry today has a great demand for personnel with technical training and experience, and companies will support a student or alumni placement program at a university that produces technically trained people. Private industry is less likely to support either a student placement program or an alumni placement program at an institution whose graduates and alumni are prepared for professions in "soft" markets where supply exceeds demand.

If your institution is in this latter category, you have an excellent opportunity to focus career programs on advisory services. With fewer jobs available in their fields, alumni will welcome advice on how to compete in soft markets. The alumni placement program at such an institution should be designed quite differently from that at an institution that trains graduates for hot job markets.

6. *Fund raising for the institution.* The alumni career placement program can provide funding for the institution, but only over the long term

and not as a direct result of day-to-day operations. Funds received by the institution as a result of alumni career placement evolve from satisfied alumni who have received help in a time of need. Satisfied alumni are better-than-average candidates to become contributors.

7. *Young alumni.* An ongoing concern of many alumni associations is the difficulty of involving young alumni. The good news about alumni career placement is that nearly 85 percent of all alumni who participate are young alumni who have been out of school less than a decade.

An alumni placement program can be broken down into two categories—referral services and advisory services. Advisory services provide education, and referral services, the practical application. You can offer one without the other, but only through referral services do alumni have the opportunity to use the skills learned from advisory services. This is where the results are measured and where the loyalty factor is implanted.

There are eight primary referral services you can offer through your alumni placement program.

1. *Open resume file.* The placement program maintains a file of resumes of alumni interested in making career changes. Companies come to the alumni placement office, review the resumes, and interview alumni qualified for their job openings. This is usually a no-cost service.

2. *Weekly job bulletin.* The bulletin, in a newsletter format, is mailed to alumni who are interested in knowing about employment opportunities. Companies generally pay a nominal fee to include a job opening in the bulletin, which is mailed first-class, free of charge. Alumni respond directly to jobs listed in the bulletin.

3. *Part-time/temporary employment.* While most alumni placement programs are concerned with permanent employment, there is a need for part-time and temporary employment referrals. While this program is generally directed at undergraduate and graduate students, alumni who are between jobs or are interested in part-time employment may also benefit. The program essentially refers individuals to companies who have temporary or part-time employment needs. These programs are usually less structured than other alumni placement ones and are often a joint venture between the student and alumni placement offices.

An additional benefit is that you are providing another service to alumni—most of the companies that take advantage of this service do so because of a particular interest of an alumnus already working for the company.

4. *Recruitment advertising.* Through alumni publications, the alumni placement office can provide the entire alumni body with information on companies with employment openings. Companies with vacancies can reach the alumni readership through paid ads.

5. *Career conference.* Only a few alumni associations offer this unique service, which is patterned after job fairs that have been in existence for years. Companies pay a fee to attend a two- to three-day conference where they can hold on-site interviews with alumni. Such a conference, held once a year, might attract 80 companies and 800 alumni. While the conference is free to alumni, the companies pay from $600 to $1,000 to attend.

6. *Professional recruiters.* For years, the college placement industry has avoided liaisons with professional recruiters, mainly because the college placement office lost control of the situation once a referral to a professional recruiter was made.

Professional recruiters can, however, provide valuable services to the alumni career placement program. For example, the placement office can create a confidential database containing resumes submitted by alumni. A recruiter can submit specific job requirements, which are then compared with the qualifications of alumni. When matches are found, the placement office releases the appropriate resumes to the recruiter. When a company eventually hires an alumnus, it pays all placement fees and interview and relocation costs. The service is usually free to alumni, but the alumni association can negotiate with the recruiting firm for a percentage of the placement fee.

7. *Computer referrals.* Yet another way to use a database of resumes is to make it available to companies with employment openings. The main difference between this program and the professional recruiter's is that companies pay for the right to search and/or for a referral whether they hire the individual or not. The fee is usually considerably less than a company would pay a professional recruiter. Recent breakthroughs in communication technology make the potential in this area virtually unlimited. The key to the success of this service is providing the companies with an easily accessible search tool.

8. *Computer networks.* In some referral services, job openings and reference materials are available via on-line computer networks accessible through a toll-free number. Most advisory and referral services also can be

entered into the computer bank for access by alumni. There are very few such services in existence, but the potential for expansion will increase greatly in the months and years ahead as the alumni population becomes more computer-literate.

The ideal complement to referral services are the four advisory services below:

1. *Career counseling.* Most universities have a career counseling center for students. Some permit alumni to participate at no cost. The service generally includes testing programs for determining career interest and offers professional evaluations by industrial psychologists. The people who evaluate the tests and advise participating alumni should be licensed psychologists.

2. *Career seminars and workshops.* These may be offered as three- to five-hour seminars or workshops on Saturday morning or as a course in the continuing education program. Whatever the format, the program usually covers the following topics: resume preparation; career planning; interviewing techniques; networking; personal evaluation; employer evaluation; and self-marketing.

3. *Career advisory program.* This service matches students and young alumni interested in gathering information on a particular career with alumni who are established in that profession. There is no cost to the participants. The program is a good opportunity to involve older alumni in meaningful activities that will help students and younger alumni. This service works best in one-on-one situations, and the amount of involvement depends on the participants. Sometimes a telephone conversation will suffice. At other times, the student or young alumnus may spend time at the workplace of the older alumnus, and the arrangement may evolve into a lasting mentor relationship or even an employment opportunity.

4. *Research Library.* The research library contains information on career planning, resume preparation, and so on, as well as information on potential employers (annual reports, industry trends). The library is usually located in the alumni placement office and may be a joint venture with the student placement office.

Most major colleges and universities provide some type of alumni career program. Universities well-known for successful career programs are Georgia Institute of Technology, Harvard University, Massachusetts Institute of Technology, Michigan State University, Stanford University, and the University of Texas. The alumni association executive who manages the career placement program is an excellent source of information and advice.

CONCLUSION

As you can see, to develop all the programs mentioned would require much more than the one and one-half people needed to initiate your program. This is a building process. Keep in mind that the success of your program depends not only on the commitment of your alumni association to fund and staff the operation, but also quite heavily on the law of supply and demand in the job market.

An alumni placement program is an investment—an investment in your institution's future. A successful program is an extremely valuable tool for involving alumni and for developing a loyalty to your institution that will pay many many dividends for years to come.

PART

3

People Management

CHAPTER
9

Professional Staff Selection and Development

R<small>AY</small> W<small>ILLEMAIN</small>

As alumni supervisors, one of the most important tasks you have is to manage the personnel for whom you are responsible. While management is a critical element in any organization, both nonprofit and profit making, it is probably the least understood. If you don't give it enough time in your daily schedule, you will have to contend with staff discontent and turnover. Besides being costly in time and resources, lack of management will hinder your efforts to develop an effective alumni program.

But when you manage your personnel effectively, you can count on a degree of stability in your staff that will make it possible to develop long-range plans as well as advancement opportunities for those whose skills have been honed through proper encouragement and support. This chapter outlines some of the factors involved in establishing a sound personnel management program.

PREHIRING PROCEDURES

When a vacancy occurs in your office, view it as an opportunity to reexamine the position *before* you advertise the opening. You should review and, if necessary, modify the job description to reflect the present and future requirements of the position. For example, you need to answer the following questions: Should any changes be made in the duties to be performed? The qualifications required by the position? The supervision necessary and the person to whom the employee will report? Think about the work station or office of the employee. Is it appropriate for the tasks to be performed or should the person be located elsewhere? You may want to consult other staff members, particularly those who will supervise or work with or for the employee, to gain their insights on how the position can be improved.

The Search

Advertise the position in professional journals, alumni publications, local papers, and the personnel department of your institution. Confer with colleagues in other alumni offices who may know of likely prospects. Be sure to take all the time you need to locate qualified applicants. *And be patient*. For this is *the* crucial step in building a qualified and dedicated staff. It is better to leave the position open for an extended period of time than to hire someone who does not fulfill the requirements. Hiring the wrong person practically guarantees that the position will be open again in the not-too-distant future—or that you will wish it were. As the saying goes, "Hire in haste and regret at leisure."

The Interview

Once you have a pool of qualified candidates, ask each one to submit a resume. Before the interview, go over the candidate's resume, noting strengths and weaknesses and developing questions you will ask. (But be sure to ask your personnel department which questions *not* to ask. For example, don't ask a female applicant how long her husband plans to remain in his present job. Don't ask any applicant how old he or she is.) Look carefully for continuity of employment in the candidate's work record and make sure each job includes the immediate supervisor and/or the manager of the business. You will need this information for references.

Schedule the interview so that you have sufficient time to meet with the applicant *without interruptions*. Have your phone calls held and don't schedule a meeting immediately afterward. It is difficult to evaluate an applicant if you are constantly looking at your watch.

Once you have selected the one or two best qualified applicants from those you have interviewed, have other subordinates in your department interview them before you make your decision. They may discover strengths or weaknesses that you did not see. And participating in the interviewing process will make them feel that they are part of the team. Because they have been consulted on this important decision, they will enthusiastically welcome the new employee to the department.

Checking References

I consider one category of references to be practically useless, namely, those who are not professional or business references—friends, relatives, the local banker or physician. No candidate is going to list someone in this category who will give a negative response.

The important references are those of previous supervisors and fellow workers. You should check these references thoroughly and always by telephone. People will speak more freely over the telephone than they will in a letter. You can tell a lot about a supervisor's real feelings from a change in tone of voice or a pause before he or she answers a question. Don't hesitate to probe until you are satisfied with all the business and professional references.

STAFF DEVELOPMENT

Training

In order to perform well on the job, your new employee must have thoughtful training. Before his or her first day of work, you should plan a training schedule that includes office procedures, institutional regulations, hours required, dress code, telephone etiquette, and so on.

During the first week on the job, your employee should visit with each member of the professional staff so that he or she understands what each person contributes to the alumni program. You should personally introduce the staff person to others in the institution with whom he or she will be interacting. This will help the new employee develop a sense of the mission of the institution and the important part his or her efforts will play in that mission.

Motivation

Most of us do not spend enough one-on-one time with the members of our staffs. All too often, we assume that they intuitively know when we are pleased with their work (and so we don't need to tell them), but we are quick to speak out when they make mistakes.

The most effective way to build staff stability and improve productivity is to tell your staff members frequently how well they are doing. Give them public recognition as often as possible, and praise each person in staff meetings when he or she completes a project.

If you hope to run a successful operation, you must hold regular staff meetings. You must make sure staff members feel free to participate with ideas, suggestions, and even criticisms. The more they contribute to discussions, the more they will strive to be the best among the best.

Recognition of special days in their lives is important. A birthday card, a personal note on the date of their employment anniversary, or a get-together of the whole staff to celebrate a good year will help establish the esprit de corps that unites a staff. These acts of appreciation are the greatest motivating tools that a manager can use. One of the most difficult things to give away is kindness—it's always returned.

Remember, most personnel surveys indicate that salary is not the most important factor in job satisfaction; the greatest priority is appreciation.

Interpersonal Relationships

Disputes will inevitably arise between staff members. The easy ones can be resolved by clarifying jurisdiction or explaining a misunderstanding. The more difficult ones require your immediate attention. The longer you delay, the more serious the situation will become. Bad feelings will fester and harsh words that are spoken will add fuel to the flame. Try discussing the situation with each of the people involved and then attempt to bring them together to resolve the issues as quickly as possible.

Safeguard against interdepartment disagreements that often arise from an exchange of angry memos when something goes wrong. It is much better to use "foot diplomacy." Make an appointment to visit the person involved and discuss the situation in a calm and intelligent way. Usually, you can resolve these problems without any acrimony remaining in the relationship.

Freedom to Grow

Give your staff members the opportunity to grow in their positions. Start out by defining the objectives and goals that are to be achieved, and then allow each staff person to approach the task in his or her own way and style. There are many ways to go about a task, and each staff member should be permitted to perform in the most productive way possible.

Encourage your employees to experiment with new ideas and programs even if they should sometimes fail. This creates an exciting atmosphere and may lead to surprising results.

You will find the role of an adviser much more rewarding than that of a supervisor who dictates all the activities and stifles creativity.

Staff Retreats

I recommend holding a professional staff retreat once a year. I prefer retreats of a day and a half, without interruptions, at a location away from the office and not including spouses.

Prepare your agenda carefully and work to establish full and open discussion of all issues and problems. The goal of professional retreats is a renewal of purpose among staff members, but they also foster lasting friendships between staff members and the development of a greater esprit de corps.

Staff Evaluations

Every employee is entitled to a performance review once a year. While you can write up the evaluation, you should go over it with the staff member. You should prepare carefully for each review. The evaluation should include strengths and accomplishments as well as problems that need to be solved. When you meet with the employee, the conversation should be candid and thoughtful. Make sure the employee expresses his or her concerns and that all the issues are resolved before ending the meeting.

Exit Interviews

An exit interview may not be possible or profitable if an employee is fired or leaves with a grievance. But when a staff member leaves in an amicable fashion, an exit interview can be very informative. Encourage him or her to tell you what was right or wrong with the job and how it can be improved. You can gain new insights into staff relationships and take steps to correct certain problems.

CONCLUSION

To build a competent and dedicated staff requires a thoughtful approach to each staff member's needs. It also requires leadership that establishes a style of management that builds and nurtures the morale of a department.

Personnel problems can be avoided through daily attentiveness to areas of distress or aggravation. Patience is essential and a willingness to listen to the concerns of employees. If managers wish to decrease turnover and increase productivity, they must make personnel requirements the number one priority on their schedules.

CHAPTER 10

Alumni Association Boards of Directors

ROBERT L. GALE

The alumni of our colleges and universities have always been terribly important to their various institutions; but as our society has become more complex and the needs of our institutions greater, the role alumni can and must play becomes more important than ever. As a result, all institutions of higher education—both public and private colleges and universities—are depending more and more on their alumni.

Our institutions need alumni help in a variety of ways—from fund raising and fund giving to lobbying at the state and federal level and helping in admissions marketing, placement of recent graduates, and general public relations. Many other partnerships between institutions and their alumni could be added to that list.

A supportive—and sometimes appropriately critical—alumni body can be marshaled effectively only if there is a well-organized alumni association led by a strong board of directors. The role of the alumni association is to advance the goals of the institution by involving alumni and providing them with opportunities to help their alma mater. And the board of directors of the alumni association acts as a catalyst to see that this happens.

What, then, are the specific responsibilities of the board of directors of an alumni association? The alumni board, working through the alumni director, can help carry out the goals for the institution as set by its governing board and president. A close working relationship here, with appropriate involvement by the president, can help the alumni board develop a program that advances these goals. But in no case should the alumni board try to usurp the powers of the governing board of the institution.

The other major role of the alumni association board is to identify the needs and desires of the alumni and to channel these desires for involvement into initiatives that advance the long-range goals of the institution. Many alumni feel a strong sense of continued responsibility to, and pride in, the institution and are prepared to help maintain and improve the quality of the institution. Many—if not most—strongly believe in the value of higher education and prefer to involve themselves in that larger purpose through their alma mater.

Alumni associations are organized in many different ways; some are autonomous but most are connected directly to the institution. Many alumni executives are selected by the administration in consultation with the alumni board; others are jointly selected; and the independent alumni association chooses on its own.

Some alumni associations are fraught with politics; others have practically none. Much of this has to do with the past history of the alumni association, the degree of autonomy, and even the personality of the current president of the college or university. If you can ignore all of those politics for the moment, here are some suggestions for improving the board of your alumni association.

ORGANIZE THE STRUCTURE OF THE BOARD THROUGH BYLAWS

The best way to improve the operating structure of a board is by carefully putting together a set of bylaws that cover the following important issues:

Size of Board

A board should be large enough so that it has the diversity to represent all of the constituencies in the alumni body and also include the kinds of skills needed to function effectively. It should be small enough for manageability so that good discussions can be held. It should be large enough to take on the many assignments needed to carry out the plan of the alumni association. It should be small enough to be a cohesive working unit. So how big should it be? Perhaps somewhere around 25, plus or minus a few.

Terms of Office

While a board needs stability, it must also have enough change so that interested alumni can get involved. There are many options, but a number of boards use three-year staggered terms with a maximum of two terms possible. A board member who has not participated fully during his or her first term would not automatically be given a second. Some associations allow the fantastic few who have served so well for two terms to be reelected after a year off. The officers, too, should have limited terms, but be careful that they are not moved so frequently that they don't have a chance to make an impact on the alumni board and its programs. For example, an alumnus who serves a one-year term as president of the association does not have a chance to develop good working relationships or to complete program initiatives. Perhaps two years would be a good compromise term for any given office.

Selection Procedures

The preferred method of choosing the board is to have a strong nominating committee that solicits recommendations from the entire alumni body, from members of the alumni board, and from other appropriate sources. The nominating committee screens the nominees and then recommends candidates for election by the board. A number of associations have open elections, but unfortunately this system tends not to populate the board with the kinds of people needed to carry out the particular programs adopted by the board. In addition, when two people are put up against each other, the one who loses is bound to feel rejected even if he or she claims otherwise. If open elections are unavoidable, however, you should try to influence the nominating procedure so that the kinds of talents needed are selected.

Committee Structure

The best way to get good participation and run good programs is to have a strong committee structure with active committee members. The committees most often used by alumni association boards include:

The executive committee.   This committee should handle only routine business between meetings of the regular board. It should always report to the full board expeditiously. It is important that the executive committee does not set policy. If it plays too strong a role, the rest of the board will feel left out. At the same time, matters that need to be settled may come up between board meetings.

The nominating committee.   This committee is one of the most important. It needs to be strong in order to work hard to put together the most effective board possible. It should have a written charge requiring members to meet on a regular basis to determine the current needs of the board, identify alumni to meet those needs, cultivate them, and orient them when they join the board. The nominating committee also reviews the performance of current board members to see if they should be re-elected and recommends appropriate officers.

The program committee. This committee is the key to all current and future activities of the alumni association. It is from this committee that the following committees spring, and it is responsible for alumni programming in the field as well as on campus.

The admissions/marketing committee. In recent years, this committee has become vitally important for most institutions. As the number of 18-year-olds has declined, the role of alumni in recruiting potential students has grown dramatically. This committee works closely with the admissions department of the institution to identify, cultivate, and interview potential students.

The placement committee. This committee is an excellent vehicle for involving alumni in the institution. Well-placed alumni can assist in finding jobs for recent graduates in cities about the country, and they can visit campus to discuss with seniors their profession or job area.

The development committee. This one has also become a vital adjunct to the regular fund-raising operation of each college and university. This committee helps plan ways to raise money from alumni and is involved in alumni deferred-giving programs, class gifts, and other efforts to bring financial stability to the institution.

The finance committee. In recent years, this committee has become much more common. Because there have been a number of scandals, many of them the result of error rather than wrongdoing, and because board members are legally liable, it has now become the practice to have a committee that oversees the finances of the alumni association.

Ad hoc committees. The bylaws should include provision for forming ad hoc committees to take on special projects. These committees should not continue indefinitely but should terminate when the particular project is completed. Including alumni who are not board members on these committees is a good way to evaluate these alumni for future membership on the alumni association board.

ENLISTING AND TRAINING AN EFFECTIVE BOARD

A board is only as strong as its individual members, and only through the use of a strong nominating committee can a strong board be built. How, then, do you build such a board? First, there must be agreement on the ideal composition of the board; then candidates must be identified and enlisted to fill the agreed-upon matrix.

Composition

The board, through its nominating committee, must decide what talents are needed. This would include expertise and experience in certain professions such as the law, banking and business, marketing and public relations, and so on. The people with these talents must also have an interest in the institution and in serving on the board; they must have the time to give (but remember that busy people tend to be the best workers); and they will need a sense of humor. In addition, collectively these people must reflect the diversity of the institution's alumni body as to age, race, sex, geographical location, and, where relevant, religion.

Identifying Potential Board Members

In most cases, too little attention is paid to finding just the right people to fill the available slots. The nominating committee should ask the entire alumni association to suggest names, and it should press the board to do the same. In the long run, however, the nominating committee usually ends up identifying most of the candidates.

There are several ways to find people who will give time and energy to board membership. Look for evidence of involvement such as giving to the annual fund, participating in club activities, serving on campus committees, visiting campus, and so on. Alumni who are parents of current students frequently make good prospects, as well as alumni who were active during their campus days. Review past yearbooks to identify those who were especially active.

Once the names have been gathered, check their past performance as volunteers: have they performed well on other nonprofit boards?

Cultivation of Potential Board Members

Sometimes the nominating committee identifies several "perfect" prospects who have never been involved in the past. Committee members may feel that these people will decline if they are asked to join the board without prior cultivation. In this case, the board should organize a campaign to cultivate the prospects to the point where an invitation would probably be accepted. For example, they could be invited to campus events, taken to lunch by appropriate officials, or invited to participate on a committee.

The Invitation

Far too often the invitation to serve on the board comes in a letter or a casual telephone call. Unless you are confident that the prospect will accept, it makes sense to select the best person or team to make the approach. This might include the president of the alumni association, the chair of the nominating committee, and the alumni director, or the president of the institution when appropriate. If at all possible, this group should make a personal call on the prospect, but a conference telephone call is an acceptable substitute if the prospect lives far from campus. The team should carefully explain the duties and responsibilities of a board member so that the prospect understands exactly what will be expected of him or her.

Orienting New Board Members

Orientation should be the responsibility of the nominating committee, but strong staff back-up is necessary. The committee should hold a training session just before the first board meeting the new member will attend. If he or she lives nearby, the training session could take place as soon as the invitation has been accepted. Orientation should include a discussion of the duties of a director, a brief review of the purposes of the alumni association, and an update on the exciting things the college or university is doing.

The new member should also receive a packet of information on how the alumni board functions (including minutes of recent meetings) and how the alumni association is organized, as well as background information about the institution so that he or she can speak knowledgeably about its strengths and needs. But don't send too much information or it won't get read. One way to prevent the new board member from being overwhelmed is to use the "buddy system" and assign him or her to a current board member who will answer any questions the newcomer may have.

Using New Board Members

New board members should be involved immediately since their first official meeting is often several months after their election. Assign them to an appropriate committee or two, particularly an ad hoc committee, so they can get involved with board activities *before* their first meeting. A telephone call, and perhaps a follow-up luncheon with the president of the alumni association and the alumni director, can make them feel involved and give them a chance to ask any questions they might have.

IMPROVING THE CURRENT BOARD

There are several methods to improve a board already in existence: You can develop better leadership, make an inactive board more active, or an overactive board more inactive. And you can work to get rid of deadwood.

Developing Leadership

It is important to identify potential leaders—and this will probably be your most difficult task—and then get them more involved. You can do this by moving them up on committees and eventually making them chair of a committee; by giving them special assignments such as chairing an ad hoc committee; and by involving them in local club activities in their part of the country. Regularly rotating officers will also give potential leaders a chance to serve at higher levels in the association. The president of the institution can help too: when he or she believes that the work of the alumni association is terribly important to the future of the institution and makes this belief clear to alumni, good leaders are more likely to be willing to serve on the alumni association board.

The Inactive Board

You can make an inactive board more active by judiciously dropping ineffective members and adding the right people. Strong leadership, especially from the president of the alumni association, can prod and inspire the board. Reinvigoration of the board might include instigating—perhaps over their dead bodies!—some exciting new programs that would catch the imagination of even the most inactive members. And this might call for the involvement of the president of the institution to show once again the importance of the alumni association to the college or university.

Self-assessment of the board and its performance can help. These assessments, which frequently use an outside catalyst from another institution as the moderator and take place in a retreat situation, can turn the entire board around. But, in all cases, an inactive board needs to have meatier agendas to consider. Too frequently, alumni board agendas are made up of housekeeping items and unexciting policy issues that can be discussed in tedious depth but have no real impact.

The Too-Active Board

You may wish you had a too-active board, but such a board can cause serious problems by continually crossing the line between policy and administration. Once again, a retreat for self-assessment can calm down the activists. Also needed is a strong alumni association president to preside over and control the board when it is in session. At the same time, and behind the scenes, the moderates on the board should be organized and an appropriate nominating committee should be encouraged to bring better balance to the board.

Dealing with Deadwood

The best way to get rid of a totally inactive board member is to have the courage not to renominate him or her. But in the meantime, proper cultivation may perk up even the least involved. The president of the alumni association might try taking the board member to lunch and talking over the apparent lack of interest. Often such a meeting turns up an area of special interest that can inspire the board member to get involved.

MESHING THE ORGANIZATION
AND THE PEOPLE
INTO A DYNAMIC BOARD

You can't build and maintain a strong board unless the alumni association is carrying out an important program that attracts the kind of people needed. This program should include:

- a network of active alumni clubs;
- well-organized homecoming celebrations and reunions;
- dynamic marketing and admissions recruitment programs;
- effective placement and counseling initiatives;
- a visually attractive and editorially sound publications program; and
- last but not least, a carefully structured program to assist the institution in raising money.

In other words, the program should help to achieve the goals of the college or university while keeping the alumni informed and involved.

The Role of the Alumni Officer in
Dealing with the Board

The alumni officer's first responsibility is to carry out the alumni association program as directed by the board. He or she should also make sure that individual board members and board committees are given appropriate staff back-up. The alumni officer should also help identify, cultivate, enlist, and orient strong board members, and work closely with the president of the alumni association to develop exciting and substantive agendas. No alumni officer should ever forget to thank hard-working board members, both publicly and privately. And, finally, he or she should have the courage to give the board as much responsibility as possible even at the risk that it may run occasionally in the wrong direction.

The Role of the President of the Alumni Association

The chief alumni officer can expect certain things from the president of the association, who serves as liaison to the rest of the board. The association president conducts productive meetings (with coaching in advance, if necessary), works with staff to develop meaningful agendas, helps identify and enlist appropriate new board members, inspires uninspired board members, and deals with problem board members. He or she also acts as liaison to the president of the institution and its governing board. But, most important, he or she participates in the continuing evolvement of a meaningful alumni association program.

The Role of the President of the Institution

If the alumni association is to attract the kind of people needed to build a strong board, the president of the institution must demonstrate that he or she feels a strong alumni program to be one of the top priorities of the institution. To do this, the president should recognize publicly and privately the importance of the alumni board and the program of the association, and he or she should devote an appropriate amount of the limited time available to working with the alumni director, the board, and the far-flung alumni clubs.

CONCLUSION

It takes planning, hard work, and a little bit of luck to develop an alumni board that performs effectively while respecting its role in the total scheme of the institution. But it is worth it if the goals of your institution are advanced and a substantial portion of your alumni feel fulfilled through their involvement with the alumni association.

Alumni Volunteers

Michael J. Koll

THE MARRIAGE

In the early 1900s, a group of classmates gathered to celebrate the success of their first class reunion—also the first class reunion ever held at the University of California. As the evening progressed, talk turned to the next reunion, tentatively scheduled to be held in five years. But having done the enormous amount of work necessary to organize that first successful reunion, the classmates were mute when the call was made for a volunteer to manage the next event. These were young, aspiring professionals already experiencing heavy demands on their time, in both their business and their family lives. While everyone expressed a willingness to assist in the planning, no one was willing to make a total commitment.

It became apparent that, if a successful program was to be established, some sort of support and leadership was needed. The idea emerged that a class member should be hired to assume the role of planning and organizing reunions, not only for this class but for all the classes. The hat was passed among this original group in Berkeley and they gave generously, perhaps out of relief as much as a sense of loyalty; $100 was collected—a sizable sum at the turn of the century.

Robert Sibley, an engineer from the class of 1903, accepted both the challenge and the $100. And thus was founded the California Alumni Association, today one of the world's largest and leading alumni associations. These events at Berkeley also marked the marriage of volunteers and professionals—a marriage that endures today. And like all good marriages, its success is based on mutual respect, the sharing of goals, a clear identification of roles, and general compatibility.

The number of volunteers who respond to their institution's needs has grown by leaps and bounds over the years. Estimates today suggest that there are 37 million; if an actual count were made, that number would probably be even higher.

Undeniably, this large number of volunteers represents a tremendous resource and one we must treat with care. We must ask ourselves: How well are we utilizing this resource? Are our volunteers being identified, cultivated, oriented, evaluated, and rewarded in the most productive manner?

Most professionals in the alumni administration field would point to the great strides that have been made in the use of volunteers during the past several decades, but they would also admit that there is room for improvement. The discussion that follows examines some of the ingredients of a successful volunteer program.

IDENTIFICATION

The alumni association may be totally committed to the use of volunteers, but its programs will not succeed unless it is able to identify those who will be able to serve the institution well. And quantity alone does not mean success; while impressive, an abundance of volunteers can do more harm than good unless they are properly cultivated and utilized. Experience teaches us that not all alumni make good volunteers, no matter how interested and dedicated they may be. Their personal traits, how much time they have available, and where they live may limit their potential. Therefore, whether you are dealing with an alumni body of a few thousand or one of several hundred thousand, you must set up a screening process to identify your best prospects.

To screen prospects, you must first determine what qualities to look for in a volunteer. I have observed that the broader the base of volunteers, the more successful the volunteer effort. Begin with the alumni association staff at all levels and encourage each staff member to identify alumni who have demonstrated a potential for service and leadership. Extend the search by asking administrators, faculty, students, and current volunteers to suggest names of prospects. To maintain continued interest in the search, be sure to extend proper recognition to those who are involved in the recruiting process.

This search should result in the development of a file that contains the following information for each prospect:

- name,
- address,
- biographical material,
- interests,

- availability,
- past service (if any),
- donor records, and
- potential areas of service.

This record will be useful only if it is readily accessible, continually updated, and periodically evaluated. If possible, establish categories that identify, for example, volunteers with current potential, future potential, and declining potential due to changes in circumstances (this might be a group you need to delete from the list).

Today, unless your alumni body is very small you will probably maintain this prospect file on a computer. As biographical information about alumni has become more comprehensive and programming in turn has become more sophisticated, the computer plays an increasingly important role in alumni record keeping. Most alumni associations now use the computer to produce lists that give data about class year, major field of study, areas of current interest, geographical location, and records of past participation. By using these lists, you can divide the alumni body into special "volunteer prospect" groups and then match them with potential areas of service. But regardless of how "high-tech" your office may be, a successful volunteer program remains dependent upon individual evaluations.

CULTIVATION

Once you have identified potentially successful volunteers, you must begin to cultivate them. Put the prospects on both institutional and alumni mailing lists. This will serve two purposes. First, the mailings will add to their knowledge of the institution and its programs and so help create or maintain interest. Second, they will be pleased at this attention as an indication that the institution feels they are worthy of special treatment. This feeling will make them more likely to respond to requests for service.

Other methods of cultivation include workshops, informational meetings, luncheons, dinners, lectures, and newsletters. Even more effective are personal approaches such as a visit, a phone call, a card or letter, small gifts (school calendars, pins), parking privileges on campus, invitations to campus events in the prospect's area of interest, purchasing privileges, and complimentary tickets to events. Each of these cultivation activities has as its goal the development of a strong identification with the institution and therefore a greater desire to serve it.

MATCHING

One area that perhaps receives the least attention nevertheless holds the key to the success of a volunteer program: matching the volunteer with the job. This means preparing an accurate description of the task to be done and then selecting the volunteer who can best meet the demands of the job. A poor match between job and volunteer can be a major source of disappointment, for both the volunteer and the professional staff.

Probably very few alumni associations have actually developed detailed job descriptions for the variety of services they expect their volunteers to perform—even my own association, the California Alumni Association (CAA), at the University of California, Berkeley, has only recently completed comprehensive volunteer job descriptions.

You probably have rather exact expectations for each specific task you assign to volunteers—from the envelope stuffer to the association president. If your volunteers fail to meet your expectations, it may be that you did not communicate precisely the responsibilities you had in mind. Few volunteers will knowingly accept more responsibilities than they can handle. It's up to you to see that they do not inadvertently do so.

Begin at the top by developing a list of the total scope of responsibilities for the members of the board of the association. While many of their responsibilities are obvious, don't forget their special involvements—meetings with committees and staff, serving on university committees, participating in university and civic events, travel and entertainment (some of which is not reimbursed). Also of importance, but not always spelled out, is time spent—often on weekends and evenings—away from their businesses and families. While most of our top leaders at CAA rise to the occasion, in moments of candor they acknowledge their surprise at the extent of their involvement. They deserve fair warning of what is included in the job before they make a commitment.

Over the many years I have assisted with the orientation of new members of our board of directors, I have found few who have fully understood the commitment that accompanied their election to a three-year term on the board. While these volunteers had a general sense of the basic function they were expected to perform, including required attendance at meetings and board functions, few realized the scope of their involvement. These volunteers were also unaware that they would be representing the university in their local communities and that they would be participating in local club, scholarship, and student recruitment activities. Also surprising to them was the total time they would be expected to give to their association duties as well as the financial commitment (in addition to expenses that would be reimbursed).

The best procedure is to give nominees for these volunteer positions full and accurate descriptions of the extent of their involvement *before* they accept the nomination. This can be accomplished by a letter notifying the volunteer of his or her nomination for a particular office or position and detailing the total commitment involved. Also in the letter should be a request that the volunteer confirm acceptance of the nomination and involvement described. We have found that following this procedure helps us avoid a great deal of misunderstanding.

Volunteers who will serve as club presidents, scholarship chairs, student recruitment leaders, and the heads of a host of other alumni committees deserve the same treatment. Before you invite volunteers to take these positions, ask yourself the following questions. Is there a clearly defined list of responsibilities and expectations for your volunteer leaders? Has a standard been established that will serve as a guide and yardstick for performance? You can't depend on previous volunteer leaders to communicate their roles and responsibilities to their successors. It is much more efficient and reliable if the alumni association itself develops detailed manuals for each committee.

Even those volunteers who are not in leadership positions and who perform only minor functions should have a detailed job description before they accept an assignment. You should be clear and explicit in regard to all volunteer job assignments. If a job requires special skills, describe them; if it is a task best described as tedious, be honest about it. You have an obligation to communicate both the positive and the negative aspects of volunteer involvement. And once you recognize the limited appeal of certain jobs, you may be able to make changes that will make them more enjoyable.

This honesty on your part may result in a few refusals from prospects, but that's better than assigning a volunteer to a job he or she will not do adequately. Not only does this leave you with a job undone or poorly done, but it also gives the volunteer a negative feeling about the association. Volunteers who knowingly accept the commitment of involvement are most likely to contribute productive services to the alumni program and to feel a sense of pride and ownership in the program.

SUPERVISION

Once the volunteer has accepted the responsibility for a particular assignment, your role is that of a supervisor. You will have to provide ongoing guidance just as you would if you had added a new member to the professional staff. The amount of supervision will vary with the extent of the volunteer's involvement and responsibility and his or her knowledge and experience in the particular area of service.

You will need all the tact and diplomacy you can muster when you are dealing with top volunteer leadership—the president of your association, board members, and committee chairs. Frequent meetings between you and the volunteer, perhaps over lunch or breakfast, are the best way to accomplish results. Make discussion rather than direction your aim; establishing rapport with the volunteer leadership is the first step in developing a productive relationship. Once you have established an open channel of communication, you can discuss freely items of procedure and action, and you can work out joint positions.

Volunteers are usually responsive to the professional staff's viewpoints when they are presented in the proper manner. In fact, most volunteers recognize the staff's experience and expertise and appreciate their guidance. Tailor the amount and kind of guidance to the specific volunteer, and this special attention will not only increase productivity but will lead to a better working relationship for all involved.

When dealing with volunteers who are not in leadership positions, you can provide more traditional forms of supervision—that is, concentrate on giving direction at the beginning of the volunteer's involvement and additional help as needed. Early successes or failures of the volunteer will have a lasting effect on his or her performance and attitude, so it is up to you and your staff to ensure that the experience is a positive one for all concerned.

RECOGNITION

Many factors motivate volunteers—among them, loyalty to the institution, the desire to contribute something in return for the university experience, and eagerness to help others, particularly students who are undergoing that same experience. But don't neglect the motivating force that comes from recognition and praise; these are always appreciated. Volunteers who contribute many hours of service to your institution deserve special recognition which can range from a simple "thank-you" and a pat on the back to a formal black-tie banquet.

Whatever the form of recognition you provide, it is important to let the volunteers know that you appreciate them for who they are as well as for what they have done. Visit their areas of service and exchange greetings and pleasantries; get to know your volunteers personally and introduce them to other staff members. Be sure to provide an adequate working area and the support they need to perform their assigned tasks. Special "perks" will also help them feel appreciated—such as parking privileges, occasional lunches, and memberships in special university organizations.

At the conclusion of the volunteer's effort, he or she will appreciate a token gift, badge, or certificate (see Figure 11.1). Perhaps more important than the gift is the manner in which it is presented. If you plan a recognition ceremony, it is a good idea to include the top leadership—if not in

FIGURE 11.1. *Certificate awarded to alumni by California Alumni Association, Berkeley, California.*

person then at least by signature. An audience of peers is equally important. If the recognition is for a volunteer who lives far from campus, you can use a club meeting or gathering of alumni in his or her community. If you cannot be present yourself, another representative of the alumni association should be there.

An annual award or recognition banquet provides an excellent format for the recognition of volunteer leadership. Grouping recognitions in one ceremony makes it easier for both institutional and alumni association leaders to participate. Schedule the date well in advance to allow time for planning and to make sure everyone can come. If you have the proper promotional support, you can expect an impressive response to your invitation. A large crowd will justify the expense of programming, commemorative brochures, and photography—you will want to take pictures of the recipients and provide other publicity in the local media to ensure success of the program.

A large gathering not only adds a special dimension to the recognition but also publicizes the volunteer program. At the ceremony, your praise of the volunteers will usually include a description of the program. Alumni who attend the event as well as those who read about it in the local papers will be made aware of the volunteer program and of opportunities for participation. Thus, the recognition ceremony becomes a recruiting tool.

At Berkeley we hold an annual joint recognition banquet to honor volunteers both for the alumni office and for the development office. This event signals, in a public way, that the alumni and development programs operate in partnership. Although each carries out a specialized mission, they operate most effectively when they work to support each other. Volunteers are deeply involved in these two areas, which both have as their primary goal the support of the university. Holding a joint recognition banquet stresses the common purpose shared by these two areas.

CONCLUSION

The role of volunteers in alumni programming is well known. Their contributions as leaders, policy makers, and energetic workers are vital to the types of programs we are engaged in. In the past few decades, their numbers have grown and so have their avenues of service. Volunteers are a key resource as we meet the demands of the future.

There is, of course, another partner in this "marriage"—one with an equally important, if less publicized, role to play—and that is the alumni association and the professionals who run it. The alumni association stands between the institution and the alumni. Whether we call these professionals brokers, quarterbacks, directors, or managers, it is their performance that determines the success or failure of the volunteer program.

How productive the volunteer program is will depend to a great deal on how wisely and well the professional uses the talents and skills of the volunteers—recruiting, training, and motivating them, and recognizing their contributions. The strengths of the professional staff will be reflected in the success of the volunteers.

As I look back on my years of experience at the California Alumni Association, I would give our volunteer program a passing grade. We have made great progress in the past 20 years, and I believe this can be said about many other alumni associations around the country. But all of us must do even more if we are to keep up with the expanding needs of our institutions. Our partnership with our volunteers must grow in strength and scope for the benefit both of our institutions and our profession.

Budget
and Records

CHAPTER
12

Budget and Funding Sources

Gayle M. Langer

"Growth is our goal, profit is our measurement, survival is our reward." While this may describe Lee Iacocca's corporate philosophy, it applies just as well to that of alumni administrators. In our roles as financial managers, we, too, are very much concerned with meeting our goals and operating within established budget guidelines.

There are two primary types of alumni association structures—dependent and independent—but as Robert Forman, Executive Director of the Alumni Association at the University of Michigan, notes:

> Many alumni organizations . . . do not fall directly in either of these two categories. There are those with separate policy boards that are funded wholly or largely by the university. There are those that have membership dues but at the same time operate as a department of the institution.[1]

Who must approve the alumni association budget, therefore, depends on the type of organization at the particular institution. The association that functions as a department of the institution traditionally works closely with university administrators to match projected program costs with available funds. In this setting, the alumni director is expected to justify and document increased costs and new programming needs.

In contrast, the alumni organization that operates independently from the institution ultimately seeks approval for its budget from volunteers elected to govern the affairs of the association. Prior discussion with university administrators, which is often required, ensures that the goals of the association complement the goals of the institution.

In both situations, once the budget is approved, the alumni director must monitor expenditures and present comparative summaries on a monthly or quarterly basis.

83

INSTITUTIONAL FUNDING

Alumni associations exist to serve the institution. Consequently, the majority receive some—if not all—of their financial support from the institution. Institutional funding provides the base required for the alumni association to strengthen the bond between the alumni and the college. Costs often borne by the institution include: salaries and fringe benefits for alumni association personnel; record keeping; publications; and involvement programs such as reunions, alumni chapters, and constituent relations. In addition, the institution usually provides an alumni office on campus without cost to the association. (Some independent alumni associations raise funds for their own alumni headquarters and retain ownership of the facility.)

The financial challenges confronting education in the last decade have prompted alumni associations to supplement institutional funding by sponsoring revenue-producing activities; the net proceeds fund new staff positions or programs that enhance the institution's goals.

MEMBERSHIP DUES

The phrase "paying our dues" has many connotations. Essentially, it suggests an obligation—the repayment of a debt or an expression of appreciation for what has been received. In an alumni association, a dues program signifies level of interest. Paying dues represents a commitment to the institution—a commitment that can be pursued and cultivated for financial giving, volunteer service, and participation in programs. A membership dues program is most effective when coordinated with development goals. If the institution does not have a well-established annual giving program, the implementation of a dues program may be confusing to alumni. Yet dues programs generate up to 80 percent of the operating budget for alumni associations at a number of public institutions.

The opportunities for funding an alumni relations program through dues are dynamic because the number of prospects increases each year. Acquisition costs are relatively low and income is unrestricted. These factors enable the association to direct funds to areas where they are most needed.

Dues are generally based on the cost of servicing the member. Because of escalating mailing costs, the association needs to review rates periodically. If you plan to use dues as a source of funding, keep in mind this point from *The Law of Associations*: "Flexibility . . . is the most desirable trait of any dues system, enabling dues rates to be changed easily so as to adapt to changing conditions and needs."[2]

Alumni administrators experienced in the long-range planning process recommend projecting an association's budget over a three- to five-year period. You should base your projections on an assumed rate and number of members. Comparing these figures to expenses often documents the need for adjustments in the member/rate structure. Annual membership dues for alumni associations vary from $10 to $40; the rate for spouse affiliation is usually from $5 to $10.

It's not easy to set a realistic rate for life membership because you can't accurately predict future servicing costs. An actuarial study can help you establish fees. In a survey of associations participating in the 1987 Big Ten Alumni Directors Institute, life member rates ranged from $175 to $600, with spouse affiliation an additional $50 to $100.[3]

Alumni associations frequently offer life memberships on the installment plan, and some offer discount rates for select categories such as new graduates, retired alumni, or graduates celebrating their 50th reunion.

Since life membership commits the organization to servicing the member for a lifetime, it's wise to invest all or a portion of the life fee. In the July/August 1987 CASE *Currents*, Dan Heinlen, Director of Alumni Affairs for the Ohio State University Alumni Association, addresses this subject:

> If your life-member program serves your organization well, you've no doubt set aside a portion of the fees in an endowment large enough to cover the costs of servicing each member throughout that individual's actuarial lifetime. Since life-member funds can easily grow into the multimillion-dollar range, they call for astute financial management and investment.[4]

Heinlen further recommends seeking the professional counsel of a skilled financial manager to establish investment goals and a formal process for evaluating fund performance. Alternatively, you may want to consult your institution's development or investment officer.

Do membership dues compete with the annual fund? Seemingly not—records at a number of institutions reflect a positive correlation between association memberships and gifts. At the Stanford Alumni Association, for example, Executive Director William Stone reports that his office conducted a random sample of several thousand graduates to track the number and amount of gifts received. Results showed a greater increase in gifts to the university from association members than from nonmembers, even among members who received their memberships as gifts while students. "That makes the case for involvement rather convincing," Stone notes.[5]

Ohio State University, the University of Wisconsin–Madison, and the University of California–Berkeley have also achieved impressive results; representatives from these institutions note that nearly 50 percent of alumni contributions are received from association members. The giving pattern at these institutions supports the theory that dues establish a link—a beginning that, when pursued, can dramatically increase support level.

Nancy Harper presents an opposing viewpoint in the November 1976 *CASE Currents*. She states that "several alumni associations began their operations with dues systems, only to reject them in later years."[6] Adelphi University, Georgia Tech, Marquette University, the University of Pennsylvania, and Texas A&M discontinued their dues programs; administrators cited as the primary reasons the difficulty of coordinating mailings and the need to communicate with all alumni—not just with those who paid dues.

SUBSCRIPTION INCOME

Closely related to member dues, which essentially underwrite the cost of mailing a publication to alumni subscribers, is the voluntary subscription program. At the University of Notre Dame, alumni readily contributed to a fund to defray publication costs. This income-generating technique was introduced by the late Ron Parent, editor of the Notre Dame alumni magazine, and has since been adopted by a number of alumni associations— Brown, Pennsylvania, and Lehigh.

Associations at Kansas State University, the University of Minnesota, and the University of Wisconsin–Madison use a modification of this approach. They invite life members to contribute an amount to help defray increased publication or member-servicing costs, and they make it clear that contributions are voluntary.

Special club memberships encourage additional support from life members. The University of Iowa Alumni Association invites its life members to contribute $350 annually to its Old Gold Club. At Indiana University, contributions from life members founded the Woodburn Guild, which helped remodel and refurbish a reception facility at Bloomington. Although the management of this fund-raising program is by the Indiana Alumni Association, gifts are deposited with the Indiana University Foundation and earmarked for use by the alumni association for program enhancement.

MEMBERSHIP DIRECTORIES

Who's Who in America is a prestigious reference book, published on a regular basis. Its sales appeal is predicated on the fact that people enjoy seeing their names in print. A directory of association members relies on this same technique and affords member-dues organizations the opportunity for membership growth and increased revenues. Varying arrangements with directory companies are available. The "no-cost" method ensures the alumni association that the directory firm will cover all costs of mailing and updating directory information.

Revenue generated for the alumni association results from the sale of the directory and from increases in the number of dues-paying members. The directory can be presold to both members and nonmembers, and the directory firm assists with a mailing targeted to nonmembers. As an incentive, alumni joining the association prior to date of publication are listed in the directory. This technique has increased paid membership by as much as 30 percent for some alumni associations, and about 10 to 30 percent of members purchase a copy.

ADVERTISING INCOME

Alumni publications can offset printing and mailing costs by paid advertisements. In developing an advertising program, institutional and alumni administrators, with the assistance of legal counsel, should establish key policy. An editorial advisory board can also provide expertise in developing advertising guidelines and setting rates. The higher the circulation, the higher the advertising rate. Per page ad rates among alumni publications range from $15 to $30 per 1,000 names. To attract national subscribers, you may want to use an advertising consortium that sells several alumni publications by region or by conference. However, alumni directors familiar with this arrangement recommend close scrutiny of contractual agreements, as consortiums may dictate placement and require that the publication take advertising that is unacceptable to the institution.

To attract advertising from business firms located within the geographical area of the institution, the magazine editor may contract with an advertising agency. The agency representative usually takes a 15 percent commission, but this is easily offset by the additional revenue generated.

Alumni publications represent an attractive medium for advertisers because of the readers' income level, job status, and lifestyle. If your association is interested in attracting outside ads, you should conduct readership surveys that include advertising-related questions. You can then use survey results to interest potential advertisers and retain current ones.

You may want to offer a special advertising rate for departments within your institution. For example, the bookstore or the athletic department may wish to market merchandise to the alumni audience.

ALUMNI CAMPS

Family camping is a tradition for graduates of Indiana University, the University of Michigan, Brigham Young University, and the University of California–Berkeley. Alumni association representatives at these institutions rate involvement opportunities at an extremely high level. The vacation environment brings families together and provides an ideal setting for continuing education. Students frequently are hired to assist the staff, and this provides yet another important tie to the institution. In addition to benefits afforded to members, an established camping program can generate 10 to 29 percent of the alumni association's operating budget.

INSURANCE

The University of Minnesota was one of the first alumni associations to sponsor a group insurance program for its members. Today the majority of those associations that have alumni mailing lists of 50,000 or more offer this benefit to their constituency. Kees van der Zee, former Associate Director of the Alumni Association at the University of California–Berkeley, suggests that you survey your alumni members to determine the level of interest in an insurance program and the various types of insurance needs. According to van der Zee, a qualified insurance broker—not the alumni staff—should administer the program.[7]

Most popular with alumni groups is term-life coverage. In this program, the sponsoring alumni association receives the net proceeds when premiums paid by participants exceed the cost of claims and promotion.

As an additional benefit to the institution, alumni may designate the college or university as beneficiary on their life insurance policy. Other types of coverage—major medical, accidental death, disability income—are structured to provide reimbursement to the alumni association for its sponsorship of the program. The greater the number of participants in the plan, the greater the income to the association. Therefore, income from the association may not be available within the first five years of the program. Mature programs experience a 4 to 8 percent penetration rate—that is, 4 to 8 percent of those eligible to enroll actually do so. The insurance program is particularly attractive to alumni, such as recent graduates, who do not have similar benefits through a current employer.

ALUMNI TRAVEL

Group travel offers increased alumni involvement and continuing educational opportunities. You can design trips that facilitate study programs or college sports or that are simply pleasure trips to international or domestic destinations. The *Handbook of Institutional Advancement* suggests the following checklist of essentials to cover when you are selecting a travel agency:

1. Itinerary: review schedule, carrier, accommodations, transportation and guides, meals, special events

2. Tour director: experience, responsibilities, procedures for emergencies

3. Promotion: brochures' printing and mailing costs, advertising policy, announcements to alumni, special promotional activities

4. Administration: inquiries, billing and receipting, information sheets, personalized items, itinerary, passenger lists, final instructions, ticketing

5. Financial arrangements: cancellation policy, complimentary passage for alumni representative, remuneration to alumni association for each tour passenger, liability coverage

6. References from the agency.[8]

In addition to earning complimentary passage for faculty members or alumni representatives accompanying the group, alumni associations have the option of including a commission payable to the association for each booked reservation. Depending on the number of trips offered and the level of participation, this program can generate 5 to 10 percent of an association's revenue.

MERCHANDISING

Many college merchandising programs had their beginning with the sale of the traditional class ring. Today, pride and loyalty of alumni for their alma maters have inspired bookstores, athletic departments, and alumni associations to develop a catalog of items featuring the institution's mascot or seal. In recent years, professional marketing firms have helped associations market limited editions of high-quality merchandise, such as watches, grandfather clocks, and commemorative photo albums. In this way, the associations earn commissions on sales, but do not take on the financial responsibility for direct mail or fulfillment.

CREDIT CARDS

Financial institutions have found alumni to be an attractive market for credit cards. A credit card that features the institution's mascot or logo is a service to alumni that also provides extra dollars for the alumni association. New graduates are frequently targeted; as an incentive, the offer may waive the annual fee for the first 6 or 12 months. The sponsoring alumni association receives a percentage of the credit card transactions as well as a percentage—from 25 to 33 percent—of the annual fee.

Fred Williams, Executive Director of the Alumni Association at the University of Kansas, offers members a reduced interest rate of 16.8 percent; nonmembers pay 17.88 percent. Williams notes that every time they use the card, alumni are reminded of the university and the need for supporting it. A number of associations encourage members to use their cards to pay membership dues and to charge merchandise and program registration fees.

SHARED FUNDING

Whatever its form of organization, an alumni relations program forms a partnership with the institution and the various departments that serve the institution. This partnership lends itself well to the co-sponsorship of projects that can benefit the institution. For example, at the University of Wisconsin–Madison, the alumni association has shared start-up program costs with alumni chapters, the Alumni Student Board, the University of Wisconsin Foundation, and many academic departments. Co-sponsored projects include faculty and alumni recognition programs, student scholarships, career counseling, publications, a speaker's bureau, and student recruiting.

At Wisconsin, the foundation and the association encourage alumni chapters to hold fund-raising events. The foundation matches proceeds that are earmarked for student scholarships. Since the program's inception in 1967, nearly 300 students have benefited from over $1 million in scholarships.

Another underwriting concept that has not yet been fully pursued is grants. Programs addressing the needs of minorities or adult students may provide an avenue for attracting outside revenue. Working closely with the development office, alumni associations may be successful in soliciting foundation and corporate funding to meet the needs of changing student and alumni audiences.

KEEPING IT IN PERSPECTIVE

You should design alumni programs to provide service to your alumni and benefits to your institution. How do you decide what activities are viable for your particular organization? What problems might you encounter if your association sponsors profit-making ventures?

To answer these questions, you must have a clear understanding of institutional goals. William Stone at Stanford notes that "probably 95 percent of what we offer has some component of Stanford academics. That is our strong suit and we take full advantage of it."[9] Knowing your market and identifying the needs of your audience can make the difference between success and failure.

When you are considering potential programs, it is important to distinguish between those that are related to the educational purpose of your organization and those that aren't. Your alumni association is probably organized and operated for educational purposes, and engaging in a significant amount of unrelated business activity may jeopardize your tax-exempt status.

A number of alumni associations have found themselves subject to tax liability on revenue resulting from activities such as alumni travel, advertising, and merchandising. To be safe, consult with legal counsel or certified public accountants before you embark on money-making ventures. Some alumni associations have established separate service corporations to isolate income and costs from significant profit-making activities not related to the stated purpose of the educational organization.

As we approach the 1990s, we need to develop realistic approaches to funding the alumni relations program. We must plan carefully to keep pace with the changing needs of our alumni market and the expectations of institutional administrators. This will help us meet the challenge of providing effective programming in concert with institutional goals.

Notes

1. Robert G. Forman, "The Potential in Alumni Stewardship," in *Presidential Leadership in Advancement Activities*, James L. Fisher (guest ed.), New Directions for Institutional Advancement, no. 8 (San Francisco: Jossey-Bass, 1980), 50.
2. G. D. Webster, ed., *The Law of Associations* (Washington, D.C.: American Society of Association Executives, 1971), 29.
3. Peter W. Yoder, ed., *A Survey of Participating Alumni Associations*, Big Ten Alumni Directors Institute, 1987. Survey prepared by Indiana University Alumni Association, Bloomington.
4. Daniel L. Heinlen, "Alumni Administration 101: The Management Basics," CASE *Currents*, July/August 1987: 53.

5. Telephone interview.

6. Nancy Harper, "Alumni Dues and Don'ts," *CASE Currents*, November 1976: 17.

7. Richard Emerson, "Designing Auxiliary Programs and Services," in *Handbook of Institutional Advancement*, 2d ed., ed. A. Westley Rowland (San Francisco: Jossey-Bass, 1986), 473.

8. Ibid., 472.

9. Telephone interview.

CHAPTER
13 ═══

Alumni Management Information Systems

JAMES A. HOPSON

The next five to ten years will be significant ones as alumni administration professionals struggle to be everything to everyone. To meet future demands upon our profession, we'll need every tool at our disposal, and electronic information processing capabilities will be essential to our overall success.

The field of electronic information processing is so vast and changes so quickly that no one can possibly be totally computer-literate. Even trained computer science professionals are finding it difficult to keep abreast of the latest revelations. So how can alumni professionals take full advantage of the most economical and efficient options available to us?

A BRIEF REVIEW

As early as the end of the nineteenth century, it was becoming obvious to college and university administrators that it was an advantage to know the whereabouts of their alumni. Ivy League schools were beginning to hold formal alumni gatherings that necessitated some form of alumni record keeping. By the beginning of the twentieth century, many institutions of higher learning had developed sophisticated manual records systems that included, in addition to address information, data on occupa-

93

tion, interests, and even salary. By 1930 there were few institutions in America that did not have comprehensive records on the majority of their graduates.

In the 1930s, something happened on the campus of Iowa State College in Ames that would ultimately astound not only the academic community but the entire human race. This was the development of the prototype of the first electronic digital computer. John Vincent Atanasoff, a math and physics professor at Iowa State who can be called the father of the modern computer, is credited with inventing the most prolific tool known to mankind. The ramifications of the electronic revolution have been far-reaching for the alumni administrator as they have been for all of us.

The Early Days

Computer technology began to impact alumni administration in the late 1940s and early 1950s. The first computers on our campuses were cumbersome and slow compared to today's electronic processing machinery. At what we then considered high rates of speed, these "batch" systems sorted IBM cards that had data keypunched onto them. We depended upon these card filing systems with no direct access to the computer file.

The batch system became less effective, however, as alumni bodies grew in number and the data on each individual became more voluminous. Computer-processing time increased and this increased costs.

The On-line Revolution

While on-line (direct terminal access) applications in institutional advancement were available in the late 1960s and early 1970s, costs were prohibitive in most instances. But by 1973, costs were coming down and data processing departments at colleges and universities were beginning to convert their databases to this made-to-order processing system. This conversion process was slow and painstaking but its rewards were numerous.

In 1967 the American Council on Education published *Computers on Campus* in which authors John Caffrey and Charles J. Mosmann refer briefly to on-line systems and predict their probable use on campuses.[1] But the change was to be sudden and profound. In 1975 less than 5 percent of all alumni offices in this country had on-line capabilities. By 1982 that figure had grown to 60 percent, and it stands at 95 percent today.[2]

As on-line costs dropped, few alumni offices could afford *not* to take advantage of this tremendous office automation device.

TODAY'S INFORMATION
MANAGEMENT NEEDS

Since those early on-line conversions in alumni offices around the country, both computer technology and the scope of alumni office operations have changed dramatically. Today we rely heavily on our database management systems to drive virtually all of our programming needs.

Efficiency

Since the beginning of alumni administration in this country, we have continually sought to improve the efficiency of both our offices and our programs. Today's technology enables us to do far more and to do it more efficiently. We are now reaching for more efficiency, and there seems to be almost no limit to what we can do.

While alumni offices come in many shapes and sizes, you can usually judge their efficiency by examining the quality of the database management system.

Accountability

Foremost among our obligations to our alumni and constituent groups is accountability. Whatever we do, we will be ultimately evaluated by these groups on the basis of our reliability and our competence. And it follows that our accountability is only as good as our attention to detail. And don't forget, even the most comprehensive database management system is only as good as the human factor—the person who provides the initial data.

Most alumni administrators are not computer experts, and you should not try to be. As Peter A. McWilliams says in *The Personal Computer Book*, you can be computer-literate without understanding the inner workings of a computer.[3] If you can intelligently enter and retrieve data, you are computer-literate. Most of us have access to competent computer experts; it is their job to deal with what goes on inside the machine.

Selectivity

We are all familiar with the phrase, "Garbage in, garbage out"—the data you get from the computer will be only as good as the data you put into it. But what if you can't even get "garbage" out? Retrieval capabilities are very important in a database management system. A good system has built into it fast turnaround and response times, that is, we're able to retrieve desired data quickly.

Whether your system is a mainframe, mini, or microcomputer, response time and fast retrieval should be high on your list of priorities. While state-of-the-art databases provide video display queries at a speed of less than one second, some of us are still living with five-second or longer response times. Equally important is turnaround time on document or label requests where hard copy is needed. This can be as short as 15 minutes or as long as several weeks.

TODAY'S INFORMATION
PROCESSING OPTIONS

While more and more software firms are offering programs for alumni administration information management needs, the majority of us still work with software programs that we developed or that our institutions provided. But today's technology offers seemingly endless options in computer software.[4]

As computer technology has improved over the years, the two major developments—batch processing and on-line processing—have been of great importance to alumni administration. The next developments appear to be distributive on-line processing and relational database.

Distributive On-line Processing

More and more alumni offices are plugging into this advance in information processing. In essence, it replaces the "stand alone terminal" and provides for network computing through time-sharing, whereby several computer jobs are interwoven. It also provides for downloading data from a mainframe to a mini to a microcomputer and vice versa.

A long-standing goal on most of our campuses has been to amalgamate all records into one database so as to eliminate subsystems that often lead to costly duplication and tend to confuse and at times infuriate our constituents. Distributive on-line processing may well be the answer to this dilemma. Through such a system, departments, colleges, agencies, and other units on campus receive data directly from an alumni master file. The data may include the full file or a portion thereof, whatever the need may be. This system may provide data for viewing only or it may offer a hard-copy retrieval option. The latter is provided by downloading up-to-date data from a mainframe, mini, or even a micro (or personal) computer. The key ingredient here is "up-to-date," especially in the case of mailing label requests. Conversely, uploading (e.g., transferring data from a microcomputer back to the mainframe) is also a possibility.

Relational Database

Many experts in the field of electronic information processing view the relational database as the computer revolution of the 1980s. Given the potential scope of this technological advance, alumni professionals may have reason to "dance in the aisles" before the decade ends. A relational database (RDB) uses an indexing structure that tends to uncomplicate and speed up previously complicated and slow processing.

RDB is already operational in some institutions in the form of such software packages as IBM Data Base II, Oracle, Ingress, and others.

If you are not familiar with RDB, check with your data processor. Early indications are that this is the database of the immediate future. While major disadvantages of RDB are not yet apparent, costs are always a concern. But it's simply too early to make a prediction. On one hand, the simplified data structure of RDB should greatly decrease processing time. On the other hand, the new resource may lead to increased workloads for processing that would negate any cost savings.

The advantages, however, are real. Here are the major ones—RDB:

- speeds up processing,
- improves turnaround time,
- makes it easier to add and delete fields,
- provides easier and faster downloading, and
- provides easier programming maintenance.

DETERMINING THE RIGHT SYSTEM
FOR YOUR ASSOCIATION

All too often, either costs or institutional policy forces you to live and work with inadequate computer and office automation systems. Nevertheless, you should realize that your database support system is the hub of all of your programs and office procedures. With anything less than adequate computer support, you cannot expect your programs to run "full steam ahead."

Here are some tips on assessing your computer support needs and capabilities:

1. Begin by reviewing and defining your needs. Give yourself a report card by comparing your system with that of colleagues whom you respect. Check with your current data processor to learn what your

enhancement capabilities are. Find out if you have options within your institution and just what they might be.

2. Once you have a good idea of what you want to accomplish with your database, determine costs. Compare them with your financial capabilities and proceed.

3. If you must work within your institution, hardware decisions may already be defined for you. You may still wish to explore available microcomputer and word-processing options.

4. Software should be of prime importance to you, and you should be the decision maker in either the purchase of new software or the upgrading of what you have.

5. If you will be purchasing either hardware or software, refer to books such as those of Peter McWilliams mentioned above, or consult your colleagues. CASE *Currents* periodically lists computer hardware/software vendors.

6. Once you make the decision to buy, know your vendor well. Ask for a list of alumni administration customers and seek them out. See the system work and be sure the package is fully documented.

7. Determine who will install and maintain the system. Prompt and reliable maintenance may very well be as important as the system itself.

8. Don't make hasty decisions. You will have to live with the system you select. Choose wisely!

A LOOK INTO THE FUTURE

Few can predict with any accuracy what the future holds for computer technology. One thing is certain, however: by the turn of the century, today's databases will be viewed as slow and awkward. If the past is any indication of the future, "We ain't seen nothin' yet!"

In the past 25 years alone, computer disc storage capacity has improved by a factor of 1,000, according to George O. Strawn, director of the Iowa State University Computation Center. And, predicts Strawn, "Disc density and performance will improve again by a factor of 1,000 by the turn of the century."[5] This should translate into good news for alumni administration professionals around the country as computer support becomes better and—we hope—cheaper.

Keep in mind that only a little over 50 years have passed since John Atanasoff introduced the first electronic digital computer. What the next 50 years might bring taxes the imagination!

Notes

1. John Caffrey and Charles J. Mosmann, *Computers on Campus* (Washington, D.C.: American Council on Education, 1967).
2. Compiled from ISU On-Line System Workshop Surveys.
3. Peter A. McWilliams, *The Personal Computer Book* (Los Angeles: Prelude Press, 1983), 36.
4. Ibid., 321–334. Peter A. McWilliams, *The Word Processing Book* (Los Angeles: Prelude Press, 1983), 282–293, includes a complete brand-name buyer's guide for both software and hardware.
5. Personal communication.

CHAPTER 14

"Dear Alumni..."
Who Are
These People?

Alumni administration involves dealing with the former students (note this vague, inclusive phrase) of an institution. As such, alumni administration is like playing chess blindfolded or fiddling with a chemistry set full of unlabeled ingredients.

Who are "the alumni"? They are an amorphous mass, well defined at the core, perhaps, but even the core can be hard to pinpoint, and the periphery is a blur without definite boundaries. A certain percentage of your alumni at any given time are lost; you have no way to contact them. Others are findable, but you have no idea what they do, what their interests are, and whether they can help you. Many of the people on your list may not even qualify as "alumni."

Your first and most basic task as an alumni administrator, then, is to build a base of solid information about those whom you serve. The scope, quality, and effectiveness of your service depends on the knowledge you have about your constituents. Researching your alumni should be an incessant, ongoing task, a low-level background hum beneath the daily noise of typewriters and telephones.

It is all too easy to overlook the need for research; it is so basic and so undramatic, we often take it for granted. It is not the urgent "thing to do today" so it doesn't get done. But the challenge of alumni research is formidable. It should be given high visibility and approached with very careful planning.

Small colleges may have only a few thousand alumni, while alumni of the largest state universities approach or exceed the quarter-million mark. Yet for all institutions the tasks and the difficulties are roughly the same. Here at Johns Hopkins University, for example, we have 73,000 alumni at this writing, but we are adding almost 3,000 new graduates a year. In a decade, at least one-third of our alumni will be people not now on the rolls. And they are mobile people: of 100 typical Americans, more than 20 will change address *next year*. Simply reaching this group is a tough job. Knowing them in depth amounts to an endless quest.

The quest is hopeless unless you have a design and a plan. Proceeding by accident and inadvertence will not do. You need to approach alumni research systematically and consciously. Above all, remember the architectural maxim that form follows function. The very first step in alumni research, as often overlooked as it is obvious, is to establish what you intend to do with your basic alumni files. What questions will you ask of the data? In order to do Project X, what information do you need? What programmatic demands will be put on the data, and what fund-raising priorities must be met?

From this basis you can proceed to the next step: determining the kind of information you want to keep regularly, the data-processing capacity this requires, how to set up your basic files, and what staff you need in order to do this. Once you have a basic concept in place—preferably written, however brief—you are ready to face the challenge of alumni research with confidence. You know where you want to go; now you must decide how to get there and then proceed in that direction.

Your first move is to define, or redefine, who your alumni are. You will certainly include degree-holding graduates, but who else? Most institutions count as alumni those who matriculated in a degree program, are no longer connected with the institution, and earned a certain number of credits. How many credits? That's up to your institution and its purposes. Some institutions require at least one year's full-time equivalent work.

Should you count these nondegree alumni? In most cases, the answer is "yes." Students who drop out, flunk out, or transfer often harbor warm feelings about the institution, or develop these feelings when time and distance have softened any bitterness or disappointment they may have felt at the time. One small, southern, liberal arts college counts as a devoted alumna (and a major contributor) a woman who, after two years, was forced to transfer (for family reasons) to her home state university. If that college had not considered her to be an alumna, both it and she would have lost all the benefits of their enduring relationship.

What are the reasons for *not* counting nondegree alumni? Some institutions, particularly the larger ones, may feel the burden of time and file maintenance is not worth the possible return. Dear Old Siwash, with over 150,000 degree holders, does not want to add to that list. Degree holders are a better target, and more likely to be interested participants than nondegree alumni. Let the others come forward if they wish, the reasoning goes, but limit the basic file-keeping chores to the actual graduates.

Once you have decided who your alumni are, you need to determine what you want to know about them. What information will you keep on file for each alumnus? Will you collect the same data for everyone or accumulate a bigger file for certain development targets? Eventually, you will have to select database software. Keep in mind that, for research to be effective, you must not only put information into a system but also be able to get it out again. There is no point in keeping fraternity/sorority membership records if you can't find a list of all the Phi Gams from 1950 to 1970 when you need it.

The list of possible research data fields is almost limitless. The system used by the alumni relations and development offices at Johns Hopkins can track over 400 elements, including job title, industry codes, student activities, alumni activities and honors, family connections, and multi-year giving histories. It uses 32 screens and more than 600 lines. It has room for narrative files, which cuts down on paper research reports and conventional files full of memos and notes. But remember that narrative files cannot be used for retrieval purposes; you have to read each one to get back the information. And many of the lines are blank for most of our alumni. Our optimum use controlled the choice of machinery and software.

You could probably use all the information you could get. The sky is the limit when it comes to what you'd like to know about your alumni. Big databases and big research projects, however, call for big budgets. Elaborate software demands more costly mainframes. Training users is more complicated. Staff to load and manipulate the information costs money, plus time to hire and train. Don't overreach. If your budget and your staff time are limited, your research agenda should be too. Good limited files are better than poorly kept ones, no matter how extensive. And bad files are a lethal liability.

A few years ago, a fund raiser from a major eastern university approached DuPont armed with some alumni research. More than 80 highly trained graduates of his university were working for DuPont. Their names were on a list in his pocket, ready to be produced when needed to convince the company to support research education at the institution. Ten minutes into the conversation the DuPont executive said brightly, "Y'know, your university has been very fertile for us. I checked our files and 137 of your graduates do research here." The development officer smiled feebly, swallowed hard, and ditched his inadequate research printout at the first available wastebasket.

Above all, on whatever scale you operate, you need a database manager to maintain the files and coordinate the mechanics of computer research. Don't spread the job around. Make it the principal responsibility of one person. While everyone from the president to the most distant alumni volunteer can be a source of information, only one person should control the technical aspects of the file. In a small shop, this person may have other jobs, too, but the key point stays the same—one person has accountability. If there are many people with the power to enter and change data, they must be carefully trained and answerable to the database manager. Uncontrolled or poorly attended files will, in time, destroy any hope of good alumni research.

At the heart of your research are basic demographic data. Some of this information never changes—date of birth, dates of attendance, major, degrees earned, sex (well . . . *almost* never), and so on. But much vital information shifts considerably—address, employment, marital status (and name with it?), children, and giving record. How do you keep your files up-to-date? The options are numerous:

- voluntary reporting;
- return mail corrections, especially from publications;
- questionnaires, including homecoming/reunion surveys;
- published sources (for obituaries, particularly), including clipping services;
- club and class secretaries;
- press releases;
- directory publishing efforts;
- lost alumni tracer programs;
- other directories, *Who's Who*, professional and telephone directories;
- opinion surveys; and
- list sharing with professional associations, fraternities/sororities, honorary societies, and so on.

Getting new information is not the end of the updating process, however. First, one change often hints at others not reported. A move from one city to another usually signals a job change, for example. Second, you need to verify the change, just in case, particularly if the source was not the alumnus. You can deal with these two concerns with one stroke. Use a simple follow-up reply card to verify the change *and* to ask for additional information. Your computer might be programmed to generate such a card automatically. Some institutions use student labor to double-check changes by phone.

If the change is an obituary, a sympathy card is appropriate and serves to confirm the news; nothing gets a faster response than commiserating on the death of someone who happens to be alive and kicking. Every database manager can tell stories of "deceased" alumni who wrote in to ask why the alumni magazine had stopped coming.

Despite your best efforts, of course, some alumni will get lost. The mail will come back labeled "No forwarding address." But don't drop these prodigals from the files. Develop codes for "inactive" or "no address." Keep the old address for now; it may come in handy. Consider doing an occasional test mailing, just a postcard, to check that the address really is no longer valid. A small college in Virginia did such a test mailing two years ago, and found that in almost 30 percent of the cases where mail had been returned, the address was still good. The Postal Service had been careless.

Tracking lost alumni is an art. Brian Gorman summarized various research methods, including use of professional "tracer" companies, in a 1981 CASE publication, *Finding Lost Alumni: Tracing Methods Used by 19 Institutions*. Note, also, that the best cure is prevention. Don't lose track of them in the first place. And the sooner you begin to search, the more you are likely to find the lost. The longer an alumnus is missing, the less likely he or she is to be found.

One important way to shore up your database and provide a service you can sell to your alumni is to produce an alumni directory. Alumni directories are standard fare at most institutions, and you probably know all the pros, cons, and pitfalls. Keep in mind that the finished volume represents less than half the benefit to you: directories are major research undertakings, and they clean up your files very effectively.

If you are going to work with an outside vendor to produce a directory, these guidelines may help you plan the research element:

- Double-check all promises of technical compatibility, data collection, and data manipulation. Some salespeople commit to more than their programmers can deliver or can deliver in a timely way.

- Be *sure* the data file given to you by the directory vendor can be *directly*, immediately loaded into your computer.

- Date-code all entries in your file and theirs. If what the directory vendor gives you doesn't match your information, who has the correct, most current data? Don't assume they do.

- Insist on speed. Data collected by the directory vendor many months (or even a year) ago is going to be pockmarked with errors by the time it reaches you.

- Take advantage of the customized features in directory questionnaires. Put in your own research questions. Take the time to plan what you want to ask; make the directory effort part of your master plan for record keeping and research.

Once the basics are squared away, you can consider some fancier fact-finding. One possibility is an alumni census, perhaps combined with an opinion survey on pressing institutional issues. An alumni census is a massive updating effort covering all (or some designated portion) of the alumni base. The most common form of census is the initial questionnaire used to create a directory. One caution: those alumni who do not wish to be in a published directory will not return the survey, whereas they might if it were part of a file-updating census. Consider the costs and benefits of a total alumni census.

A careful census helps you find the fit between your institution's needs and the expertise and interests of your alumni. For a detailed look at the whys and wherefores of a full census, see Mary Pendel's fine CASE *Currents* article, "Beyond Gallup." She lists 16 kinds of information, beyond demographic basics, that a good census can provide. See also one of her sources, *Surveying Your Alumni* (compiled by Barbara McKenna and published by CASE).

One of the most fruitful areas of research and record keeping is activity coding. Start by keeping records of who participates in which alumni activities. As staff hours are available, research past alumni participation and enter that, too. In time this creates a research base for marketing your travel and merchandise, identifying volunteers, and deciding who your best prospects are for any given alumni activity.

These records also make good background material for development contact. They document your worth and pinpoint areas of program weakness. They allow you to quantify how many attendees are "repeaters" and how many represent new blood. They show you the demographics of your participants so that you can either play to the existing pattern or develop strategies to change it.

In addition to your research on alumni activity, you need to do background work on student activities. Start with current seniors. Then use yearbooks, organization records, survey questionnaires, commencement and awards ceremony programs, and whatever else you can find to build a file on the past student activities of alumni. The benefits are similar to those of alumni activity records.

Records of student involvements give you a research base for special-interest reunions. These reunions are built on student activities, not graduation years. Athletic teams often have their own reunions, and the concept works well for other activities as well—choirs, junior-year-abroad programs, theater groups, the possibilities are limitless. Institutions that do special reunions report that a large percentage of those invited actually come, and among these are many alumni who have been unresponsive to general programs and class-year reunions. The roots of such fruitful and imaginative programming are in sound alumni research and record keeping.

If your demographic base is solid, you can do some fairly sophisticated survey research on alumni attributes and opinions. The methodology of survey research is precise and can be elaborate, but the basics are reason-

ably simple, and the literature to help you through the process is extensive. In addition, most campuses have faculty in statistics, psychology,
sociology, and marketing who can provide technical assistance. Here are
some fundamentals of survey research:

- Sampling really works. If you have a large population to survey, a
  truly random sample with a high percentage of return will yield
  strikingly accurate results. You can assess 10,000 people, for example, to an accuracy of plus or minus 3 percent, with 965 responses
  (again assuming your response rate is good, say 40 percent or better).
  If you will settle for plus or minus 5 percent accuracy, you need only
  380 replies. Professional survey specialists say a homogeneous, self-
  identified, highly educated group like institutional alumni can yield
  survey response rates of 60 percent, maybe even higher.

- Survey research can yield four general types of information. In as-
  cending order of uncertainty and susceptibility to error, these are:
  attributes (what the respondent is); behavior (what the respondent
  does); beliefs (what the respondent thinks is true); and attitudes
  (what the respondent prefers).

- The biggest pitfalls to avoid in survey research are sample error or
  bias (including failure to cover key subgroups), poorly worded questions, and response levels too low to assure accuracy. True random
  selection is your best insurance against sample error. You can field-
  test questions on a small group for clarity, or ask them in several
  different formulations. The most concrete answers are obtained from
  closed-ended questions with ordered responses—that is, you offer
  distinct response options to the question and array them from one
  extreme to the other (for example, "strongly agree," "slightly agree,"
  "strongly disagree"). From there you can move to closed-ended questions with unordered responses, or partially closed-ended (you
  provide several choices and one write-in line labeled "other"), or
  completely open-ended responses. These last are tough to quantify,
  but in small batches they can yield interesting narrative results.

- Response rates to surveys depend principally on two things: the
  survey instrument and its attendant literature (such as a cover letter)
  and the mechanics of distribution and follow-up. The questionnaire
  should be interesting, not too long, and attractively presented. For
  example, why begin with the tedious demographic questions? Start
  with substantively interesting items and save the name-rank-serial
  number questions for last, when the respondent has already made
  an investment in the survey. The cover letter should be clear, persuasive, and convince the respondent that the survey is important.

- Always make it easy to return the survey, and always follow up with
  reminders at selected intervals.

A telephone survey is another option. It works best for specific information items. Opinion surveys by phone require precise wording of questions and careful training of volunteers. Professional market survey firms are available to help if you can afford them. You can sometimes piggyback your research on the calling that your institution is doing for fund-raising purposes. Keep your questions few, brief, and concrete, and remember that your sample is not random; most phonathons address targeted groups of prior givers or prospects who have not responded to mail solicitation.

Survey research is an essential building block of marketing, a subject beyond the scope of this chapter (but see Chapter 21 by Margaret Carlson and James Day). It is worth noting, however, that the success of efforts to market the institution and its products and services is directly tied to the quality of the alumni data your office has gathered and maintained.

Your files and all that can be done with them are an invaluable resource to the alumni association and its related staff, which are committed to speaking for the alumni and serving them according to their needs. Indeed, alumni record keeping and research contribute to the very survival of the entire institution. Colleges and universities are not clusters of buildings and equipment. If the buildings burn down, the institution remains. Colleges and universities are associations of men and women engaged in a common intellectual, pedagogical, and educational pursuit. Within that group of men and women, the largest component is the alumni. Their lives have been touched by alma mater, and they have left their imprint upon her in return. The relationship of the alumnus to the institution is a vibrant and significant one, and it is in your care. Your record keeping and research mean nothing less than that.

The days of the alumni director who kept all the key data under his or her hat are gone. Alumni relations is part of the global metamorphosis toward an information society. Knowledge is power, and your research will empower you to serve your constituents with skill, sensitivity, and impact.

Programming

CHAPTER
15 ═══

Alumni Clubs

KEITH A. WILLIAMS

Alumni clubs are relatively recent developments. Alumni relations, however, began during the early years of the American university when individual alumni, and then groups of alumni, compelled by nostalgia and the desire to rekindle fond ties with their college experience, returned to campus for commencement. For many decades these visits were made in the absence of any formal structure or arrangement. Then gradually, in order to accommodate increasingly greater numbers of returning alumni, class secretaries were appointed to plan activities and to make arrangements for the graduates. In these emotional yet modest happenings is found the essence of today's comprehensive alumni programs, no longer administered by volunteer class secretaries but by professionals operating with well-defined management objectives.

ALUMNI CLUBS: DEFINITION
AND PURPOSE

During the early years of the alumni movement, providing opportunities for alumni "to promote the welfare of alma mater" was the raison d'être proffered by the organized groups.

Gradually, as the growing alumni movement became enfolded within the broader institutional advancement effort, alumni programs took on another purpose—serving the needs of the alumni. And today, alumni relations as an integral part of institutional advancement continues to embody these two purposes.

As the alumni community began to extend beyond the immediate university campus to the far reaches of the city or to the surrounding state or states, alumni relations began to focus on the need to accommodate alumni removed from campus activities. Thus was born the alumni club. While reunions brought alumni to the campus, alumni clubs brought the campus to alumni.

In essence, therefore, alumni clubs are centers of an extended university community, and their purpose is part of the institutional advancement effort of promoting the institution to its external constituency. Alumni clubs create communities of university support and spirit and thereby extend the boundaries of the university community to the far reaches of the state, the nation, or the world—wherever the institution's alumni are found. Consequently, the role and purpose of an alumni club must be consistent with the goals of the university and of the alumni association.

Club purpose must be derived from the perspective of the institution as well as from that of the alumni served by the club. The institution gains from alumni involvement and support, both financial and normal. Alumni gain from a heightened awareness of the vibrant extended university community whose reputation affects their own; they also benefit from networking, exposure to professors, and the opportunity to serve the institution that served them.

A Worthwhile Investment

While an alumni club network is not an inexpensive undertaking, the money expended to cultivate a supportive community is well invested. The cost of alumni clubs should be considered in terms of their value as part of a comprehensive institutional advancement program. Capital campaigns, for example, depend on well-organized local alumni structures, and an alumnus who maintains strong emotional ties with alma mater is more likely to contribute to it.

Essential Features

Each club should be viewed as functioning independently within a network of clubs. While each club retains its individual character, the network concept fosters the sharing of ideas. This, in turn, enriches services to the overall alumni population.

In order for the alumni club network to function at its best, certain essential features should be shared by all the clubs. Club organization should consist of four officers, an 8- to 12-member board of directors, and committees that implement the club's various activities.

Success of the Club Network

The success of the regional club network is determined to a large extent by the attitude the alumni association adopts towards the individual clubs. The regional club must perceive the central office as being, above all, cooperative, dependable, and having the club's best interest as a high priority. Alumni club leaders are volunteer agents in the achievement of the association's goal of establishing an extended university community. They must feel confident that their volunteer efforts fit into a well-thought-out scheme and that they are in partnership with the association. In other words, club leaders must perceive the central office as having clearly defined, worthwhile goals about which it is enthusiastic. And association leadership must be able to inspire club leaders with this enthusiasm.

Alumni must perceive club programs and activities as appealing and substantive as well as fun. Club programs should be broadly conceived to reflect a membership of individuals of diverse ages, backgrounds, beliefs, and education, who have a variety of social, intellectual, and athletic interests. To plan club programming only to satisfy social interests while at the same time ignoring educational and other purposes destines the club to an early demise.

STARTING AN ALUMNI CLUB

If you are a club administrator—whether you devote all of your time to this activity or have many other duties—you need to be a multitalented manager of volunteers, flexible enough to function in a myriad of situations with persons of various beliefs and backgrounds. In your hands falls the responsibility of interpreting issues for the alumni club and dispensing a range of services that will ensure the club's continued life. You are also the guiding force in the formation of new alumni clubs.

You need to decide whether a minimum number of alumni should be required to organize a club and whether this minimum should vary depending on the location. Normally 10 to 20 percent of the alumni population will be active in alumni events; therefore, you should consider how many active members will be needed to make the club workable. The minimum may vary according to the kinds of events the club undertakes. For example, 10 is enough for a sit-down dinner but not for a lecture or reception. Also, remember that in any organization a handful of individuals provides the driving force. The more enthusiastic and energetic the individuals who comprise that handful, the smaller that group need be. In an alumni club, that group should consist of the officers and the board of directors. Enthusiasm then radiates from the club leadership to the club membership.

Following are the three stages of organizing a club: defining boundaries and identifying leadership; holding an initial meeting; and holding a general organizational meeting.

Defining Boundaries and Identifying Leadership

First, you need to define the club's geographic boundaries and identify local alumni who can help with the organizational effort. Perhaps you are organizing the club in response to a request from an interested alumnus in the area who might be willing to lead the organizational effort. Otherwise, you will have to seek alumni contacts through the mail. Send a brief letter-survey to solicit interested volunteers. A one-page flier with a tear-off response form will enable alumni to express interest in holding office or serving on a committee and may also help you identify a principal alumni contact.

Once you have located interested alumni, ask them to help you identify community boundaries and determine the club area. ZIP codes or county lines often provide convenient boundaries.

The Initial Meeting

Invite all interested respondents to the initial planning meeting. If there is a principal alumni contact, he or she will probably become the first club president and, therefore, should conduct this initial planning meeting as well as the general organizational meeting that will follow. Take as much time as necessary to prepare the alumnus to answer questions that might arise concerning the relationship between the association and the club, the activities undertaken by other clubs, and the benefits of membership in the association. He or she should have a good sense of the "how" and "why" of club operations.

If there is no alumni leader at this time, you will have to convene and conduct the meeting. An alumni leader may then emerge through the interplay of group dynamics at this meeting. The earlier the leader is identified, the better. The lack of such a leader might suggest that the driving force needed to organize and continue the club is also lacking.

At the initial meeting, you (or the alumni leader) should explain the organization procedures. Three tasks should then be accomplished:

Writing bylaws for the club.   Club bylaws should include the name of the club, its purpose, a definition of its membership, and procedures for electing officers and a board of directors. The bylaws should stipulate the terms of office and the frequency of general elections and meetings.

Identifying a slate of officers and board members.   There should be four officers—a president, vice president, treasurer, and secretary—and an 8- to 12-member board of directors. The board assists the president and officers in deciding the club's policies and its general direction. By serving on the board, alumni gain the experience necessary to manage club affairs as officers or as president. Normally, board members are recruited from the general membership to serve for two years; they are assigned major responsibilities in the club's committee structure.

Alumni are elected to the board in a staggered fashion so that new members join every year, but a measure of continuity is provided. So that the whole board is not replaced at the end of the club's first two years, half of the first board should serve two years and the other half three. Thereafter, elections should replace half the board every year.

The nominations committee should nominate candidates for officers from the board of directors and then present the slate to the general membership for its vote.

Committee chairs may be selected from among the board members at the initial meeting or later at the organizational meeting. Committees are the club's action groups. They provide the framework to carry out the club's programs and at the same time offer involvement opportunities for club members. The activities committee plans all programs undertaken by the club—not only the club's major annual event (dinner, golf outing, or speaker's seminar), but also informal social gatherings and receptions.

The activities committee may include other subcommittees that plan aspects of the larger activity such as program format, decorations, welcoming, and so on. The newsletter or communications committee produces the club's newsletter and may also announce club events. The student recruitment committee is the club's liaison with the university's admissions office; it provides supplemental recruitment assistance in the region by calling prospective students or making college night presentations at the local high schools. The membership committee monitors the club's membership numbers, recruits new members, and reports address changes to the alumni records office.

Setting a date for the general organizational meeting.   The date should allow adequate time for announcements to be printed, mailed, and delivered two to three weeks before the meeting.

The General Organizational Meeting

All alumni in the area should be invited to this meeting. After an informal reception, the principal alumni contact should preside over the meeting, introducing the slate of officers and board members and the plan of action developed during the initial meeting. Each candidate for office and for the board (if time permits) should stand and say a few words. Nominations can be sought from the floor before the vote. The agenda should also include a report on the university and the alumni association.

The meeting can end with questions and answers and the presentation of the alumni association's charter to the club to certify it as an organized affiliate of the alumni association. The new president should see that an announcement of the club is carried in the local media and that the minutes of the meeting, including a list of those present, are forwarded to the alumni association.

ISSUES AND POLICY

The size of your budget will determine how much money—if any—you can allot to the clubs for financial support, services, and visits by you or your staff.

Travel to Clubs

It is difficult, if not impossible, to coordinate alumni clubs by telephone or newsletter. While telephone calls, newsletters, and memoranda suffice for the most part to convey information from the central office to the club, periodic visits by association representatives are essential to the overall plan for club administration. Some clubs by virtue of their size and political importance merit more frequent visits than others. And clubs that have fallen into inactivity may benefit from the visit of an association representative.

A rating system, based on factors such as club size, political importance, and need for guidance or morale boosting, can help you determine a visiting schedule. Look for ways to save money by scheduling visits to several clubs on one trip.

Financial Support

If your association is a dues-based one, you can allocate a portion of the dues to each club. This provides a regular source of operating funds during the start-up period when the club is not ready or able to raise its own funds and later if, for some reason, its fund-raising productivity falls off. A club that receives a portion of dues has an incentive to recruit actively, as new members from its area will increase its budget. Sharing revenue through a dues reimbursement policy also fosters a bond between the association and the individual club. It makes the local club an integral part and partner of the national association. But even if the clubs share in the dues, the club administrator should encourage them to develop programs and activities that will lead to financial self-sufficiency.

SERVICES

Once the alumni club is organized and chartered, you should continue to provide services that will enhance its ongoing operations.

Building Club Leadership

No service is more important than establishing a mechanism to identify and secure strong club leadership and providing leadership orientation, training, and recognition. When you are screening candidates, use position descriptions for officers and board members that specify time requirements as well as duties. Once the initial officers and board members are in place, the nominations committee should take over the responsibility of ensuring a strong leadership. Club leaders should be encouraged to cultivate promising club members for leadership by asking them, for example, to serve first on committees, then on the board.

Alumni who contribute their time and effort to make alumni clubs succeed should be thanked sincerely and often. Expressions of appreciation can take many forms, such as a small gift or tickets to a campus dramatic production or athletic event. Invite volunteers to leadership workshops as a token of appreciation for the time and effort spent for the club, and enclose a note of thanks with the invitation. Whenever possible, invite—in addition to the club president—other officers, board members, and former club presidents, especially those who have contributed significantly during their terms of office.

You cannot express too often your appreciation for a job well done.

University Speakers

Alumni enjoy visits of university representatives—faculty, administrators, and athletic personnel—who bring news about the university or a particular area of the university. Providing a speaker service will greatly strengthen club programming. Encourage the clubs to plan events well in advance. The earlier they plan, the better the chances of having a favorite speaker attend. Ask to receive itineraries of university personnel from the institution's travel office or, if necessary, from each department. With this information in hand, you can coordinate travel plans with scheduled club programs or even plan special events to capitalize on the visits of the university representative to the area.

Alumni Lists

Computer lists of alumni who reside in the club area constitute the lifeblood of an alumni club network. The alumni association or the alumni records office has lists of donors and of university publications subscribers, among others. These are probably the best source for current addresses. If possible, provide lists categorized by region, major, year of graduation, or extracurricular interest. In return, the clubs should report changes in the data to the association so that records can be updated.

Promotion

Include club news, highlighted with lively photos when possible, in the alumni magazine. Publishing club news is an important promotional activity, so be sure club presidents know publication deadlines.

Consultation

If you have had many years of experience with alumni clubs, you should be able to provide a consultation service to the regional club leaders, either answering inquiries directly or referring them to other experts.

Idea Sharing

Expertise on many alumni club matters lies within the club network itself. Thus, the good ideas of any one club should be shared with the others. Establish a mechanism to identify successful ideas and to spread them throughout the network. Putting the clubs on each other's mailing lists is one way to foster the sharing of ideas.

Monitoring and Evaluation

The activities of the local alumni club can enhance or tarnish the image of the institution and the alumni community. This makes it essential that you monitor and evaluate all aspects of the alumni club network. You need to know to what extent goals are being attained. The club must articulate its goals, and progress toward their attainment must be measured or lack of progress explained. You should review the annual reports that each club is required to submit to the alumni association.

Setting goals to correct existing problems is an important part of planning; it is equally important to set short- and long-range goals to deal with anticipated problems. For example, if a reduction in next year's annual budget is imminent, then you need to set more stringent spending goals. The various factors on which the success of the club program depends— cost-effective measures, the number of programs offered annually, and an increase in membership, for example—should routinely be the subjects of goal setting. If you list the goals to be achieved in each area and then monitor the attainment of these goals, you will have a good grasp of the state of each club as well as the condition of the overall club network.

Clubs should themselves set goals and regularly evaluate the success of their efforts in achieving the goals. Goal setting and evaluation are the means to find out what works and what does not work within a defined context so that planning for the next phase of action will produce a result nearer the goal.

The Alumni Club Handbook

An alumni club handbook is a valuable orientation tool for new club leaders. You can probably organize the many memoranda you have already written to club leaders and prospective club leaders into a handbook that sets forth the information needed to set up a club and to foster the best in club operation. The material should be organized into three sections (and perhaps a "miscellaneous" section, if needed).

Organization.   This section contains all the information needed to take a club from definition of its boundaries to the granting of its charter. Include the association bylaws, which describe the functions and rules governing the alumni association and which provide a model for defining the club bylaws. Sample club bylaws should contain blank spaces so that club organizers can write in the specifics of their own club.

Include the association's objectives for a regional alumni club. For example, club leaders should know if the association has decided that clubs should not promote political candidates or conduct private business.

Outline the steps required to organize a club so that they can be easily followed by a reader with little or no alumni club organizing experience.

Include position descriptions for club officers and board members so that the duties and responsibilities are clearly understood. This will help prevent the club president from failing to delegate when necessary. Although the president is a volunteer in a labor of love, he or she still needs to use management techniques that have proven successful in the business world.

Conclude this section of the handbook with miscellaneous but necessary information such as procedures for opening a club bank account and an explanation of tax-exempt status and incorporation status. To make sure this information is complete and accurate, consult experts such as the university's legal counsel, the local bank, credit union, and advisers at the United States Postal Service.

Operations.   This section deals with the day-to-day tasks of the alumni club. These include step-by-step procedures for planning an event, be it the club's annual function (requiring extensive advanced planning time) or a spur-of-the-moment activity.

Outline a sample schedule with task objectives at the end of each one- or two-week period. List the dates in reverse order to show the time remaining before the event. For example, you might suggest that six weeks before the event, announcements be designed, written, and printed; labels ordered; and the site for the event selected and reserved. (If the site is a popular one, the club may need to reserve it as early as six months to a year in advance.)

Briefly describe the committees needed. Include a description of the services the association provides to the clubs, annual activities put on by the clubs, and alumni association activities such as special reunions, Alumni Day, and homecoming. This gives a sense of the variety of the annual activities planned throughout the entire alumni community and shows peak activity periods when the demand for university speakers and association services is high.

Reference materials.   Include miscellaneous reference documents and forms such as the following:

- An up-to-date list of regional club presidents so that club presidents can communicate with each other. The list should be alphabetical by club name and include each president's name, address, and home and business phone numbers.

- Regional club totals. Include totals for association members and nonmembers for each region. These figures will enable club leaders to set membership goals.

- A list of the alumni association's board of directors. Club leaders should at least know the names of the association's board of directors. Accompanying the list should be position descriptions, applications, and a statement of the criteria and the procedure for election to the board.

- Awards. List all the awards granted by the association and the institution for which alumni qualify; include descriptions and applications.

- University speakers and topics. Coaches are the most popular speakers. A list of other campus speakers and their areas of expertise may suggest a broader range of speakers and subjects.

- Films and videotapes. List all the films available to clubs including those from the institution's library, public relations office, athletic department, and academic units. Include order forms and a statement of loan policy.

- University spirit merchandise. Include various premium items offered by the association and the campus store, plus order forms and ordering information.

- Sample printed materials and forms. These materials will give club leaders an idea of the fliers and newsletters produced by other clubs. Include sample blank forms used by the association and the regional clubs to communicate with each other, such as athletic ticket request forms, annual report forms, and activity report forms used to report club news to the association's editor.

THE CLUB PRESIDENT

In coordinating the alumni club network, you and the club president should work as a team. It is important that there be a clear understanding of the president's role as it differs from that of the club administrator. The club president is the association's agent in the field. He or she is responsible for the continued life and growth of the alumni club and for carrying out locally all the tasks related to alumni club operations. The club president is responsible for planning and implementing a program of club activities for alumni in the area. He or she provides leadership for the officers, board of directors, and various committees of the club. This individual must be a person of action, able to motivate all those who serve the club.

The success of the club president will reflect the extent to which good management techniques are practiced. Above all, you should encourage the club president to delegate responsibility and keep careful club records. Both are essential to the life of the alumni club. Delegation minimizes burnout and allows a large number of alumni to have a vested interest in the success of the club. Careful record keeping ensures that future club presidents will have readily available a historical map of the club's development, showing both its successes and its failures.

While delegation may be recommended but difficult to require, record keeping on the other hand can be ensured by requiring clubs to make annual reports to the association with both a summary of activities and a financial statement of the club's income and expenditures. The club should keep a detailed account of its transactions, all of which should be approved by its board of directors. In addition, the club should keep a record of its activities—how many attended and who they were, costs, quality of the food and setting, effectiveness of announcements, and other aspects that might guide next year's planners.

The club can serve the association by reporting regularly any corrections to alumni records. The club may want to use an address form developed specifically for this purpose with the advice of the alumni records office. One of the club committees—perhaps the membership committee—should be in charge of forwarding this information to the association.

The club president should set up a procedure for regularly submitting club news to the association's publication; he or she should develop a reporting format and keep a schedule of deadlines. The president may also assign the reporting job to one of the officers or to another alumni volunteer. Alumni seeking news about alumni events and activities will look to the association's publication. If alumni don't read about a local club, they won't know it exists.

CONCLUSION

As club administrator, you must manage both ideas and people (volunteers). As a manager of volunteers, you need to review and redefine when necessary the roles assigned to the alumni leaders in the club network. As a manager of ideas, you must monitor the club concept to make sure it represents the university community as it really is, not as it was when the clubs were first organized. You should attend professional conferences to exchange ideas and discuss concepts, procedures, and strategies of club administration.

To manage volunteers effectively, you need a good understanding of volunteer organizations. The best way to develop this is to be a volunteer yourself. If you volunteer in an organization (not your institution), you will learn how volunteers are treated and how they are made to feel—or not made to feel—that their efforts are worthwhile and appreciated.

In preparing for the future, you cannot ignore the role of the computer. You can use the computer in every phase of alumni club operations. Information files soon become unwieldy and impractical, but the computer facilitates the storage and retrieval of club data. Word processing greatly enhances communications to club leaders. Programs designed to hasten the composition and design of announcements and newsletters will become standard fare in the alumni office. On the other hand, you must never lose sight of the personal needs that first brought alumni back to campus. Computers should give you the time and energy to meet the personal, intellectual, and social needs of the alumni and of alumni volunteers.

The alumni association is the vehicle through which the alumni community relates to the university. Thus, as alumni club administrator, you should attempt to integrate into the activities of the alumni clubs as many aspects of the university community as possible, for alumni clubs are the focal point of interests as diverse and varied as the alumni they represent.

CHAPTER
16 —

Professional School Organizations and Other Constituent Associations

MARY RUTH SNYDER

The largest constituency of a college or university is its alumni. The alumni constituency is itself composed of various categories: classes, geographic locations, academic majors, professions, extracurricular activities, and ethnic groups. In order to tailor programming and publications to the interests of alumni, alumni administrators have identified large numbers of alumni by these categories or constituencies.

Class-year reunions and national alumni clubs are traditional alumni programs. These serve well when the groups are small enough that the 10 to 30 percent who participate will fit into a restaurant or lecture room or can travel to a game in two or three buses. In the 1940s, when the classes of large institutions started bulging—and in 1950 when the graduating class was larger than the whole university had been in 1935—it became apparent that other subdivisions would be necessary.

The alumni office identified those alumni with similar academic and professional interests and offered programming that featured the professors from their past and the research of the future. Band alumni unpacked their instruments and took to the field again—just for fun. As soon as "two or three were gathered together," an alumni organization was formed.

123

But once these groups were formed, they needed two things to survive: a purpose and organizational support. Constituent organizations of alumni with similar academic and professional interests or with a continuing concern for the band or glee club or hockey team find purpose in supporting the "parent" school or group and its activities. And they need organizational support from the alumni relations staff. Alumni organized to promote and support an academic program can be of great value to the dean or department head of that program; consequently, deans, coaches, and activity sponsors also seek the organizational support of the alumni staff.

Once an alumni department undertakes support of the first professional school alumni association, all other academic units will want an alumni organization. Unfortunately, not all academic units have equal appeal. A typical undergraduate college offering a variety of majors in liberal arts and sciences does not provide the long-term professional loyalty characteristic of a professional school. The alumni department may need to identify subconstituencies within the college—departments, class years, housing units, extracurricular activities—for which to undertake programming.

It is tempting for deans of professional schools, particularly, to view the alumni organization as their financial support group. Although general support of the school should be the primary purpose of the constituent organization, alumni staff should ensure that programming is broadly cast so that it appeals to all alumni, not just to potential major donors.

Another pitfall—which may also be an advantage—is that many groups are quite small; while the intimacy often encourages loyalty, a very small group may demand as much staff time as a large constituency, so the alumni administrator must consider the cost-effectiveness of his or her efforts. It is hard for a small group to be self-supporting; the economies of scale aid larger groups. You may want to combine smaller constituencies or provide special programming for small groups under the general association umbrella. Support of constituent organizations is staff-intensive, and you should not undertake it unless you are committed to meeting this demand.

In spite of these caveats, there are many benefits of maintaining organizations related to the academic units or specific interests of alumni. In the *Handbook of Institutional Advancement*, Stephen Roszell, then Executive Director of the University of Minnesota Alumni Association, wrote, "Of all the alumni programs to emerge during the last twenty-five years, the constituent program represents the greatest challenge for alumni directors. . . . The ability of a university or college alumni association to respond . . . in a professional, service-oriented manner may ensure the future for alumni associations as we know them today."[1]

UNIQUE BENEFITS OF
CONSTITUENT ORGANIZATIONS

Benefits to the School

By identifying the alumni of a school and forming an organization of just those alumni, you can focus communication and programming on the mutual interests and needs of the school and its alumni. Newsletter articles can include professional jargon, details of esoteric research, and the latest doings of good old professor Jonah. Everyone will be happy, including the readers of the general alumni publication who will be spared those mysteries. The ability to target messages not only makes it possible to give them more personal appeal, but saves considerably in costs by limiting mailings to those most likely to respond.

The focused organization can offer involvement opportunities for alumni who have resources and expertise needed by the school. Deans' curriculum advisory groups, student career advising programs, profession-exploration opportunities for current and prospective students, contributions of laboratory equipment from alumni businesses—all are possible benefits of constituent organizations.

Concentrating attention on a limited population of alumni enables you to identify outstanding professionals for recognition, for special service to the institution on governing boards and advisory committees, and for advocacy of the school with legislators, corporations, and foundations.

Benefits to the Alumni

Alumni appreciate the special attention of constituency programming. Many alumni who are not normally attracted to general alumni programming may be "turned on" when they are approached by their school. One institution found alumni were much more likely to respond to requests for biographical information from the school than from the university. Alumni are more likely to attend an event when they know that the other participants—alumni, faculty, and students—share their special interests. Also successful are alumni receptions hosted by the constituent organization at national professional meetings; there's nothing like meeting a friend from "home" when you are away from home.

Although big gatherings of alumni are impressive and inspiring (especially to alumni directors and their administrative superiors), alumni really do more professional and personal visiting in small groups; the constituent organization offers these opportunities.

HOW TO ESTABLISH AND MAINTAIN
CONSTITUENT ORGANIZATIONS

Getting Organized

If you currently have no alumni organizations based on academic/professional or special interests (band, glee club, Hispanic origin, geology, etc.), you have the luxury of defining your future. If you decide to form constituent organizations, you have the problem of deciding which groups to favor—"fitting in" has to be done if you already have some professional school alumni organized, but don't want to support the small ones. It may seem inconsistent to support selected ones. It is difficult to tell eager alumni and deans that their groups aren't "important" enough (large enough, homogeneous enough, wealthy enough, etc.) for special attention. Establish organizational criteria before you begin.

A Model Organization

Some questions to answer . . . and some answers.   Unless you have a death wish, you will involve your alumni leaders and deans from the start. While there is no "ideal" organization, there are some good models that will suggest the questions you need to answer—such as the criteria for forming such organizations, financial and staff support needed, goals, priorities, accountability, and alumni involvement.

Here are some of the characteristics of a model constituent organization:

1. A charter document details the structure and obligations (it may be formalized as articles of constitution and bylaws); all the constituent organizations within the institution should adopt a similar format for the charter to ensure fairness in terms of support and obligations.

2. Alumni interest meets the minimum requirements. The organization should be chartered only upon the signed commitment of at least 25 alumni who agree to attend meetings, serve on committees, and encourage others to join. In fact, don't even consider forming a constituency organization unless there are a certain minimum number of alumni of the school or activity "within driving distance." Generally, we expect 10 percent to be really active and 1.5 percent to be leaders, so an alumni constituency of fewer than 500 may be too small to organize and maintain.

The organization should have at least three officers and a board of five to nine members. Restricting the terms of officers and board members prevents a few leaders from dominating the organization for many years. Someone should represent the dean's office at the board meetings but, in general, staff of the school (even if they are also alumni) should not be on the board. While it might improve efficiency if they were, it could mean that the school would dominate the organization rather than the alumni.

3. Minimum activity is required to qualify for staff support: one annual meeting, one annual newsletter to all eligible alumni encouraging them to participate, and one annual program or activity that supports the school or special-interest group.

4. Financing of the organization takes one or more of several forms: it may be funded by the alumni department, the dean, the university foundation, dues, an endowment, or it may be self-supporting (funded by its own projects). If the general alumni association is supported by dues, a portion of the dues is allocated to the members' constituent organizations. Often the dean wishes to communicate with alumni and will share the cost of a newsletter, provide speakers, and otherwise encourage the constituent alumni organization.

Since special-interest organizations do not attempt to "cover" all alumni, as do organizations related to schools, their funding is usually provided by the alumni of that group.

5. The constituent organization undertakes programs and projects that meet priority needs of the school. These programs and projects are not limited to fund raising or providing unrestricted funds to the dean, nor do they cater to a small group of alumni to the exclusion of other interested alumni. The funds provided to the organization—however they are provided—are used to communicate with alumni and to promote programs that are self-supporting, if possible. The programs may include efforts to seek funding for scholarships, special equipment, library needs, and so forth. Dues or other money taken in for operating the organization, however, should be used for that purpose—not as if they were gifts.

6. Provision is made for excess operating funds. Some very large dues-paying organizations soon find that the per-member allocation for the constituent organizations is more than they can use in a year. In some instances, excess funds are pooled and the constituent organizations can apply for "grants" to fund special projects. For example, a constituent organization gained funding to sponsor receptions at professional meetings for three years to see if the receptions could become self-supporting (they did). Another received seed money for a newsletter that the dean liked so much he funded it thereafter. Another organization received funding for a school centennial celebration.

Some alumni departments operate on a "use it or lose it" basis. Any excess funds revert to the general budget, which may be used to provide additional services to all the constituent organizations, such as funding leadership conferences.

If constituent associations are allowed to solicit their alumni for dues, the process should be centralized in the alumni department for efficiency and coordination.

7. Responsibility of institutional staff for the constituent organization is clearly defined. The shepherding of multiple organizations takes a great deal of time, and you should not undertake this project without considering other staff commitments.

Staff members assigned to constituent organizations should try to keep board meetings to a minimum (three or four a year) and to encourage the formation and activity of project committees and the involvement of alumni on committees and in leadership positions. The staff member has primary responsibility for the quality and timeliness of publications and promotion of programs. Since institutions with large numbers of alumni are those most likely to need constituent organizations, the alumni staff is usually large enough so that one staff member can bear the primary responsibility for all the constituent organizations. Or several staff members might handle two or three organizations along with their other duties.

Moving Right Along

Once you've done the groundwork, the formation of organizations begins—a few at a time. Depending on the number of academic divisions in the institution and the interests of alumni and the dean (or other academic head) in becoming involved in such a venture, you may have some 10 to 40 constituent groups. When it all shakes down, some groups will be very active and productive while others will just limp along. My informal survey of 50 alumni departments indicates that the schools that usually have active groups are business/management, agriculture, law, and medical (especially nursing) schools; the least active are liberal arts and social sciences. If you are asking several staff members to share in the supervision of the organizations, you may want to balance their assignments with active and inactive groups. And you might also shift assignments every few years just to keep perspectives fresh.

Staff who supervise constituent organizations should meet regularly, and the presidents of the organizations should also meet once or twice a year, with their respective deans if possible. A council of presidents can help solve mutual problems, share program ideas, and provide mutual support. The council can also determine the use of excess funds (awarding grants) or present a united front to appeal for additional support. Some activities can be held jointly; at one university, the school of science alumni sponsored a ''run,'' and the school of nursing alumni offered blood pressure tests and cool drinks. At another institution, all the constituent organizations have tables at the homecoming luncheon and vie for prizes for the most informative and most attractive displays.

Special-interest Groups

Although every alumnus can be identified with an academic program, not every student has a "special interest," and some have several. If the alumni department provides funding and staff support to constituency organizations, all alumni ought to benefit equally. Support for band alumni excludes a lot of alumni. Support for band and glee club alumni provides services to the clarinet-playing tenor but neglects Johnny One-note. But alumni often have greater loyalty to their special-interest group than to their class year or academic program. How then should the alumni department provide support to special-interest groups?

Many alumni departments encourage the activity of alumni of special-interest groups by giving staff advice and assistance; they also provide address labels and other mailing assistance.

Some departments budget a fixed amount for the support of selected special-interest groups. Otherwise, the groups have to be self-sufficient. Some charge dues, publish newsletters, and sponsor events. Some are "adopted" by departments or by academically related constituent organizations. Alumni of performing groups are often invited to perform at events on campus. Some ethnic interest groups plan activities for their alumni concurrently with other general alumni programs, such as homecoming, and focus their programming on student recruitment and retention and career networking.

Planning Ahead

When I asked alumni directors of institutions with constituent organizations about their plans for the next five years, the operative word was "more"—more staff, more organizations, more involvement with the schools, more programming (continuing education, legislation advocacy, and reunions). Areas singled out for development were young alumni and members of fraternities and sororities.

To make sure constituent organizations are on target with their programming, you should establish mechanisms to identify top priority needs of the school. To supplement the information supplied at a board meeting of the organization, the president of the organization and the alumni staff member could meet with the dean over lunch or dinner; they should review the department's long-range plan, read the dean's messages and news releases about the school, and talk with other school administrators, faculty, and student leaders. The dean needs to meet with alumni to get a realistic view of what alumni can and want to do—and an understanding that those things may not happen to be his or her top priority.

It is important that alumni leaders of constituent organizations have abilities and interests that are compatible with the current needs of the school; avoid, if possible, "preservationist" alumni in leadership roles.

Some alumni will inevitably object to school policies; they may try to rally the constituent organization to oppose the dean. There should be a process for informing the dean of alumni concerns (such as sending a letter to the dean with copies to the dean's advisory committee or forming an ad hoc study committee to produce a resolution), but the resources of the constituent organization should not be tied up in controversy with the entity it is supposed to be supporting.

As with any organization, the constituent organization must have a plan. A three-year plan that is projected annually will help maintain continuity through the officer/board turnover that involves many alumni in leadership roles over the years. Each annual plan—usually finalized in the spring for the next academic year—should include a schedule for the year of all major activities and appropriate resources for them.

Every planning process should begin and end with evaluation. Each year a monitoring group of alumni and staff should measure the plans of the organization against the outcome. Accomplishments should be recognized and failures analyzed. Publishing an annual report of the total alumni program can provide a means of giving recognition; some alumni departments give certificates, gavels, or plaques; others invite officers of outstanding programs to make presentations at leadership meetings. Sharing "how-not-to" as well as "how-to" information can help others learn from their mistakes.

Conflicts of Interest and Other Pitfalls

When you establish constituent organizations related to academic majors, some alumni will be eligible for membership in several. This is really a record-keeping problem; it is important to establish which organization the alumnus is interested in. When you are setting up the constituent organizations, ask alumni to specify their "preferred" school—usually you can consider the undergraduate college to be "preferred" unless they tell you otherwise. But plan your records to accommodate the possibility that alumni may wish to support more than one constituent organization. Then you can send them all the appropriate mailings and record their multiple dues payments. For example, the current president of one general alumni organization has degrees from three schools within his institution, and he served all three on his way up.

A more serious problem arises if the constituent organization becomes too narrowly focused. Because their resources are usually modest, especially at the beginning, and staffing may be a lower-priority assignment for the alumni department, such organizations can manage only a few programs. Thus, the selection of the programs is critical to the future of the organization. Programs should appeal to and involve as many alumni as possible and serve the school in a way that will gain the recognition of the dean. On the other hand, if the dean sees the organization only as a fund-raising group and wants top donor cultivation to be the primary focus, the nature of the programs will exclude many alumni. Becoming "too development-oriented" was one of the biggest pitfalls mentioned by several experienced alumni directors in my survey.

Many alumni directors also pointed to the need for more staff to service constituent organizations. Successful programming requires staff input; as programming grows, so does the demand on staff time. In many schools with well-developed constituent organization programs, the most successful programs are so valuable to the school that the dean assigns an assistant to aid in the staffing of the organization. The dean's staff person generally has responsibility for fund raising, student recruitment, public relations, or other advancement tasks. These "school advancement officers" become an important part of the alumni staff team and should be included in staff meetings that relate to constituent organizations.

At other institutions, a development staff member assigned to the school can be enlisted to help with events of mutual interest. In a few cases, the alumni staff member assigned to the school is housed in the dean's office but reports to the alumni director. Whatever the reporting relationship, the alumni director needs to maintain a high level of staff responsiveness so that the dean or development director doesn't feel so ill-served that he or she attempts to take over the alumni organization.

Strong alumni leaders, who have expectations that are not met by alumni staff, may decide to keep membership records on their home computer and do their own mailings for last-minute programs. Centralized services (mailings, records, accounting) provided by the alumni office should be efficient and effective; this will release staff to work with deans and alumni boards, but is an added demand on clerical staff.

As the number of constituent organizations proliferates, so do the number of mailings and activities. Centralizing mailing enables you to monitor activities to make sure they do not conflict with similar activities of the general alumni association or with other university functions.

Although you have established constituent organizations to provide more involvement opportunities for alumni, you and your staff will have to find and nurture these alumni. Your existing cadre of alumni leaders may see this as a threat to their own positions and to the attention you can give them, and it certainly represents more work for the alumni staff. An experienced alumni director of 43 constituent organizations warns that the constituent organization "competes" with the general alumni association for alumni involvement, staff, and other resources.

Alumni programming involving constituent organizations requires highly professional and energetic staff support. Staff members must know how to communicate with deans in reassuring ways and how to motivate volunteers to do the necessary tasks; they must cheerfully attend a dozen more committee meetings; and they must keep alumni focused on institutional priorities. This type of programming does not get easier as it goes along—in fact, if it is successful, it gets more difficult. As one alumni director said, constituent organizations "can overwhelm you." So, before you begin, be prepared for success.

CONSTITUENT ORGANIZATIONS CAN CONTRIBUTE TO OTHER ALUMNI RELATIONS PROGRAMMING

As the programming of established constituent organizations matures and leadership identification progresses, you will begin to explore the opportunities for alumni involvement and service not only to the related school or activity, but to the institution as a whole. You will discover alumni who can serve as speakers, performing artists, volunteer fund raisers, student recruiters, advisers, and trustees. One constituent organization may identify a project that will appeal to other groups—such as landscaping the quad, adding computer equipment to the library, or offering an issues forum. Regular communication about general alumni association programming in the constituent organization publications may encourage more alumni to participate.

But the most important contribution of the constituent organizations is that they greatly expand opportunities for alumni involvement with their alma matter. And that is just what we want.

Note

1. Stephen W. Roszell, "Alumni Chapter and Constituent Organization," in *Handbook of Institutional Advancement*, 2d ed., ed. A. Westley Rowland (San Francisco: Jossey-Bass, 1986), 448.

CHAPTER
17

Reunions

M. LANEY FUNDERBURK, JR.

At most colleges and universities, there were reunions before there were formal alumni programs. Reunions are an American phenomenon, as natural to the American character as community organizations and associations.

The first recorded meeting of Duke alumni took place at the college in 1851, just 13 years after the institution's humble beginning as a one-room schoolhouse for the sons and daughters of poor farmers and Methodist preachers in rural North Carolina. These alumni were present for commencement exercises, to hear and make speeches, and to renew friendships with each other and with the college.

This desire to renew friendships, to maintain ties with each other and with the institution, is the impetus for that truly quintessential alumni program—the reunion.

Any poll taken of alumni administrators would reveal that a very high percentage of their associations sponsor reunions. The level of commitment to, and the amount of support for, reunions, however, would vary dramatically among the institutions.

Alumni administrators everywhere need to pay more attention to reunions, to support them with staff and money, and to make an organizational commitment. The reason is simple: the potential "return" is excellent. Wonderful things happen to alumni when they return to campus. As they walk about the grounds and into the buildings, they experience the old and the new: fond memories and familiar faces combined with exciting changes and new ideas. Something else often happens: alumni undergo a renewal of interest in the institution. A well-designed reunion program offers alumni who are ambivalent about the institution a chance to clarify their feelings.

This is why we must organize a diverse reunion program and then promote it—to compel our alumni to return to campus periodically. Alumni magazines, class agents' letters, solicitations, order forms for football tickets, watches, chairs, T-shirts, and world travel all have a place in the scheme of things, but the trip back to campus is magic. Nothing else can quite equal it.

But once you have decided that you want to bring your alumni back for reunions, you must ask yourself, when do you want them to come and what do you plan to do with them once they are there? There is an almost infinite variety of answers to these questions.

SCHEDULING: WHEN DO YOU
WANT THEM TO COME?

Some institutions have no particular reunion schedule but simply invite everyone back at the same time—for homecoming, for example. This technique is self-defeating, however, because the interest and enthusiasm necessary for a successful reunion cannot be sustained year after year. Reunions held on this basis quickly lose their special quality.

The most common scheduling technique is the quinquennial, or five-year, plan. In a calendar year ending in "0," graduating classes for all the years ending in "0" and "5" have reunions. The following year, classes who graduated in years ending in "1" and "6" have reunions, and so on.

Professor Robin Robinson (Dartmouth '24) of Dartmouth's mathematics department, upon the request of the Alumni Council, devised a variation on the quinquennial schedule. The Alumni Council hoped to attract classmates on either side of the quinquennial reunion classes. For example, the classes of 1959 and 1961 were invited to join the class of 1960 for its reunion. Significant reunions, such as the 5th, 25th, 40th, and 50th, were excluded from the multiple-year plan—that is, no other classes were invited to these special reunions. Professor Robinson's plan was copyrighted by Dartmouth in 1948 and is still used by the college today.

If your institution has a small staff and limited budget, you may feel that you can't manage or sustain the comprehensive programs of the quinquennial plan. In that case, you might specialize instead in significant milestone reunions—the 25th or 50th, for example—to coincide with some major campus event.

What time of year should the reunion be? Reunions may be held at commencement, at homecoming, in the summer when essential dormitory space is available, or at any time that best suits your institution's particular circumstances.

What better time for reunions than commencement? Commencement, the institution's significant celebration of itself, is the traditional setting for reunions. But commencement is also the time when the campus is at its busiest, when area hotels are booked, and when university officers and administrators are most harried and often have little time for alumni. On many campuses, there is just too much activity at commencement.

Some institutions seek a less hectic time when alumni will receive more attention. On the other hand, you do not want to schedule a reunion when nothing else is happening on your campus.

Alumni of Johns Hopkins University enjoy that institution's perennial success in lacrosse. For this reason, reunions take place in the spring so that returning alumni can see the team in action.

The Stanford Alumni Association schedules reunions during football season as do many other institutions that enjoy success on the football field. But at the University of Illinois, the alumni association recently decided to move reunions from the fall to the spring. With huge crowds on football weekends, there was too much competition for hotel space, and football tickets were hard to get.

At Purdue, the Gala Weekend in the spring continues to draw large enthusiastic reunion crowds.

Most Ivy League schools continue to hold reunions at commencement, in spite of conflicting schedules and workloads, because of their strong institutional commitment to the value of reunions. It is not a coincidence that the Ivies continue to enjoy a position of leadership in alumni giving and participation.

ESTABLISHING THE
REUNION TRADITION

It is vital to establish a winning reunion tradition for your institution, and the seeds of that tradition should be planted when alumni are undergraduates. Now is the time to prepare and to encourage senior class leaders to continue their leadership role after graduation, at least until the 5th reunion. The class leaders should be responsible for the first reunion, and they can best do this by organizing a committee before they graduate. Periodic class newsletters and communications will keep the class informed and involved. Another way to do this is to hold a minireunion at a game or special event 12 or 18 months after graduation.

It may be up to the alumni office to prod and nudge class leaders initially. After the process works several years, it quickly becomes traditional and accepted practice.

The most successful reunions occur at institutions where the tradition is present, class officers and committees have been active since undergraduate days, and reunion "ownership" is vested in class volunteers rather than in institutional staff. If there is no institutional or association support, an individual alumnus or a small group usually decides to do it.

With only a minimum of support and assistance from the institution, many of these bootstrap reunions are highly successful. The moral is that, while a reunion can succeed without formal institutional involvement, it *must* have strong volunteer leadership.

ORGANIZING THE REUNION

How a reunion is organized, planned, budgeted, and coordinated can also take an infinite variety of forms as can the amount of institutional or association support. When there is more institutional involvement, the alumni office usually assists with scheduling, mailings, and registration. It takes at least 12 months, and preferably 18, to plan, organize, and implement a reunion. There are no magic formulas. It depends upon the institutional commitment to the reunion program and the traditions that have been established over the years. But the following is a basic timetable for a major reunion, such as a 25th or 50th.

- 18 months: Alert class officers and leaders. Begin the process of selecting committee chairs and setting dates for committee meetings.
- 15 months: Hold the first general planning meeting of class officers and key reunion committee chairs. The president of the institution or a significant officer should host a dinner or social occasion during this meeting.
- 12 months: Invite the class president and reunion chair to attend the reunion of the class of the preceding year to get the feel of things.
- 10 months: Hold a full meeting of all officers, committee chairs, and other significant class and staff people to determine a specific schedule of events and promotional activity.
- 8 to 6 months: Individual committees should meet as necessary to carry out their assigned responsibilities.
- 4 months: Committee chairs should meet or schedule a conference call to confirm all arrangements and details.
- 3 months: Send all reunion alumni the first mailing with reservation form to return.
- 6 weeks: Send a final reminder for reservations.

Committee structure

What committees should be appointed? Enough to do the job! These should include:

A general chair. This may be the class president or a classmate appointed by the class president or, in the president's absence, incapacity, or indifference, the alumni staff may make the appointment. The chair provides leadership, serves as a motivator, prods when necessary, and keeps an eye on all aspects of the reunion. Above all, he or she must be enthusiastic—a cheerleader for the whole undertaking.

Attendance chair. This is perhaps the most important person in the entire structure. If people don't come to the reunion, it's a failure. The attendance chair should be well known to the alumni, and he or she should be prepared to use any means to communicate to the class and establish the network necessary to get out the troops—letters, telephone calls, and/or personal visits. Try to make sure that every identifiable group or constituency within the class is represented on the attendance committee. Each person should take the responsibility of contacting his or her particular group of friends. Ideally, each classmate would get a call from a fraternity or sorority member, someone from his or her freshman dorm, and someone from an activity such as student government or newspaper.

Local arrangements chair. This is usually someone who lives near the reunion site. Responsibilities include working with hotels and caterers and handling decorations and entertainment. The arrangements committee must follow the guidelines established by the entire committee in terms of the kinds of events, the costs associated with them, and the schedule for them.

Publicity and registration chair. This chair works with local arrangements to be sure that plans are made and expenses are covered. The registration committee oversees the preparing and mailing of reservation forms; receives and records reservations; and produces lists, packets, and name tags.

Program chair. He or she is responsible for arranging a well-balanced program which may include: faculty seminars, student life panels, admission sessions, presentations by well-known classmates, a "state of the university" report by the president, tours, athletic events, and recreation. A major decision involving programming is whether to plan an adult weekend or one that may include the whole family. Alumni need to know how the *institution* views this reunion so they can plan adequately.

Class gift chair. A reunion provides a wonderful opportunity for the class to do something special and significant for the alma mater. If the institution has a well-staffed annual fund office, it usually coordinates the class fund-raising effort.

There really aren't any hard and fast rules about reunion organizations. The key to success is discovering what works for your institution and doing it. A poor plan well executed is better than a good plan poorly executed. Just about anything will work if it works!

PROMOTING THE REUNION

Budgetary considerations often dictate how you will promote the reunion. Approximately a year before the event, you should begin a carefully scheduled series of mailings and promotional activity. A reunion piece should appear every two months or so. You may want to follow this suggested promotion countdown schedule:

- 12 months before: Publish a class directory with full names (maiden names for married women), addresses, and telephone numbers. The cover letter or inside message should state the reunion dates and ask classmates to hold those days.

- 10 months: Send a nostalgia piece, perhaps in newsletter form. It might include photos of campus life then and now, lists of faculty and administrators still around, and classmates' children enrolled or graduated. Good sources for this material include the archives and back issues of campus newspapers and yearbooks. Be sure to include an invitation to attend the reunion.

- 8 months: The general reunion chair sends a letter that gives details of the reunion and includes lists of committee members, an invitation to serve on a committee, and an invitation to attend the reunion.

- 6 months: Send a general university or campus publication—but not one that alumni normally receive—that highlights cultural or sports events on campus.

- the December preceding the reunion: The reunion chair sends a "Seasons Greetings" card. It contains a campus scene and the message, "Seasons Greetings—Hope to see you at the reunion on [date]."

- 3 months: Send complete details on the reunion—dates, times, places, speakers, costs, accommodations—along with a comprehensive reservation form to be completed and returned with a check. The mailer should include an invitation to attend.

- 6 weeks: Send a final reminder, a list of classmates registered to date (but only if the list is impressively long). A telephone committee organized by the attendance chair should be hard at work calling people who have not yet registered.

Many institutions are beginning to realize that reunion class giving is the major growth area for the annual fund. As a result, development, annual fund, and alumni offices are working together as never before to improve the quality of class organizations, of reunion planning, and of support for these efforts.

AFFINITY REUNIONS

The traditional class-organized event need not be your only reunion effort. Affinity reunions represent a major opportunity for alumni programming. Athletic teams; fraternities, sororities, and other living groups; musical and military organizations; cheerleaders; editors; and members of scholarly organizations make wonderful audiences for periodic reunions. At Duke in 1986–87, affinity reunions attracted nearly one-third of the 4,000 who attended reunions.

You cannot do this kind of reunion without a good database and records. Usually, someone on campus—a teacher, coach, or adviser—has names and addresses, although probably not current ones, of former participants. At some larger institutions where many classmates have never even met each other, affinity reunions may be the only logical area for major reunion emphasis.

Affinity groups should play an important role in traditional reunion programs as well. The attendance committee should include at least one member of each affinity group. He or she is responsible for contacting all the other members of the group and encouraging them to come to the reunion. In this way, you can provide reunions within reunions. At Duke we have found that affinity groups provide the most substantial impetus to good attendance.

Finally, it is fair to ask how one measures the success of a reunion program. Is it attendance or the size of the class gift? Is it the process of increasing loyalty and affection for the institution? Is it for the short term or a longer term? My view is that reunions are a long-term, tradition-building, loyalty-engendering process. A well-orchestrated and adequately funded reunion program is an investment in the institution's future. Reunions should provide for a time of renewal, of celebrating significant events and accomplishments, of reaffirming strong bonds of friendship, and of cementing bonds with the institution and its traditions and values.

CHAPTER
18

Alumni-in-Residence: Programs for Students

Nancy Morse Dysart

Helping active students follow a natural progression to become active alumni—that is the challenge that faces us all. We see in our student bodies the future alumni leaders and financial contributors who will continue the traditions of the past and enrich the commitment to the future. How then—and when—do we begin the cultivation process?

As long ago as 1947, F. Hill Turner addressed this question when he spoke at Vanderbilt University:

> The basis for loyalty is to be found in the college experience of our undergraduates. It is at that time that their ideals are formed and their attitudes developed. The treatment they have received . . . the associates they have found . . . determine their loyalty in later years. [1]

If we look to our alumni for support, we must begin the cultivation process long before they graduate. The old days of defining our alumni responsibilities solely in terms of those who have completed their matriculation are long gone. Now we must look to our most precious resource—our "alumni-in-residence" as we call them at the University of Maine—to see how we may enhance their academic opportunities and enrich the living-learning experiences that add dimension and meaning to their lives.

An undergraduate program provides the environment to stimulate an enriched undergraduate experience. It creates unique opportunities for meaningful dialogue and shared experiences between students, alumni, and administrators. The feeling of "oneness," the sense of "family," the participation in traditions, and the commitment to continue "the long blue line" at the University of Maine—this is what we strive to create with undergraduate programs and services.

When, then, do we begin building the young alumni habit?

THE ADMISSIONS OFFICE LINK

Alumni Ambassadors

For the University of Maine and many other institutions, alumni ambassadors serve as the admissions office link between students and alumni. Recruited and trained by the admissions office, these alumni extend the reach of that office by serving as official representatives of the institution at college fairs and college nights.

Alumni ambassadors visit high school guidance counselors to provide updates on curriculum offerings. In addition to interviewing students assigned to them by the admissions office, they also identify potential candidates—children of friends or business associates; leaders in local church, scouting, 4-H, or other youth activities; and students identified in local newspapers as honor roll candidates. Finally, they host accepted students and their parents at home dessert parties.

In every instance, they provide the networking at the local level that lets students and their parents know they are a part of a very special collegiate "family." It is the beginning of the cultivation process.

Student Ambassadors: A Peer-Group Success Story

If students are the "product" we develop at our institutions, then we can do no better than to send the best of that product into the high schools to recruit their younger counterparts. Student ambassadors represent the peer-group success story of college recruiting.

The program at the University of Maine begins with a sign-up period when students indicate the schools they are able to visit during semester break—usually a hometown high school and those of neighboring communities. The director of admissions sends a letter and a form (see Figures 18.1 and 18.2) to the guidance counselors in each of the high schools to invite them to participate in the program.

Meanwhile, the prospective student ambassadors undergo an intensive four-week orientation. They attend lectures by administrators and faculty covering topics that include academics, student activities, residential life, athletics, and financial and admissions office policies and procedures. An additional seminar in audiovisual techniques instructs ambassadors in the use of slide projectors and videotape equipment.

UNIVERSITY OF MAINE

Alumni Activities

GENERAL

ALUMNI ASSOCIATION

November, 1986

Dear Guidance Counselor:

The decision to go to college is one of the most important decisions your high
school students will ever make. The advice and counselling they will receive
from you will affect the remainder of their lives.

We, too, wish to help in this important decision-making process. For the past
eight years, members of our Student Alumni Association have presented a program
of peer-group counselling known as Student Ambassadors. These University students are prepared to relate their personal college experiences to your interested juniors and seniors during the first week of January. Our ambassadors
discuss:

1. What college life is like on a medium-sized campus of
   10,000 students.

2. How college differs from high school.

3. What support groups are available to help your students
   make a successful transition to the college experience.

All ambassadors come well-prepared to answer the type of questions which are of
greatest concern to future college students. It has been our task to assist
these ambassadors with their preparations, and we do not hesitate to endorse
their program.

Every effort will be made to send students who have recently graduated from your
school! We are excited about this program, and share with you a letter received from a fellow guidance counselor who participated in last year's program.
We hope we can be of equal service to your students.

If you have college preparatory juniors and seniors who would like to be included in this year's program, please indicate your preference on the enclosed
form and return it to us as soon as possible. Because of the amount of time put
into this program by our ambassadors, we ask you to schedule meetings with a
minimum of 10-15 students. The most successful visits have included two meetings with 30-40 college preparatory students, one for juniors and one for
seniors, in a classroom situation. If you have any questions, please do not
hesitate to call us.

Sincerely,

William Munsey '60
Director of Admissions

Nancy Morse Dysart '60
Director, Alumni Activities

Joanne Monsen '87 President
Student Alumni Association

"Serving the University of Maine for 112 years"
Crossland Alumni Center ● Orono, Maine 04469-0147 ● 207-581-1132

FIGURE 18.1. *Letter to guidance counselor about student ambassador program.*

Students visit participating high schools during semester break. Sometimes these visits include a day of one-on-one peer sessions. Or the student
ambassador may address an assembly of college-bound students. More
frequently, the format includes a classroom presentation followed by a
question-and-answer period.

```
Please return, as soon as possible to:

Student Ambassadors
Crossland Alumni Center
University of Maine
Orono, ME  04469
207/581-1132


High School_____Guidance Counselor_____

Address of High School_____

Telephone Number of High School_____Best Time To Call_____

Location of High School (if possible, please give general direction or area)

_____

One of the two following dates would be most convenient (Student Ambassadors will be
available from January 5, 1987, through January 9, 1987).  Please indicate the dates you
prefer:

( ) Mon., Jan. 5    ( ) Tues., Jan. 6    ( ) Wed., Jan. 7    ( ) Thurs., Jan. 8

( ) Fri., Jan. 9

More students could attend the presentation if it were given _____ in the morning or
_____ in the afternoon.

Approximate number of students attending presentation _____ (minimum of 10).

What kind of presentation would best fill the needs of the students at your high school?

( )   A formal presentation to an assembly of students.
( )   An informal presentation and discussion with a class of students
( )   Slide show presentation (school must provide projector and screen).

Any additional comments or questions: _____

_____

_____

For Office Use Only:

Date Received: _____          Time Scheduled: _____

Date Scheduled: _____          Confirmation Date: _____

Other Schools Scheduled for this Date:     Names of Ambassadors Sent:

_____                _____

_____                _____

_____                _____

_____                _____
```

FIGURE 18.2. *Form to sign up for student ambassador program.*

The purpose of these presentations is to provide the prospective college student with a realistic picture of:

- what college is,
- how it differs from high school,
- the need for self-discipline at college,

- the increased expectations of professors,
- the differences in class size and schedules, and
- the opportunities for both social and academic enrichment.

Ambassadors encourage students to visit the institutions they may be interested in, to schedule interviews with the admissions office, and to meet the dean in the academic discipline of their choice.

The student ambassador program produces double benefits: as they cultivate others, the student ambassadors not only develop leadership and communications skills that will serve them all their lives, they also increase their own commitment to their alma mater.

PROGRAMS FOR NEW STUDENTS

"Off-to-Maine" Receptions

Designed for accepted students, this program teams local chapter alumni and current students at an event designed to welcome prospective students into the "family." This program, which was "liberated from" a similar one at Bowling Green State University, usually focuses on a dessert-party social hosted by the local alumni chapter. Accepted students and parents are invited to attend and to bring along friends who might wish to learn more about the university.

After a 30-minute social (a "build-your-own-ice-cream-sundae" party), attendees are presented with the formal part of the program:

- alumni office welcome;
- slide-show presentation;
- student speakers (five minutes each) on the following topics: "Academics: Achieving Success," "Residential Life: The Living-Learning Experience," "Student Activities: Growth Beyond the Classroom," and "Athletics: The Winner's Way";
- speaker from the financial aid office;
- admissions office wrap-up; and
- alumni testimonials.

Without a doubt, the most successful part of this program is the peer-group question-and-answer sessions that follow the alumni testimonials. While parents, alumni, and administrators stay in their seats, the high school students and college students move into another room where questions can be asked and answered without the inhibiting influence of parents. Parents can ask the university administrators questions of greatest concern to them, such as, "What are coed dorms really like?" and

"How can we be sure our daughter or son will get the right classes?" Students have their own concerns, such as, "What are coed dorms really like?" and "How can I be sure I get the classes I want?"

Whatever the question, the peer-group environment encourages a spontaneous, open discussion. In the process, the feeling of "oneness" is developed so that parents and students alike begin to understand that the experience they are about to encounter is a shared one, nurtured by alumni, administrators, and students.

Freshman Welcome and Legacy Recognition

In midsummer, a freshman packet, which includes letters from the presidents of the alumni and the student alumni associations (see Figures 18.3 and 18.4), is sent to all entering freshmen. Brochures describing the Maine Mentor Career-counseling Program and the student alumni association are included, along with a student ID card from McDonald's, which entitles the bearer to a free soft drink with certain food purchases.

Legacies (children of alumni) receive a special welcome letter, inviting them to stop by the alumni office with their parents to pick up a legacy welcome gift (the gift may be a freshman coffee mug, student calendar, or painter's cap).

Working closely with the office of student affairs, we help promote the "Maine Spirit" Project during new student orientation. This freshman welcome begins with first-day floor activities designed to introduce new students in each residence to their floormates. Posters are created to proclaim the unique characteristics of each floor.

Second-day residence hall activities bring all floor residents together to make banners for the dorm. Third-day events include unit activities where residents learn cheers unique to their complex.

The ever-widening circle of cultivation culminates in a freshman parade and bonfire. The president of the university, the alumni association president, faculty, coaches, team members, the band, cheerleaders, the Maine black bear mascot, and local alumni join the torchlight parade down the mall from the library to a bonfire near the football field.

It is here, at this event, that the freshmen are first introduced to the full impact of the Maine Spirit (see Figure 18.5).

STUDENT ALUMNI ASSOCIATIONS: BUILDING TOMORROW'S ALUMNI LEADERS

A chapter on undergraduate programming without a discussion of the impact of a student alumni association (SAA) would be like a classroom

---

UNIVERSITY OF MAINE

ALUMNI ASSOCIATION

Dear Member of the Class of 1991:

As President of the Alumni Association of the University of Maine, let me welcome you to campus.

We are an organization of 68,000 former students who have attendend UMaine since 1865. We are the alumni who, over the years, have been responsible for the building of such facilities as the Memorial Gym and Fieldhouse, Fogler Library, the Alfond Arena and the Maine Center for the Arts, to name a few. We are the individuals who, like yourself, share a common bond. . .a deep sense of loyalty and pride for the University of Maine.

We're glad you have chosen the University for your college experience. We know you have selected an outstanding institution. You will be well prepared to enter the job market after graduation to pursue your chosen profession. Our alumni records confirm this.

In the meantime, we wish you the best of success during your years as an undergraduate. If you wish to enrich your college experience and develop important new leadership skills, I encourage you to read carefully the enclosed material regarding the Student Alumni Association. It is the members of this group who have arranged for you to receive the enclosed membership card from McDonald's. You will also find a "Good Stuff" box of toilet articles from SAA waiting for you when you arrive on campus and receive your room key.

Remember, you and your folks are always welcome at Crossland Alumni Center. The door is open, and coffee is waiting! If there is anything we can do for you, just call on us. Our offices are located across the street from the Alfond Arena. "There are no strangers here, only friends you have not met!"

Good luck; and keep in touch!

Sincerely,

UNIVERSITY OF MAINE
ALUMNI ASSOCIATION

Fred Tarr '53
President

"Serving the University of Maine for 112 years"
Crossland Alumni Center ● Orono, Maine 04469-0147 ● 207-581-1132

FIGURE 18.3. *Freshman welcome letter.*

without books. Surely no recent movement in alumni administration has done more to cultivate future alumni leaders. While some institutions, such as Indiana University, can document more than 20 years of SAA or student foundation (SF) sponsorship, it is in the more recent ten-year period that this movement has gained widespread international recognition and endorsement.

WELCOME!

STUDENT ALUMNI ASSOCIATION (SAA) would like to welcome you to your new home, the UNIVERSITY OF MAINE

"Who", you ask, "is the STUDENT ALUMNI ASSOCIATION?

We are the student group on campus that attemps to unify ALUMNI and STUDENTS through the ALUMNI ASSOCIATION.

Our philosophy is that you're as important BEFORE you graduate as you are after. We serve as the link between YOU and the 68,000 alumni who've already attended UMAINE.

When you arrive on campus for the fall semester, you will receive a "GOOD STUFF" box of toilet articles from SAA. We also work on ANNUAL FUND PHONA-THONS, HOMECOMING, TAILGATE PICNICS and REUNION; conduct CAMPUS TOURS and serve as STUDENT AMBASSADORS visiting high schools for the Admissions Office.

If you're interetcd in joining the STUDENT ALUMNI ASSOCIATION, please call or stop by to see me or any of the SAA members at the Alumni Center. We're located in Crossland Hall, across from the Alfond Arena   (1132).

"There are no strangers here - only FRIENDS you have not met."

Again, welcome to Orono and best wishes for a successful freshman year!

Michael Lynch, President
Student Alumni Association

"STUDENTS HELPING STUDENTS. . .Past, Present and Future."

FIGURE 18.4. *Student alumni association freshman welcome.*

At the second CASE conference on "Student Alumni Programs and Foundations," held in Des Moines, Iowa, in September 1979, Richard Emerson, then CASE Vice President for Alumni Administration, shared these thoughts with conferees:

> Good advancement programs don't just happen. And good alumni don't just happen. Upon receipt of a college degree, an undergraduate doesn't mag-

ODE TO ORIENTATION
OR
A TORCH LIGHT TROMP
DOWN THE MALL

MOVE IT TO THE MALL.
MARCH IT TO THE FIRE.
COME ONE AND ALL.
MAINE SPIRIT'S FLYING HIGHER.

WEAR MAINE BLUE
SPIRIT OF THE BEAR.
RAISE A TORCH TO MAINE
ADD EXCITEMENT TO THE AIR.

BE THERE, ALOHA!

FRIDAY NIGHT BON FIRE
September 4
Fogler Library
8:00 PM

JOIN MAINE MARCHING BAND, ALL CAMPUS COMPLEXES, THE
UM GREEKS, UM ALUMNI & FRIENDS, FACULTY,
STAFF AND MORE . . .

FIGURE 18.5. *Freshman parade notice.*

ically become an alumnus eager to give his or her time and money to alma mater. The transformation of a graduate into a good alumnus or alumna requires hard work. That process should start right on campus during the undergraduate years. Those years spent earning a degree are crucial in setting the stage for future alumni involvement and support.

Unfortunately, many undergraduates don't know the alumni association or foundation exists. Most don't know what it is they do. Most couldn't find the alumni or development offices if they had to! Yet these are the alumni-to-be to whom we will be appealing for service and support.

The cultivation of these future alumni is critical to the future growth and success of your association. Your association-sponsored student alumni association will help you create an environment for the development of student loyalty and affiliation.

At the University of Maine, the motto of the student alumni association is, "Students Helping Students: Past, Present and Future." The guideline we follow for SAA programs is, "By your deeds you shall be known."

The biggest factor in developing the success of your group may well lie in the public recognition of its contributions and achievements. Once the academic and alumni communities are aware of the organization's work, your students will begin to receive official acknowledgment of the value of their services, and they'll respond accordingly. Visibility is critical, and it is up to you and your group to "show and tell" its worth.

Serving Students Past

In serving this constituency, SAA members must be encouraged—and provided with opportunities—to play significant roles during class reunion and homecoming weekends. For example, they might:

- serve as student hosts assigned to individual reunion classes,
- serve as campus tour guides during alumni weekends,
- serve as authors of homecoming spirit projects.

At the University of Maine, two days before homecoming every year, SAA members paint 28-inch paw prints on a path from the Black Bear statue around the entire campus to the football stadium. Although the students receive administrative permission for this project, they do it secretly at night, under cover of darkness. Thus, the campus community awakens to discover that the Maine Black Bear has laid claim to the scoreboard just in time for the traditional homecoming football game. The paw print project engenders a strong sense of shared pride between SAA members and alumni.

SAA members can be effective public speakers at local alumni chapter meetings, and you should encourage them to attend these meetings with staff representatives. SAA officers will have the leadership and public-speaking skills that qualify them for these assignments. This type of positive reinforcement will add to the motivation and loyalty of your students.

Be sure to include the SAA president and some other SAA members on the board of directors of the alumni council. These students should have full voting privileges. SAA officers and members should also be appointed to serve on all alumni association committees. If students are to serve your goals and objectives, you must extend to them full recognition of their importance to the alumni association, both now and in the future. Committee assignments with full voting privileges acknowledge their stature within your organization.

An alumni association award for students is part of homecoming festivities at the University of Maine. The presentation of the Student Alumni Service Award offers an opportunity to recognize and honor outstanding contributions by undergraduates.

Serving Students Present

Perhaps the greatest importance of the SAA cultivation process is that the programs and efforts of the student members enrich the collegiate experiences of their fellow undergraduates. The diversity of programming opportunities in this area is almost unlimited. At the University of Maine, the following programs have been particularly effective:

*   Distribution of *Campus Voice* "Good Stuff" boxes of toilet articles to all residence hall students at the opening of school. Whittle Communications of Knoxville, Tennessee, provides the boxes, and SAA members deliver the appropriate number to each dorm. Tucked inside each box is a welcome message from the SAA (see Figure 18.6).

THE STUDENT ALUMNI ASSOCIATION

brings this "Good Stuff" package with our very best wishes for a successful school year!

If we can be of help to you during the year, please call on us at Crossland Alumni Center.

"SAA—STUDENTS HELPING STUDENTS: PAST, PRESENT, FUTURE"

FIGURE 18.6. *Welcome message for "Good Stuff" boxes.*

- Final exam survival kits. This project provides the best of fund- and friend-raising opportunities. Parents, who pay for the delivery of the kits, are particularly pleased with this idea. As one parent put it, "It's nice to know the University of Maine is not too big to care!" (See Figures 18.7–18.8.)

- Maine Day. This day in the spring is set aside for campus service projects. A 7 A.M. parade sounds reveille for the morning service

 Student Alumni Association

UNIVERSITY OF MAINE

CROSSLAND ALUMNI CENTER, ORONO, ME 04469, PHONE 207-581-1132

October, 1988

Dear UMaine Parents,

FOR THE COLLEGE STUDENT, FINAL EXAMS MEAN STRESS, WORRY, LONG HOURS, HARD WORK, HEADACHES......

You can help relieve these exam blues - NOT by taking their exams (that's against the rules!), NOR by giving them a hug (you're too far away for that!). Introducing the FINAL EXAMS "SURVIVAL" KIT - a personalized package filled with delicious, nutritious "BRAIN FOOD" and a special surprise "TENSION RELIEVER."

The members of the University of Maine **Student Alumni Association** have designed this kit to SURPRISE and DELIGHT your LOVED ONE at the most difficult time of a college career. Don't miss this opportunity to show your special student how much you care!

> **NOTE: THIS IS THE ONLY OFFICIALLY SANCTIONED ON-CAMPUS SURVIVAL KIT PROGRAM!**

Monies raised from this project will be used to provide programs of direct benefit to **University of Maine** students only.

Please see our enclosed brochure for complete ordering information. Orders will only be accepted until November 28, 1988. On behalf of the University of Maine and the Student Alumni Association, we thank you for your support.

Sincerely,

Rodney Mondor
President

Mark Kosakowski
Treasurer

Enclosures

"STUDENTS HELPING STUDENTS: PAST, PRESENT AND FUTURE."

FIGURE 18.7. *Letter to parents about final exam survival kit.*

WINTER "SURVIVAL" KITS

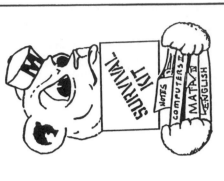

Contents:

Fresh Orange
Granola Bar
Fritos Corn Chips
Sugarless Gum
Fresh Apple
Peanut Butter Crackers
Malted Milk Crackers
Hot Cocoa Mix
Banana
Orange Juice
Raisins
Instant Cup-a-Soup
Two-Pack of Twinkies
Pineapple Juice
M & M's
Reese's Peanut Butter Cups
Pen
Surprise Tension Reliever

COLLEGE:
A TESTING OF TIME!

Q: What is a "Survival" Kit?

A: It is a surprise package containing nutritious snacks, study aids, and an encouraging note from you.

Q: Why give a "Survival" Kit?

A: Hours of intensive studying are exhausting. A surprise package from home boosts morale and rewards your student's efforts.

Q: How do I order one?

A: Please see our enclosed brochure. Any questions or correspondence may be directed to:

        Final Exams "Survival Kits"
        Crossland Alumni Center
        University of Maine
        Orono, ME 04469-0147

Q: When will the kit be delivered?

A: Kits will be delivered to the residence halls and fraternities on Saturday, December 10, 1988. **Off-campus students must pick up their kit** at CrosslandHall on Monday or Tuesday, December 12 or 13 between 9 a.m. and 3 p.m..

FIGURE 18.8. *Both sides of final exam survival kit flier.*

projects. Classes are cancelled, and students, faculty, and administrators work side by side cleaning up the campus, painting, raking, building sidewalks, erecting service buildings, and so on. At noon, an all-campus outdoor barbecue is held, followed by an "Oozeball" Tournament, a form of volleyball played in several inches of good "clean" mud. An evening concert/dance rounds out the day's events.

Last year, Maine Day saved the university nearly $10,000 in spring clean-up costs. The Oozeball Tournament raised $2,000, which was used to send a 4-year-old leukemia patient to Disney World.

• National student phonathon. A program of the annual alumni fund, the spring phonathon encourages student participation in a five-week effort to solicit contributions from lapsed and nondonor alumni. Not only are students highly successful in securing new pledges, but the effort raises their own level of awareness of the need for alumni support.

• Senior Challenge. This four-year pledge program of the senior class challenges all seniors to "take stock in Maine" and begin active support of their alma mater. Although this was originally an SAA program, all student organizations on campus now actively endorse and participate in Senior Challenge.

• Senior Information Night (SIN). Alumni experts are invited back to campus to discuss "the real world" with graduating seniors. Topics include "Investing for the Future," "Banking Wisely," "Dressing for Success," "Decorating on a Budget," "Financing a New Car," and "Real Estate: Buying or Leasing?"

Not only does this program enable alumni to share career expertise, but it also gives students an opportunity to recognize and appreciate the career achievements of graduates who continue to care about their alma mater.

• Senior packets. Just before commencement, SAA students distribute "Welcome Home" packets to graduating seniors. (The packets are passed out with caps and gowns to make sure graduates receive them.) The packets contain alumni travel and insurance information, a biographical information form, the Maine alumni magazine, and "Welcome Home" (an alumni association booklet describing the services available to graduates through the alumni office).

These packets remind our graduating seniors that, although they will soon be gone, they will not be forgotten, and that the alumni office is ready to welcome them "home" whenever they return to campus.

Serving Students Future

Student participation in the admissions office–sponsored programs includes student ambassadors, campus tour guides, and program speakers at Off-to-Maine receptions. The students who serve as effective recruiters are themselves the ones most dedicated to the mission of their alma mater and likely candidates for future alumni leadership roles.

SAA/SF Network

Any discussion of the impact of the SAA movement would be incomplete without attention to the development of the SAA/SF Network, a coalition of student alumni associations and student foundations from colleges and universities throughout the United States and Canada.

In 1977, at the national SAA/SF convention at Virginia Polytechnic Institute, participants voiced the need for a formal structure that would continue and enhance the achievements of the annual conventions. Dialogue between participating students, their advisers, and Richard Emerson of CASE led to the formation of the SAA/SF Network at the 1983 University of Minnesota SAA Convention. The Network was headquartered at the University of South Florida, and an executive committee was formed which included student representatives and advisers from eight districts in North America (patterned after the eight districts of CASE). A network chair and adviser, both from the University of South Florida, were elected.

The first meeting of the executive committee took place a year later at the University of South Florida. At that time, total membership in the Network was 94 institutions. In 1985, network headquarters moved to Indiana University and then to the University of Maine, and the terms for officers were increased to two years. Headquarters for 1987–89 are at the University of California, Santa Barbara. The CASE vice president for alumni administration serves as an ex-officio member of the Network advisory committee.

Since 1984, membership in the Network has increased to 224 colleges and universities. Yearly dues of $45 entitle member institutions to substantial delegate discounts at the district conferences and national convention of the Network. A newsletter, published three times a year, continues the exchange of information begun at the conferences. District newsletters are also being developed to enhance idea exchange and to facilitate the mentoring of new-member schools. (For more information about the SAA/SF Network, contact the CASE office of alumni administration: 202-328-5900.)

In 1984, five district representatives (from Districts I, II, III, VI, and VIII) were elected to serve as student appointees on their respective CASE district executive committees.

The influence of the Network on the commitment of students to the mission and ideals of their alma maters is measured in both the quality and quantity of the student leaders who serve their institutions as SAA or SF officers. They carry the torch of future alumni leadership.

SCHOLARSHIPS: THE GIFTS
THAT KEEP ON GIVING

Perhaps one of the most effective ways for any alumni association to impact on students' lives is through their pockets—namely, through scholarships. The financial assistance program of the University of Maine's alumni office focuses on two programs: one is designed to encourage academic excellence among dormitory students, and the other recognizes the special achievements of off-campus, nontraditional students.

The scholarship program for nontraditional students recognizes achievement in two areas: academic success and perseverance in spite of adversity. Funded by the Senior Alumni Association, which consists of all previous 50-year classes, this program grew from a $3,500 commitment in 1985 to $17,500 in 1987, and it is still growing. Working closely with the offices of financial aid and student affairs, our senior alumni are instrumental in the selection and presentation process. The nurturing link between our nontraditional students and our oldest graduates has proven to be a winning combination.

MAINE MENTORS:
CAREER COUNSELING THAT
PAYS BIG DIVIDENDS

Co-sponsored by the alumni and career planning and placement offices, this program recruits alumni to serve as career counselors to undergraduates. It is designed to provide students with opportunities to explore career options before they make career decisions. Again, the program provides alumni with opportunities for service, while students become the beneficiaries of alumni experience and knowledge.

ACHIEVING OUR GOALS: SUCCESS
THAT SPEAKS FOR ITSELF

In each of these areas, our primary consideration is the cultivation of our alumni-in-residence—helping our students develop attitudes, establish relationships, and form ideals that will determine their loyalty in years to come.

The SAA/SF Network creed sums up what we hope to instill in our students:

> WE BELIEVE that as students, we have a special relationship with our Alma Mater that represents a life-time commitment in the fulfillment of our dreams and aspirations. As students, we are the focus of her goals and objectives. As alumni, we will represent the result of her mission and the embodiment of her spirit in the world. What she is, we are; what she becomes, we become. Because we are the emerging essence of our institution, we will strive to enhance this special relationship between students, alumni and others so that the heritage of our Alma Mater will always be a part of our lives—for the present as we follow our dreams, and after graduation as we make them come true.[2]

If we can reach the point where all our undergraduates subscribe to this creed, then our success in cultivating the alumni leaders of tomorrow will be assured!

Notes

1. Quoted by Jon Keates, now Vice President for Development at Claremont McKenna College, at CASE District I Conference in Portland, Maine, January 1977.
2. The SAA/SF Network Creed from "Student Alumni Association/Student Foundation Network."

CHAPTER
19 ⸺

Locating, Organizing, and Developing Minority Constituencies

RICHARD E. CARTER

In ever-increasing numbers, institutions of higher education are showing an interest in organizing their minority alumni. Although the factors driving this surge of interest are not clear, it may be the alumni themselves who are expressing a desire to get involved, or it may be that the institutions are recognizing that minorities, as an increasingly larger segment of the alumni body, have a role to play in advancing institutional goals. Possibly it is some combination of the two. Whatever the cause, this growing resource is here for those who would use it.

GETTING STARTED

If you want to start a minority alumni program on your campus, the best way to begin is by assessing the past involvement of minority alumni in both the alumni association and the institution. You can do this by finding key individuals within your college or university who have a good grasp of the institution's history. Ask them to tell you what, if any, activities minority alumni have been involved in (some of these efforts may have been independent of institutional sponsorship and/or involvement). Not only will these initial contacts give you some appreciation of this constitu-

157

ency's history, but they can also provide a sounding board for staff ideas. And at the next stage, they can help you identify alumni volunteers.

When you are developing minority-related programs, it is prudent to seek some minority alumni perspectives. However, more often than not, too broad an interpretation is attributed to this perspective. The phrase "minority alumni perspective" can be misleading. What these first contacts tell you will provide some insight into the minority perspective. But be careful to avoid the pitfall of assuming that any individual or group can speak for everyone sharing a particular genetic trait—unless the person or group has been authorized to do so in some democratic process. The important thing is to gain an appreciation of the group's history. If a history of past involvement does exist, it could serve as one of the building blocks from which to establish a tradition.

Organizational Philosophy

Before you begin efforts to locate and garner the support of minority alumni, the alumni association should develop a mission statement that answers the following questions:

- How will this minority constituency fit organizationally into the association?
- What level of staff support must be provided?
- What are the appropriate budgetary considerations?

If these questions are not answered ahead of time, staff members may get bogged down in sensitive discussions with potential volunteers. In addition, the answers to the questions will provide direction for the kinds of programs to be developed. And perhaps most important, by resolving these issues the alumni association takes a proactive rather than reactive posture.

At the University of Michigan, we considered these three questions and answered them as outlined below.

Organizational Fit

In 1975 the Alumni Association of the University of Michigan began efforts to organize black alumni. We wanted the association to reflect and serve the entire alumni body. We knew that, traditionally, black alumni did not participate in our programs. We also recognized that in the past this constituency had been, for the most part, disenfranchised by the university. As a result, when these students left the university, they took with them no feeling of ownership in the institution and did not, in the aggregate, return to campus.

As we began our organizational efforts, however, black alumni who *had* been involved in the alumni association and the university raised serious concerns over the possibility of creating two separate associations. They felt that the formation of an organization of black alumni was in direct conflict with what they were trying to accomplish and, in the long run, would not serve the alumni association well.

Therefore, it was particularly important that both alumni and the university's executive officers understood that we planned to treat and serve this constituency in the same manner as all of our affiliated organizations. We made it very clear that we would not organize or reproduce alumni programs to the extent that we would, in effect, create a black alumni association.

Nevertheless, as we began to develop various activities, we received many inquiries addressed to the "Black Alumni Association." We took great pains to educate our alumni to the fact that there was no black alumni association, but the idea persisted. One of our first activities was called the "Black Alumni Reunion." When we learned that alumni were referring to this program as the "Black Alumni Association," we changed the name to the "Reunion for Black Graduates." While this name confusion may seem incidental, people tend to think of themselves in terms of the names or labels applied to them. We felt it was important in the early stage of development that we articulate clearly and accurately what we were planning.

Staff Support

The alumni officer who undertakes the effort to organize minority alumni must be willing to absorb and manage the historical legacy of the institution as it pertains to minorities. To do this effectively requires some knowledge of the university and its treatment of minorities in the past. More important, however, is the staff member's interpersonal skills and his or her understanding of group dynamics. A senior alumni officer is perhaps the best choice for this position.

The obvious question is, should the alumni organizer be a member of the minority group? I firmly believe that there is no assignment in the field of institutional advancement that can only be handled by a person belonging to a certain racial or ethnic group. But I am also aware of the truth in the old saying, "You can buy merchandise in any language, but in order to sell it, you need to speak the buyer's language." A minority professional will certainly have a better understanding of the problems minorities face and will facilitate the integration of this body of alumni. But no matter who is selected, there is no substitute for sincerity and dedication, coupled with direction and support from the executive officers of both the alumni association and the university.

Budget Considerations

What sort of budget you can provide for a minority alumni program depends on your alumni organization's resources. In the first year of building our program, we did not make this cost a line item in the budget, but "found" the money. In fact, most of the expenses that first year were for planning meetings and thus were quite manageable. As we entered the implementation stage for our initial programs, we were in a better position to cost out those programs. In the early stages of organizing a minority constituency, however, the main expenditure is staff salaries.

Organizational Structure

Although we all know that most programs involving volunteers take on a life of their own, it is important that you and your staff have some perspective on what the minority programming should accomplish. And the types of programming developed should reflect organizational goals. These goals don't have to be lengthy or complex. Staff should consider including this item in the organizational philosophy statement or creating a separate statement.

Initially, your minority programming should achieve two objectives: bringing alumni back to campus and acquainting them with the idea of being of service to the institution. Although you may have in mind a particular program to accomplish one or both of these purposes, the alumni volunteers should have considerable input in developing the program. A senior professional, however, should know how to persuade volunteers to embrace his or her ideas as if they were their own. With forethought and planning, the staff can provide the leadership essential to the advancement of these objectives.

Locating Alumni Leadership

Now you need to form a planning community of alumni volunteers. Start by identifying a core of minority alumni leaders. Get the names of a few minority alumni from those key people who filled you in on the historical perspective and from other sources on campus such as student organizations, staff, faculty, and alumni. When you contact these first leads, they may be able to suggest others. Particularly good prospects are alumni leaders who have already demonstrated interest in supporting the institution. Every effort should be made to meet individually (one-on-one) with each alumni prospect.

This initial group of alumni leaders should be, as much as possible, a cross-section of the alumni body, with different class years and fields of study and both sexes represented. I suggest that there be about nine alumni in the group.

If a few in your core leadership have some experience and understanding of the method by which your institution is governed, their counsel can broaden the perspective of the committee. In any event, it is important that the group share, in principle, the aspirations of the alumni association and that they be willing to help organize a few basic programs.

The alumni staff should take the lead in organizing the first meeting, which should be held on campus. Executive officers of the alumni association and representatives of the university should attend to welcome participants and to express their support. The result of the meeting should be that the alumni decide to organize formally into a committee.

Let us assume that the staff is effective in their one-on-one meetings with alumni and a decision is made to organize an official committee. The next step is to establish temporary leadership that will work with staff to develop an organizational structure for the committee. While I favor a three-year, staggered-term model, it makes sense to organize this committee in the same way as other committees within your alumni association.

Staff should work very closely with temporary leadership to get the committee organized. At the same time, they will be able to familiarize themselves with the leadership skills of those involved and assess how long each person might be willing to serve. This will help you determine the terms of office during the initial three-year cycle (if the staggered-term model is used).

At the same time that the organizational structure is being developed, staff, with the assistance of alumni, should draw up a document (a constitution) that prescribes the procedures for bringing new members onto the committee. This document should be consistent with the governing document of the parent organization. It is not essential that the constitution be developed *before* the committee begins to plan its first activities, but it does ensure that both committee members and the alumni association understand how the committee functions and what its purposes are.

It is this stage of organizing the committee that requires the greatest level of staff professionalism. During the discussion of the committee's purposes, alumni should articulate their own priorities and the issues they feel should be addressed by the committee. You and your staff, however, should have gained from earlier discussions a good idea of the kinds of programs that alumni would like, and you should have already laid the groundwork for the programs at meetings with the appropriate institutional and alumni association administrators.

You will need as much support as possible from key institutional officers. Develop channels to accommodate input from these important administrators and make sure that they recognize the significant role that alumni—both majority and minority—play in helping the institution meet its goals. The challenge to you and your staff is to facilitate the kind of environment conducive to developing programs that fulfill the mutual interests of the committee, the alumni association, and the institution.

Developing a Mailing List

Once the committee is organized and has begun to plan programs, you must notify minority alumni. For this you will need a good mailing list. There is no quick way to build a large, accurate mailing list. One way to begin is to ask student organizations for their mailing lists. The registrar's office, appropriate publications, and contacts on the alumni committee can also be good sources of names and addresses.

At various times in the past, legal constraints have mandated against identifying students by race, and this will make it difficult to locate minority alumni, particularly those from classes before 1960. Fortunately—at least for the purpose of developing a mailing list— minority alumni in that period formed tightly knit groups on campus and tended to remain in contact with each other after graduation. With a little research, you can find a few alumni from most decades. And this core group will generally be willing to provide names of fellow minority graduates.

I have not found it cost-effective to do large numbers of general mailings. Once you have compiled your mailing list, I suggest you do no more than two mailings. After two mailings, the response rate decreases considerably.

The majority of the addresses on your list may be out of date. You should request that your letter be forwarded to the alumnus. Even when it reaches the alumnus, however, you cannot be sure the letter will be read— particularly if it's been sent bulk rate. That's one of the obstacles of our profession. It may help to put a catchy phrase or something clever on the front of the envelope so the recipient will at least open it. A postcard can also be effective.

After you have put on a few successful programs, participants will give you names of other alumni who might be interested. You can encourage them to do this by distributing address cards which they can fill in with the names and addresses of interested friends and acquaintances. Word of mouth is also an effective way to get new names.

When we started our first program for black alumni, we had about 315 names on the mailing list. In the first few years, we added an average of about 400 new names a year. Our mailing list now has over 4,000 names and is about 95 percent accurate.

As you work with your mailing list, keep these three points in mind:

- the key to developing a sound mailing list is cost-effectiveness;

- the initial efforts to establish a basic mailing list are generally more expensive than follow-up efforts; and

- it takes a number of years to develop a large, accurate list.

PROGRAMS AND ACTIVITIES

Building a minority constituency involves alumni at two levels: activities and policy development.

Participating in Activities

A reunion activity is an excellent start-up program to foster alumni involvement in service programs. It brings alumni back to campus to renew their ties to the institution and, at the same time, gives the association and the institution an opportunity to acquaint alumni with various programs and to provide them with an array of information. We were very much aware of these benefits when we held the first annual "Reunion for Black Graduates" at the University of Michigan.

The Alumni Association of the University of Michigan, like those at most of our sister institutions, recognized the need to organize activities that would establish a pattern of black alumni returning to the university and encourage a greater number of blacks to participate in alumni activities. Unless minority alumni feel that they are a part of their alma mater, the university and the alumni association will not be able to draw upon this valuable alumni resource.

To accomplish this goal, the alumni association organized a committee and sponsored the first annual all-class "Reunion for Black Graduates." This all-day affair included a tailgate party, football game, reception, award ceremony, and dinner dance.

We held the tailgate party in a tent on a field within walking distance of the stadium and invited alumni, staff, and faculty to attend. During the party, we registered participants and distributed game tickets, name badges, and tickets to the dinner. In this way, we avoided the expense of mailing and the possible mix-up or loss of materials.

The football game was a big attraction for alumni who had not been back on campus for some time. We felt that the reunion would stand a greater chance of success if it was tied in with some other activity, especially in the first few years. We made a special effort to ensure quality in all the reunion events in the hope that the program would soon be able to stand on its own—and this is what eventually happened.

The reception, which took place in the black student house, served several purposes: it provided a place for alumni to freshen up after the game; it brought them to a facility many had not seen before; and it provided a congenial atmosphere in which to relax and interact. But there were two drawbacks to having sections of the programs at several campus sites. Parking facilities were inadequate, and alumni complained of feeling rushed as they went from one event to another. The next year we had all the activities (except the game) at the hotel.

The dinner was held at a facility that could accommodate only a limited number of people. This was intentional. It was our first event, and we felt that quality was more important than size. Also, we had no previous experience to give us an idea of how many alumni would attend, and, of course, we had to book the facilities in advance. If people had to be turned away, we hoped that they would be sure to get their reservations in earlier next year.

A distinguished black alumnus, George Crockett, Jr., the first black graduate from the University of Michigan Law School, a former judge and current United States Representative, was the guest speaker at the dinner. It was particularly important the first year that the guest speaker be a drawing card. The university president also addressed the audience, and the executive director of the alumni association made some timely remarks.

The Leonard F. Sain Esteemed Alumni Award is given to commemorate the career of Dr. Leonard F. Sain, a professor of Education, an alumnus, and the first director of the Minority Opportunity Program at the University of Michigan. Dr. Sain overcame tremendous physical adversities to become an outstanding educator and a credit to both the university and his profession.

Today, some 13 years later, the reunion committee has been instrumental in raising over $150,000 in scholarship funds and has awarded approximately 40 freshman scholarships. In recent years, the reunion committee collaborated with the development office to produce a video of the history of black students at the University of Michigan. The video has become an effective student recruitment tool.

The reunion is not our only program for minority alumni. The alumni association has initiated nationwide networks that focus on minority student recruitment, alumni mentorship, job networking, and alumni-student exchange. Each of these programs reflects the desire of minority alumni to get more involved with the university once they are reconnected with their alma mater.

Policy-level Participation

Alumni are in a unique position to assist the institution in the policy-level, decision-making process, and, increasingly, universities are beginning to take advantage of this potential. More and more institutions are creating "visiting committees" within various policy areas. These are essentially advisory committees. The same framework that accommodates visiting committees could also facilitate minority alumni policy-level participation.

Institutional administrators—particularly those who have had no experience with alumni advisory committees—often respond with some anxiety when such a group is set up to serve their area. However, this method of alumni involvement meets the institutional goal of increasing minority alumni "ownership" in the institution and thereby helps the institution meet its diverse agenda. For this reason, the alumni association should encourage and support minority alumni involvement at the policy level.

CONCLUSION

Working in the minority alumni area has been one of the most professionally challenging assignments that I have undertaken as an institutional advancement officer. Minority alumni are just as interested in the institution as their majority counterparts. They want their college or university to reflect diversity, excellence, and equity, and they are willing and able to help create the environment that nurtures these qualities.

If you are beginning a program to weave minority participation into the fabric of alumni activities at your institution, remember that the procedure outlined in this chapter is just one of many possible ways to proceed. Examine the needs of your institution and its minority alumni, and keep in mind the Chinese saying: "The longest journey begins with the first step."

PART
6

Communications

CHAPTER
20

Publications and Periodicals

Andrew W. M. Beierle

THE STATE OF THE CRAFT

University periodicals may have a reputation for being repositories of nostalgia, trivia, and gossip, but they can—and should—be more than that. Indeed, in these days of fiscal constraint, they *must* be more or they waste precious resources that could be better spent elsewhere. The best university periodicals are intelligent, interesting, and inviting. They stimulate an interest in higher education in general—and in their institutions in particular—by communicating something of the life of a university, its problems as well as its programs, its students as well as its alumni.[1]

The number of periodicals published by American colleges and universities today is staggering. Most institutions of higher learning have at least one publication; some have a half-dozen more. And while the audiences for these periodicals and publications are diverse, it is safe to say that one of the largest groups—if not *the* largest—is alumni, the group you are most concerned with relating to effectively.

The quality of these periodicals varies widely. Some are, sad to say, little more than the proverbial "fishwrapper," the very worst journalistic efforts. But some are remarkable; they can hold their own with any of the thousands of magazines that find their way into American homes each week or month. Careful observers of the genre suggest that, in general, the quality of these publications is rising. Indeed, university periodicals that few people had heard of a decade ago are now regularly finding their way to the head of the class.

And the rising tide of quality appears to be buoying many—if not all—in the field. The high quality of CASE workshops on writing, design, pho-

169

tography, and publishing may be responsible for some of the improvement. The increasing sophistication of readers may share some of the credit: editors know that their readers have limited time to spend with any one publication. To compete with glossier newsstand publications, to say nothing of television, they must produce eye-catching periodicals with something important to say about their institutions.

How are high-quality publications produced? What makes the best periodicals better than the rest? And how can you guarantee that the periodical *your* alumni receive is one of the best?

There is no magic formula for success. And while having enough money to spend on a publication makes the job easier and a lot more fun, you don't have to be rich to be good-looking or intelligent—and neither does your publication.

NEEDS VERSUS RESOURCES

Before you begin a new publication or make changes in the one you have, you must first evaluate your needs and reconcile them with budgetary constraints and your other resources. Ask yourself the following questions:

Who is my audience, what do I know about them, and what do I want to say to them? Commercial magazines, particularly those that appeal to narrowly defined groups (bicycling enthusiasts or photography buffs, for example), tailor their editorial content and design to serve the needs and interests of their readers. You should do likewise. For example, as alumni of your institution, your readers by definition are well educated, so the tone of your periodical should be intelligent. If your institution has strong ties to its region or is affiliated with a religious denomination, topics related to those areas would be appropriate.

How often do I want to be in touch with my readers? If your periodical is the only communication they receive from your institution, is it better to have a quarterly magazine or a bimonthly newsletter?

Is there enough news and feature material available to fill a magazine with interesting and substantial articles 6 or 9 or 12 times a year? (At smaller colleges, that may be difficult, although any institution of higher learning should provide a wealth of material.)

Do I have a large enough staff to turn out the requisite amount of copy? It takes approximately 20,000 words to fill a 32-page issue of a magazine; generating that much copy every two months is a bigger job than you might think. If you are not able to fill a magazine—or a periodical of any format—with interesting material on a regular basis, reconsider your format and frequency. A bad publication is worse than none at all.

MAGAZINE, TABLOID, OR
NEWSLETTER: WHICH IS
RIGHT FOR YOU?

Some institutions don't have to make a choice among these types of
periodicals: they can afford any or all of them. But if your institution, or
the program for which you are responsible, is not so well endowed, an easy
answer to this question is often found in your checkbook or financial
ledger. Magazines, with their slick cover, glossy paper, and option to use
color photography, are more expensive than tabloids or newsletters. If
money were no object, almost everyone would opt for a magazine. But the
easy answer is often not the only answer, or the best. Instead of asking
yourself, "How much money do I have to spend, and what can it buy?" ask
what it is you are trying to say to your readers. What image are you trying
to convey about your institution? Marshall McLuhan was right: the medium often *is* the message.

The following observations on the nature of the various periodicals may
help you decide which route is best for you.

Magazines

Magazines tend to be more formal than other types of periodicals. They
can be produced at a more leisurely pace than tabloids; partly because
they cost so much, they usually appear less frequently. Thus, magazines
often are able to explore topics in more depth, to examine trends and not
merely report on events. Readers are more likely to keep magazines, so the
content must be able to withstand the test of time. Does this format meet
your needs? Are you, or those above you, willing to sacrifice some of the
timeliness of a tabloid for the depth and detail of a magazine? Does that
suit your institution's image or the communications needs of your alumni
program? If it does, magazine format is right for you.

Tabloids

Tabloids can often be more "fun" than a magazine. Their graphics are
brighter, splashier, more exciting because their pages are bigger and allow
designers to "shout" to call attention to something. Because tabloids are
cheaper, they often can be published more frequently. Thus they can be
"newsier." Perhaps your institution is undergoing a period of unprece-
dented growth, and high-level administrators want alumni to know about
the myriad new programs the university is offering or the abundance of
new buildings rising on campus. If frequency of contact and newsworthi-

ness are important to you, a tabloid might be the communication vehicle you need.

Magapapers

Magapapers, a relatively new breed of periodical, combine the qualities of magazines and tabloids but, because they are usually printed on less expensive paper, they share more of the physical characteristics of tabloids. As a hybrid, they are somewhat more difficult to categorize and describe. You can think of them—without, one hopes, derision—as "a poor man's magazine."

Newsletters

Newsletters, a breed unto themselves, are generally aimed at small, specific groups within larger alumni bodies. A university may use a magazine or tabloid to communicate with the alumni body in general and a newsletter to inform graduates of a particular school or division of events taking place in those areas. Generally less expensive per page than a magazine, newsletters still have a quieter, more formal sense about them than tabloids. If your particular constituency is a subset of a larger alumni body, or the dean you report to wants his or her own communications vehicle (as they are wont to do), you might consider a newsletter.

Again, bear in mind that the communications needs of any institution are subtle and complex. A successful communications effort might require several different types of periodicals. But if you are forced to choose just one, or you want to design a program that addresses a number of specific concerns, these guidelines may be helpful to you.

THE COMPONENTS OF A
SUCCESSFUL PERIODICAL

Production of a periodical is generally divided into two categories, editorial and design. Both are important to a successful periodical, although writers and editors tend to place more value on words, and designers on compositional elements. As an editor, I believe design should *serve* the editorial component rather than dictate it.

A third component of success is a skilled and knowledgeable general editor who can combine the editorial and design elements into a harmonious whole.

Editorial

The type of writing best suited to a periodical depends on its format and audience. Magazine writing is different from that found in tabloids, for example. Some types of feature writing are best presented in a magazine format; "news," in the strictest sense of the word, is more appropriate to tabloids. Make sure your editorial approach is consistent with the message you want your periodical to send.

Most editors value clarity above all. An English teacher at Deerfield Academy leaves his charges with this golden rule: "Love words. Be precise." There is no doubt that clear, uncomplicated writing gets its message across. If nothing else, strive for this.

Be substantial. Few readers—if any—want to know that everyone in the class of 1928 now wears dentures. Approach your work as if you were a newspaper reporter and your university was your beat. A major university can be a microcosm of the world; you should be able to select your stories from the broad range of disciplines.

Be careful, be grammatically correct. Nothing ruins a publication more quickly than faulty grammar, poor punctuation, and sloppy spelling. This may seem obvious, but in too many university periodicals the language is mightily abused. Understand the power and the beauty of the language and use it well.

Encourage variety in writing styles. Don't make all of your articles sound the same.

Make sure you have a variety of topics in each publication. There should be at least one article in your magazine that will appeal to any reader who picks it up. At Emory, we keep a story mix graph that lets us know not only how well we have balanced each issue but also if we have neglected one particular school or division of the university for too long.

Pay attention to detail. Even the smallest parts of your magazine—your cutlines or your contents page synopses—should be well written.

Take yourself seriously, but not too seriously. Your publication can be fun to read. Be playful from time to time.

Be organized and consistent. Develop departments into which you can group stories—briefs, sports stories, and so on—and always present them in the same place. You'd be surprised at how many people fail to follow this seemingly obvious guideline.

Design

The main elements of a publication's overall "look" are design, illustration, and photography. Once again, appropriateness to the particular publication is the key element. Your institution has a distinct personality; what works for you may not work for someone else. Consider your audience as well. If your alumni body is relatively young (at some institutions, 50 percent of the alumni graduated after 1970), your publication should reflect that. The same holds true if your audience tends to be older or your institution has a conservative tradition.

In general, design should organize the presentation of the material; it should guide readers, not confuse them. Clarity in design, as in writing, is to be highly prized. Limit the number of typefaces you use, and if you choose more than one family of type (the same face in Roman, italic, and bold, for example), make sure they are compatible. Make sure your body type is large enough to be readable. Get rid of distracting elements—unnecessary visual geegaws that clutter the page.

Don't overdesign. Don't make the package more interesting than the contents. Your readers will see through this very quickly, and they will resent it. They will wonder why you are spending so much money making trivia look important or interesting, and they will soon stop reading your publication. On the other hand, don't expect good design to rescue you either. Good design is not a substitute for good writing or good editing; it invites your readers into your publication, but it doesn't absolve you of your responsibility to be a good host once they are there.

Don't sacrifice substance for style. If you can afford either good quality paper or two colors of ink on your inside pages, use the good paper and go for a rich, simple black-and-white look. Likewise, don't spend a lot of money on four-color covers if it means you have to sacrifice someplace else. Interesting black-and-white photography, well printed and offset with a single color for your logo and other editorial material, can be very effective. And if you can afford some frills, don't go whole hog. Just because you can afford a second color to highlight headlines or other design elements, don't feel you have to "get your money's worth" by tinting your halftones. Nobody looks good with a blue face. Unless you use sepia tones—and even then it should be for a purpose—avoid tinting halftones.

You don't always have to spend a lot of money to make your publication look good. I have been just as happy with an illustration for which I paid a student $25 as with one by a professional artist costing $500. That may not be something that happens all the time—perhaps I was lucky. But good staff photography, reproduced well, interestingly cropped or occasionally manipulated with screens or mezzotints, can be as interesting as an expensive illustration.

Doing the Job Right

If, as an alumni administrator, it is your task to hire and supervise the editor of an alumni publication, what should you look for in a prospective employee? The CASE Periodicals Publishing Advisory Committee, on which I served from 1983 to 1987, considers the following 12 skills essential to the successful periodical editor:

1. the ability to write coherently, accurately, creatively, and persuasively in a range of editorial formats such as features, news, and personal profiles;

2. verbal skills to communicate persuasively and effectively to constituencies and professional colleagues on campus and off;

3. the ability to work effectively with campus constituencies and to maintain credibility when dealing with conflicting priorities; the ability to communicate the purpose and nature of your periodical so campus constituencies can make effective contributions to its success;

4. issue-planning skills, including the ability to develop and/or recognize good story ideas and provide direction to writers; the ability to develop long-range plans and adapt plans to changing circumstances;

5. understanding visual communications, such as typography, graphic design, photography, illustration, and printing; the ability to communicate effectively with professionals in these areas;

6. understanding basic communications principles, including identifying and analyzing audiences, selecting appropriate communications methods, and stimulating readers;

7. understanding institutional operations, including the ability to recognize and interpret the missions and needs of the institution, and supporting these through unbiased reporting;

8. understanding basic reporting, including gathering and organizing information, effective interviewing, fact checking, and editing;

9. familiarity with issues and trends that affect education and campus life and the ability to present issues fairly;

10. management skills to facilitate interaction with the entire publishing staff, as well as to motivate and evaluate effectively;

11. financial management skills to plan and operate within annual budgets, to forecast costs, to manage advertising and circulation incomes, and to develop other sources of financial support; and

12. knowledge of distribution and mailing procedures (including regulations) and the ability to work effectively with mailing houses.

THE CLASS NOTES QUESTION

It's a sad story but true: "When I get my university alumni magazine in the mail," most people will tell you, "the first thing I do is turn to the class notes section to see what all my friends are doing.

"Then I throw the magazine away."[2]

Editors hate to hear stories like this, and the result is that they often hate class notes. "If we didn't have to run these class notes, look at all the extra space we'd have," they say. But the fact is, class notes do draw readers into a periodical. After that, it's the editor's job to keep them there.

Don't be afraid of class notes. Welcome them. Try, however, not to let them get out of control. Edit them tightly but brightly (there's plenty of room for warmth here), display them attractively, and they can be a valuable part of your publication. They can also be a gold mine of story ideas. Read them to find out which alumni might make interesting candidates for profiles. You might select a few alumni who are interesting but not worthy of major stories and do thumbnail sketches of them in the class notes section.

EDITORIAL ADVISORY BOARDS

University periodicals appoint advisory boards for a variety of reasons: to provide a critical eye from a vantage point somewhat removed from the day-to-day operations of the periodical; to provide article ideas; and to give faculty, administrators, or alumni a sense of ownership in the publication. All of these are sound reasons. As editors we sometimes get too close to our work and tend to lose the long view; advisory boards give us perspective. Our time and energy are limited, so we cannot ferret out all the good story ideas; boards can let us know what is happening outside the confines of our offices. As egotistical as editors can be, we sometimes lose sight of the limits of our relationship to our periodical; boards remind us that we are not in this for ourselves alone. But don't give your advisory board editorial control. If too many cooks spoil the soup, "editing by committee" can result in a similarly disastrous concoction.

EDITORIAL CONTROL: THE
RELATIONSHIP TO FUND RAISING

What is the purpose of publishing an alumni periodical? Easy, you say: keeping alumni informed. Why? Most editors don't like to admit it—in fact, the thought is heretical to us—but we want to keep alumni informed about our institutions because we want them to continue to feel that they are a part of the institution so that when a development officer makes a call on them, they will respond positively. While the editor should never forget that his or her ultimate goal is the advancement of the institution, in my opinion the most effective university periodicals are those that operate with a strong sense of mission not directly tied to fund raising.

Bernard R. Carman, Director of Public Information at Lafayette College in Easton, Pennsylvania, and a periodical editor for 26 years, makes several relevant points in an article entitled "Beyond Control" in the March 1987 CASE *Currents*.

> Regardless of what they may say, few schools, colleges, or universities publish alumni magazines out of disinterested regard for the exchange of ideas. They publish because they believe that a magazine yields a return on an investment.
>
> I used to offend my colleagues in development by describing our partnership as what's known on the streets as a sandwich: I jostle the mark while you lift the wallet. My colleagues were offended because, though that came near the truth, it was stated too frankly. . . .
>
> You'll have fewer hang-ups about editorial independence if you recognize that you . . . are engaged in something like a commercial operation. Your job as a campus editor is to attract the interest of people from whom your institution hopes to make a profit by converting that interest into active support of one kind or another, most often financial. If you can't accept that, perhaps you should consider another line of work.[3]

This raises some interesting questions. For example, who really controls the publication? The editor? The alumni director? The vice president for university relations or development? The president of the university? Carman suggests that in academic publishing, as in commercial publishing, it is the publisher—in this case, your institution—that is in control.

> Unless they happen to be publishers as well, editors have no true freedom of the press. Publishers have the freedom for two reasons: It's their money, and they have every right to spend it on the kind of periodical they want. Perhaps more significant, their money, not the editor's, will be on the line if a libel suit or other legal action is brought against the periodical.[4]

But even if the buck stops at the president's desk, it is (or should be) rare that he or she is actually involved in the day-to-day activities of publishing. More than likely the locus of control is found lower on the administrative ladder—at the level of vice president or director. At the best university periodicals across the country, the *editor* is responsible for making the day-to-day editorial decisions about what to run and what to omit and how to approach sensitive topics. If he or she continually makes the wrong decisions, that editor will soon be out of a job. But it should be left to each editor to understand the institution's needs and address them professionally.

Candor and credibility in university periodicals go a long way toward helping your institution. Your readers—your alumni—will respect your institution for treating them like adults, for giving them the facts and letting them make the decisions. But editorial freedom should be tempered with common sense and responsibility. In a university setting, editorial freedom does not mean muckraking; it *does* mean honest reporting about sometimes controversial subjects. It means not having to run grip-and-grin check-passing photos. It means your boss understands what you are trying to do and will allow you to map out an editorial strategy and select individual stories that are interesting and substantive.

STATEMENT OF ETHICS

Since it is clear that editorial control and responsibility go hand in hand, we should look at the ethical concerns of editors. The following statement of ethics for editors has been approved by CASE:

- Periodical editors represent their profession as well as their readers and their institutions.

- Editors have a responsibility to observe ethical standards and present material accurately, striving for truth, good taste, and fairness in their periodicals.

- They base the content of their magazines and newspapers on skilled research and mature interpretation of background. When appropriate, editors assume the responsibility of presenting opinion from diverse points of view.

- They protect the right of individual privacy and respect confidential information.

- They respect the rights of fellow editors and writers and provide credit for ideas and words borrowed from others, honoring copyright and other privileges.

- They publish no material other than advertising in return for payment or exchanges. Editors do not allow advertisers to influence editorial content and refrain from accepting special consideration for influence on the content of their periodicals or on organizational decisions.

- They treat fairly in words and in images the various races; religious, national, and ethnic groups; and the sexes.

- Editors observe these ethical standards and in so doing set a good example for others in the field to follow.[5]

CONCLUSION

What makes a superior university publication? Intelligent writing? Tight editing? Compelling photography? Clean design? All of these things contribute to a quality publication. But before the various professionals who can produce such a magazine can be gathered together, there must be a commitment to quality on the part of the university administration.

And administrative commitment ought to be forthcoming. Quality periodicals are cost-effective. Both of the periodicals I have edited have paid for themselves many times over because they attracted attention to the institution they represented. If your periodical provides a strong, positive, and credible image of your institution, your admissions office might want to use extra copies of your magazine as a recruiting piece, your news bureau could send the magazine to local and national media outlets, and your development office might use magazine articles to explain complex issues or programs to potential donors. Who knows how many ways a quality periodical could help your alumni program?

Bernard Carman had this to say about the complex and subtle relationship of an editor to his or her institution: "The key word here is not independence, but interdependence. If your joint effort is to succeed, you must each be prepared to recognize the legitimate part played by the other."[6]

Notes

1. Adapted from text by Emory University President James T. Laney in *Excellence in Communications: 1983* (San Francisco: International Association of Business Communicators, 1983), 37.
2. Jeff Herrington, "New Lessons: Emory Magazine," in *Communication Illustrated*, May 1984:13.
3. Bernard R. Carman, "Beyond Control," CASE *Currents*, March 1987: 26–27.
4. Ibid., 26.
5. Council for Advancement and Support of Education, "Statement of Ethics for Periodicals."
6. Carman, "Beyond Control," 27.

A Voice for Alumni: The Role of Alumni Research and Surveys in Alumni Relations

MARGARET SUGHRUE CARLSON
JAMES HARDWICK DAY

We college and university administrators are often accused of living in an ivory tower with our heads in the clouds—or worse. It is ironic that, although we work for institutions that produce research to expand our understanding of the real world, until recently we have failed to do research designed to improve the management of our advancement efforts and to increase our understanding of the needs and perceptions of our many constituencies. For these are times in which we must compete—and compete hard—for students, for money, and for attention. We compete among ourselves and in the public marketplace with other important societal needs for public support.

But as administrators of educational institutions committed to research and scholarly inquiry, we have displayed a surprising reluctance to ask tough questions about ourselves. We haven't regularly measured our performance or the perception of even our closest constituents—our students, faculty, and alumni. And yet, as every successful corporation in America knows, this is the most obvious, informative, and productive thing we can do to identify problems, craft solutions, and build better institutions.

At the University of Minnesota, alumni research led to major program innovations and membership growth for the alumni association. This research also contributed to proposals for reforms designed to streamline the university and make it one of the top five public universities in the nation.

ESTABLISHING
RESEARCH PRINCIPLES

Before embarking on our marketing research program, we worked with research directors of several Twin Cities–based corporations who volunteered to help us establish a foundation of research principles. As a result, before we did any research, the staff and the association board of directors had made several commitments:

1. We would report the results of all research fully and objectively. This would apply to alumni attitude research as well as opinion polls on such topics as university investment policy vis-à-vis South Africa.

2. We would be prepared to accept research results. In other words, we would follow the marketing researcher's first commandment: perception is reality. Perceptions, even incorrect ones, guide behavior and attitudes.

3. We would be equally open to criticism and analysis of research methodology and results. Inevitably, marketing research and polling raise questions about the methods of inquiry. By being open to criticism and analysis, we would give our constituents a further, useful involvement with the university, and we would strengthen our research program by sharpening the interpretation of results, improving methodology, and expanding the scope of research.

4. We would understand that any poll or research project has limitations. As a rule, the more statistically accurate or projectable the results of a poll, the more costly the research. Thus, the more important the decision hinging on the research, the more should be spent to get projectable, objective data. On the other hand, focus groups, which are much less expensive than marketing surveys, can provide a lot of useful, although subjective, information.

5. Finally, we would be committed to research as a continuing organizational value. Perhaps the greatest benefit of research is its ability to track changing attitudes and, therefore, to monitor the success of previous research and efforts to inform and involve alumni.

As we began our research, we understood that a research program was a big investment that would pay big dividends. When alumni realized the association was representing them and presenting their views on important university matters, they began to perceive the association as a meaningful vehicle for involvement with the university. And the university, in turn, began to understand that it could improve and profit by listening and responding to its "customers" and "shareholders."

RESEARCH MEASURES
ALUMNI ATTITUDES

Here is how this all came together at Minnesota. Our efforts began when association membership plateaued after five years of steady 10 percent growth. We theorized that we had already reached those former students who had a strong personal commitment to the university. Was this true? And, if so, what attitudes and perceptions, if any, characterized both the committed and the unaligned? Was there anything we could do?

All marketing research begins with informed hypotheses. With our volunteers and the highly regarded research firm of Frank Magid and Associates, we agreed to a set of research objectives and designed a 20-minute phone survey to measure alumni attitudes and perceptions about the university and their experience with it.

Results confirmed long-standing suspicions. The University of Minnesota is a big commuter-oriented campus in an urban area. In general, alumni reported extremely positive feelings about the university as an institution; yet they felt personally disconnected from it. They cared about the university, but felt powerless to affect it. The time they spent as students was a fair and completed trade. They had paid their tuition, put in their four years or so, and received an education; they considered the transaction to be a satisfactory one, but now it was completed. Neither alumni nor the university owed much to the other.

While most alumni were willing to send their children to the university, which was encouraging, they didn't have any real commitment to it. For example, when they attended a university event—and because 60 percent of the total alumni body live in the immediate area, many do attend university events—they didn't really think of the event as a product of the institution.

We could see that the university was not being credited for its successes and its many contributions to the state and the nation. Like telephone poles, the university's many parts were essential and omnipresent but practically invisible to most of its alumni.

Beneath this perceptual problem was a "product" problem. The university was not giving students a sense of community. We were doing too many things, and not enough of them well, especially at the undergraduate level. Aware of this problem, the university had initiated two efforts, and we shared our research results with the people involved. A task force had been set up to improve the student experience, and University of Minnesota President Kenneth H. Keller had developed a plan, "Commitment to Focus." This plan would pare enrollment and the scope of university programs to strengthen educational quality and to make Minnesota a top-five public institution.

ACTING ON RESEARCH RESULTS

To address the perceptual problem, we formed our own volunteer all-star advertising/public relations committee. We covered all the bases by including an account executive, a creative director, an art director, a research director, and a publisher. We shared our research with them and gave them our communications challenge:

- How can we make the university "top of mind" with its constituencies?

- How can we instill pride and awareness and ensure that the university receives credit for the many successes of its disparate units?

- How can we get alumni to notice the many telephone poles of the university and reestablish their connection to it?

The committee created an image-building ad campaign, improved the alumni magazine, and focused our research program on alumni opinion polling. This polling became the centerpiece of a larger public policy program.

The ad campaign, which was nominated for an international Clio award (it won a CASE Gold Medal), featured alumni who had made significant contributions to their fields and to the nation. Some of the ads were fun, others quite emotional. Astronaut "Deke" Slayton, one of the original seven astronauts, is just one of many Minnesota alumni who has "the right stuff." The caption of the advertisement featuring Slayton read: "Some of our graduates turned out to be space cadets." For civil rights leader Roy Wilkins, the ad read, "Some of our graduates walked with Kings"; for Hubert Humphrey, "Some of our graduates live forever"; and for actress Linda Kelsey of the "Lou Grant" show, "Some of our graduates served with Grant."

Further Research Reveals Misperceptions

The committee also conducted a series of alumni polls—the results of which were reported to the regents and university officers—on three issues: divestment of stockholdings in companies doing business in South Africa, student financial aid, and university athletics.

These polls were shorter random sample telephone surveys designed to measure alumni awareness of university issues and assess alumni opinion. For example, did alumni perceive that the university had a problem with student loan defaults? Opponents of funding for higher education often use this argument to defeat education funding measures. In this case, we found that alumni shared the popular perception that our default rate was unreasonably high. In fact, it is quite low. In reporting the poll results to alumni in *Minnesota* magazine, we began communication efforts to correct this misperception and to educate our readership about the issues surrounding student financial aid policy at both state and federal levels.

Public Policy Study

As the poll topics suggest, these surveys were part of a larger alumni association foray into public policy affecting the university. By far the association's most significant venture was its politically sensitive sponsorship of an independent study by a blue ribbon panel of state leaders, including distinguished former regents, of the process by which regents are selected to govern the university.

These efforts led to a new respect for the alumni association within the university. As a result, the administration became more active in the effort to involve alumni meaningfully in the life of the institution.

Keeping Alumni Informed

The committee of communication professionals guiding our ad campaign, research efforts, and our foray into public policy did not neglect the main communication vehicle available to us for informing alumni of our new ventures. It recommended significant changes in *Minnesota* magazine. The publication took on more substance, including reports of poll results and discussions of university and national issues relating to education. *Minnesota*, too, received national recognition from CASE and publishing trade associations.

GROWTH FOR THE PRESENT, HOPE FOR THE FUTURE

Where are we today, four-and-a-half years after our first major alumni attitude survey? Membership is growing again. The university began a $300 million capital campaign in 1986 and surpassed this goal with five months remaining in the campaign. "Commitment to Focus" continues to energize the university's planning. And the legislature has passed a bill that adds a "search" component to the process by which regents are selected. The reformed process virtually guarantees that partisan political affiliation will be an insufficient qualification for election as a regent. During the legislature's debate, the bill was endorsed by both the Minneapolis and St. Paul newspapers.

The alumni association has increased visibility and credibility within the university and the community. Our volunteer corps has never included so many prominent community leaders as it does now. Today we are an association of substance, providing increasingly valuable information, leadership, and support to the university.

Where do we go from here? The answer lies in the attitudes and perceptions of our constituency. Next year we will repeat the survey of alumni attitudes toward the university to see how alumni views have changed. On the program front, we have begun new projects. We will soon complete a student recruitment film to help attract high-ability students. In the last two years, our annual meeting has grown from an intimate group of insiders to a gathering of more than 2,000 alumni and friends—we have had to hold it in the university's indoor football practice facility instead of a hotel banquet room. Taking their cue from our earlier efforts, our affiliated collegiate alumni groups have begun their own programs of alumni research and advertising.

At Minnesota, we will continue to use the latest research methodology to test the perceptions of our constituencies. The results of our initial research efforts have already led to a stronger performance by both the university and the alumni association. We have come down from our ivory tower to find that the air is clear and the future bright.

Using Electronic Communications to Stay in Touch

KENT D. ROLLINS
JAY M. ROCHLIN

Television, radio, and computers are an important part of our daily lives, both on the job and, for many of us, at home. For the alumni professional, they are destined to play an even greater role in the future.

Today 90 percent of Americans receive most of their news from television. Studies show that many Americans watch television for as long as seven hours a day! As cable, videotape, and satellite TV increase the offerings, this figure will surely rise. Yet, in spite of overwhelming evidence that the printed word owns an ever-decreasing share of information dissemination, we alumni professionals still commit nearly all of our communications budgets to paper, postage, and ink.

Any communication that uses a device to transmit words, pictures, or sounds electronically is considered an electronic communication. No matter how small your alumni association or staff, you can take advantage of the options offered by the world of electronic media: You can use television, video, radio, and personal computers to enhance your alumni communications program.

TELEVISION: THE NEXT BEST THING TO BEING THERE

Since 1985, the University of Arizona's alumni office has produced a monthly television program called "Arizona Alumni Forum." It airs on the ABC affiliates in Phoenix and Tucson and in northern Arizona on commercial independent stations. So far, the project has been a success.

At first we thought TV would be prohibitively expensive, but we learned that with some initiative and imagination, a simple, monthly, half-hour show could be produced for under $2,000 a year. And the impact could be great.

TV is no substitute for personal contact, but a program showing your campus, scientists doing research, and students and faculty interacting could do a lot for your relations with your constituencies. A series of frank discussions with faculty about current topics could make both alumni and the community at large come to know the institution better and to feel positive about what the institution and the alumni association are doing. Additionally, copies of many of your shows could be used as programs for alumni clubs around the country, luncheon meetings, and student recruitment sessions.

Options Offered by Television

The half-hour talk show, the documentary program, and the 30- or 60-second public service announcement (PSA) are the primary ways to reach people via television. The talk show is the most convenient and inexpensive. The documentary, while an excellent way to present an idea or a subject, takes a lot of time and money to produce.

The PSA is an advertisement for, by, or about a noncommercial organization; PSAs urge you to give to the United Way, to quit smoking, not to drink and drive. Local television and radio stations air PSAs to support their communities and because the FCC strongly encourages them to. A PSA for your institution will probably get the most play on the air, especially if you are able to produce a series. You can probably get some help from a local television station in producing a PSA.

While you will probably need outside help—both expertise and equipment—to produce a documentary or a PSA, a half-hour talk show is well within your reach.

Planning a Talk Show

If you decide to create a talk show, you must decide:

- Who will produce it? The producer chooses the show's topic, lines up guests, locates supporting video materials, does some research for the host, and prepares a script. These tasks should take about 10 hours for each show. You may be the producer yourself, or someone on your staff, or a free-lancer. You may want to recruit someone from your institution's journalism or electronic media department—

producing a monthly talk show would be an excellent independent study or internship project. Or you might contact the news department of a local television station. TV news departments are deluged with resumes from young people looking for some "real life" experience. Finally, an alumnus with experience in news or public affairs may be willing to produce the program.

- Who will be the host? The host must be interested in the many subjects featured on the show, pleasant to look at, an excellent conversationalist, and able to make guests feel comfortable. If you are the alumni director, you might be the best choice. Higher visibility for you brings higher visibility to the association, and it saves money too.

- How much will it cost? You can spend as much or as little as you like when you work with television or video. For example, the Arizona Alumni Association had very little money to put into our television effort, but we did have important contacts at local television stations. Tucson's ABC affiliate agreed to donate two hours of studio and production time per show and to make copies of our program for any other station that would air it.

Our budget for producing our first 12 half-hour programs and airing these in three Arizona markets was under $1,000—about half of what we had expected to pay. A good portion of that money went for the videotapes ($20 each) we sent to stations airing our show. Although the ABC affiliate made the copies for us, we had to supply the tapes.

Getting on the Air

Next you must find a television station willing to commit both production and air time. Contacts help. If you have alumni or trustees who work at a TV station in your area or state, they can help you sell the idea to station management. It may not be easy. Public affairs programming is a very low priority in the minds of some station managers. They're in business to make money, not to give away air time to civic or nonprofit organizations. But the FCC puts considerable pressure on stations to devote time to "programming in the public interest." Each station schedules programming about community issues such as crime, education, and transportation.

When we were developing our program, we approached the general manager of the local station that had the best reputation for community involvement. Some of the key people at this station are University of Arizona alumni. We had two strong points to offer. First, the university had faculty members who could discuss topics the station identified as community needs. Second, we would use, at most, two hours of studio time per show to tape the program.

Here are some points to help in your dealings with a TV station:

- Don't be too picky about what time your show airs. At first, just getting on the air is important.

- Provide as much preproduced location video as possible to make the program visually interesting.

- Provide tape for copies of the program. It's inexpensive, and the station manager will appreciate it.

Preparing and Taping the Program

In the weeks before you tape, the show should be completely in the producer's hands. He or she must decide on an interesting topic that meets the needs of both you and the TV station, and then locate a guest who is a good speaker on that subject. Both the topic and the guest should showcase your institution.

The video that shows your viewers what you're talking about is an important part of the show. The producer must locate the appropriate tape, which more than likely already exists on campus, or prepare one if necessary, and then determine how to integrate the tape into the show.

The producer designs the set, which could be simple (two chairs and a table in front of a curtain) or more elaborate (a nicely decorated living room or an outdoor spot in front of your institution's library). Finally, the producer prepares the script. This should include about 20 questions on the topic, anticipated answers, and follow-up questions.

As host, you must be familiar with the topic and the script; you'll have less than a minute to introduce yourself, the program, the guests, and the topic. You should also be familiar with—and keep close at hand during the show—the questions prepared by the producer. You may not need all of them, but you never know. One of the guests on the "Arizona Alumni Forum" was a student who was a first-class musician, but clammed up in front of the camera, answering every question either "yes" or "no." Remember, you will not be able to edit the program after it is taped; if you run out of questions before the time is up, you'll have to improvise.

Plan your clothes and make-up to look professional but friendly. A woman can use regular make-up, perhaps a little heavier than usual on the eyes. A man may need to powder his face, especially the forehead and nose. After our first program, we got more comments about the host's shiny forehead than about the interview.

Your producer needs to keep in close touch with the program's technical director, an employee of the TV station who is responsible for getting your show on tape. At least one day before the taping, the director needs to know how many guests you will have, where in the show your video will fall, and the approximate length of each segment of the show.

On taping day, the producer should arrive at the station as early as possible to make sure the director has a copy of the script, the host's introduction (this will appear on the teleprompter), props, and any tape or slides you will be using in the program. The director will also need a "super list"—names of the host and guests to be superimposed on the screen to identify the speakers. You may also want to include credits to run at the end of the show. We list everyone in our office, including records and clerical people, because each one contributes materially to the success of our program.

As host, when you arrive at the station on taping day, you should first check with the producer to see if there are any last-minute changes to the program. He or she should introduce you to the guests if you don't already know them. Use these few minutes to try to make each guest feel comfortable; let them know you're sympathetic and easy to talk to, and ask them what points should be covered in the program.

One of our best shows came from the considerable advance work we put into addressing a thought-provoking topic—what garbage tells about the way people live. Before we taped the show, we found a video of our guest (an anthropology professor) and his team going through some of the garbage of Mexico City. Before the tape started rolling, we told him what questions we planned and which video we would show for each segment of the program. The result was a fascinating show.

Just before taping, sit in your chair for a light check, teleprompter practice, and microphone test.

Once the tape is rolling, the producer sits in the control room with the director, clarifying any instructions in the script that are not clear, and making any necessary on-the-spot decisions, such as whether to let a segment run longer than planned.

After you open the show, ignore the cameras. If you look at them or glance off the set at the floor manager's time cues, you will look nervous and shifty-eyed. Pretend you are in your own living room, talking to some very interesting people.

Although it is unlikely that huge numbers of people will sit in front of the TV at 10:30 on Sunday morning to see your program, it will contribute to your institution's image. And the longer you are on the air, the more people will watch the show as the word spreads.

RADIO

In spite of everything we read about new communications technologies, radio is still one of the best ways to keep in touch with large numbers of people with only a small commitment of time and money. While television is the medium for your eyes, radio gives you the world of the intellect. In radio you must think more about what you say and how you say it. It is the electronic medium of ideas and imagination.

Public Service Announcements

All radio stations put PSAs on the air. During our Centennial Celebration in 1985, the University of Arizona produced a series of one-minute spots on important points in the history of the university. They were a big hit at stations all over Arizona. Two years later, the stations were still playing the spots and asking for more.

In 10, 30, or 60 seconds, you can only explore one subject. Your script should be conversational. Include music or other sound effects if you can. And don't forget to let the listener know who is responsible for the spot— your institution or your association should get credit for the work.

Most radio stations are generous about donating production time for PSAs. Or you can hire an audio production studio to create the spot. In either case, you will have to decide who will write the script, what it will say, and who will read it. You can hire a producer to do all of these tasks or do it in-house if your staff has the time and talent.

The Miniprogram

The five-minute miniprogram is a good compromise between the PSA and the half-hour show. You can't get much depth in a five-minute show, but you can get in a lot of information, use one or two "actualities" or quotes on tape from an expert, and add some music or special sound effects if appropriate. You can use this miniprogram to share useful information such as tips on financial aid, how to choose the right university, whether to invest in IRAs, and special exhibits or events on your campus.

The Half-hour Talk Show

A half-hour program offers flexibility, prestige, and, believe it or not, ease of production. In a half-hour you can cover one or more subjects in depth, include news and calendar segments or other features of interest to your audience, and share information about your institution. But it can be hard to find stations willing to donate that much air time every day or week.

We have found radio station managers to be flexible and willing to give new ideas a try. Since 1985 "Arizona Magazine," a half-hour radio program with a yearly budget under $2,000 and a staff time commitment of fewer than five hours a week, has taken the message of the University of Arizona to the listeners of about 30 radio stations all over the state.

We began by approaching a local radio station with an idea. They responded favorably and within a month we were on the air in Phoenix and about a dozen smaller cities around the state. The following year the program went on the air before the pre-game show on the network that carries University of Arizona sports.

It does not take much time to produce a half-hour radio talk show. If you are the host and you have an outside producer, an hour to review the written material provided by the producer and an hour for the taping should wrap it up. Producing the program yourself will add another three hours.

If you have the budget for a producer or can find a capable volunteer, then you can include "on location" audio, music, and other sound sources that will enrich the program and its information content.

To get your show on the air, first try stations with which you already have contact—for example, those that broadcast your institution's sports programs. Approach the general manager or the program director with the idea of airing a weekly program. Be prepared to answer two questions:

- Will the program be on a seven-inch reel or an audio cassette? While most stations prefer a reel, the cassette is much cheaper.

- What is the total running time (TRT) of the program and how many commercial breaks does it have? The TRT of a program is exactly how long (to the second) it actually runs. The half-hour evening news program on TV, for example, has a TRT of about 22 minutes. A TRT of anywhere between 22 minutes and 29 minutes 57 seconds is acceptable, depending on the radio station's needs. You may want to tailor your program to the TRT acceptable to the station that is most important to you, and ask other stations to conform to that format.

As in a TV show, the producer arranges for taping, dubbing, and distribution of the program every week. He or she also chooses the topic for the program; selects the guests; "pre-interviews" them about the topic; and prepares the script, questions, an "open and close," and transitions.

During taping, the producer keeps the program on time by watching the clock and giving the host accurate time cues. The producer writes a program information sheet giving the taping date, name and title of the host and guest, and a description of the topic discussed. The topic should relate to one of the areas the station has identified as a "community need." He or she also prepares a timing sheet that gives the exact times of each segment and the TRT. Include the timing sheet and the information sheet when you send dubs (copies) of the program to other radio stations and to people who may be interested in the topic.

VIDEOTAPE

Videotape has replaced the fancy brochure as the best way to convey a message to great numbers of people, not only in pictures and words but in music as well. A video can be used in civic programs, alumni club meetings, fund raising, student recruitment, and volunteer training.

Although it costs much more and takes more time to produce a good videotape than to produce an interview-style radio or television program, the tape serves as an important communications tool for several years. The radio and TV programs are more topical and have a shorter useful life.

Production Options

If you are already producing a television program, taped reruns of the show are the least expensive way to share your story through videotape.

A vidcotaped production can be simple—set up a camera in front of your desk, turn up the lights, turn on the recorder, and start talking. You can send greetings to an out-of-town alumni club function you couldn't attend, or appear "in person" via the TV screen to thank a group of alumni volunteers.

Or you can hire a professional production crew out of Hollywood or New York to come to your institution and create 12 minutes of the most dazzling pictures you've ever seen. Of course this may very well eat up your entire budget for the next two years, but at least you'll have a good video to show for it.

In all likelihood, you will opt for something in between—hiring the expertise and equipment you need to create a credible videotape within your budget. But before you begin considering outside help, ask yourself these key questions:

- Who will write the script?
- Who will provide the talent (the on-screen person)?
- Who will set up location shooting? Choosing sites, getting permission to use them, and coordinating schedules are time-consuming.
- Who will "visualize" the written script—selecting what to show for every paragraph in the script?

We visualized a new computerized class registration program at the University of Arizona by showing "before" and "after" scenes. First an all-too-familiar "before" scene of bored and irritated students standing in long lines. Then we showed "after," a student in her dorm room discussing her schedule with friends and then picking up her touch-tone phone, dialing the computer, and registering. Finally, as a narrator explained how to use the system, we showed students pushing buttons, the computer reacting, and the confirmation of class assignments appearing on a screen in the registrar's office.

Distribution

Most educational institutions, as well as civic clubs, TV stations, cable systems, and so on, have access to, and use, 3/4-inch videotape recording and playback equipment. (A 3/4-inch video cassette is about three times as big as a home video cassette.) Your master tape will probably be on this format. Your institution's audiovisual department or any TV station or production company can make copies for you.

If you plan to distribute your videotape to individuals or alumni clubs, you will have to copy the tape to VHS format—the format used by most VCRs. A consumer-oriented video store will be your best bet for getting copies made. TV stations generally do not have home video equipment available.

COMPUTER MESSAGE BASES
AND BULLETIN BOARDS

A quarterly alumni magazine can't contain "the latest news," nor, with rapidly rising printing and mailing costs, is it a particularly economical form of communication. It cannot meet all the needs of our many audiences. Social analyst Alvin Toffler maintains that we live in a "demassified" society in which the number of common denominators—the basis for mass media—is declining. New miniaudiences, created by this demassification, form a large and active market. While special-interest magazines and newsletters appeal to those miniaudiences, electronic bulletin boards can convey information more quickly, more economically, and in greater volume.

At the University of Arizona, we use an electronic bulletin board system. An electronic bulletin board is a computer system by which people at remote locations can use computers and phone modems to call our computer and share information, usually in text form.

When you sign on to an electronic bulletin board, you are shown a menu of choices such as a message section, files section, and bulletin section. Each of these has sub-menus that give you more choices. You make your choice and push another key and the information you asked for appears on the screen. If you choose the message section, you can send and receive mail from other users of the system.

Establishing an Electronic Bulletin Board

To put together a remote bulletin board system, you need a system operator (SYSOP), software, and hardware. The SYSOP can be an employee, a student, or a volunteer from the community. He or she is responsible for maintaining and updating the system.

The software is the program that instructs and allows the computer to act as an electronic bulletin board. There are many commercial and public domain software packages available. The quality and features of available programs change almost monthly. At the time of this writing, programs called RBBS-PC, FIDO, and OPUS are popular. They are considered "shareware." The best way to obtain a copy is from an electronic bulletin board in your hometown. You can also go to a computer store and purchase a commercial program for between $75 and several hundred dollars.

For hardware, you need a personal computer, a phone modem, and a telephone line for the computer. Just about any personal computer will do, provided the software you choose will operate on it. However, you should get as much computer memory as possible to hold the information you will eventually want to share.

When we were developing our system, Mark Anderson, a University of Arizona employee and computer enthusiast, helped us develop some guidelines that might help you select your electronic bulletin board program.

1. *The system should be easy to use, both for the user at home and the people in your office who are running it.* Assume that the person calling the bulletin board is a novice, intimidated by the computer. Include a friendly welcome message on the screen—in English, not computerese. A sense of humor is appropriate here. Electronic bulletin boards have a "small town," friendly feel; this is why they are becoming so popular.

2. *Allow the establishment of special-interest groups (SIGs) that have their own electronic mail subsystems within your bulletin board.* One of the most popular features on bulletin boards is conferencing. You establish message bases where conversation is restricted to a certain subject—such as club activity, sports, student recruitment, and so on. We have about 50 conferences on our bulletin board, and they range from poetry, creativity, and astronomy to German, computers, and psychology.

3. *The program should allow for expansion so that the system can grow with user demand and institutional goals.* When more people call than your system can accommodate, many callers get a busy signal. This creates a very poor image for the bulletin board. Be sure

you select software that can accommodate more than one incoming call at a time and monitor usage carefully so that you can expand to meet demand.

4. *The program should allow for exchange of information with other bulletin board systems around the country.* Communications programs exist that enable computers all over the country to call each other and exchange data. This can be an important service to your alumni. You can set up mininetworks with key volunteers around the country and keep them up-to-date on what's happening at the institution. Volunteers can have instant access to written information about the institution, such as copies of admissions and financial aid applications. A student from out of state can leave a message on the bulletin board for his or her parents. In the middle of the night, the computer sends this message to the system in the student's hometown. The next morning, the student's parents check in for messages on the local electronic bulletin board. Similarly, they can send a message to the student.

5. *The program should be well-known and in wide use around the country.* A new user will feel much more comfortable signing on to a bulletin board if he or she has operated a similar system or has friends who frequently use your system.

6. *The bulletin board should be flexible.* You may want to keep some areas private or restrict their use to certain people, develop a specific message for new users, or restrict the number of people who can send material to you. Be sure the software you select provides enough choices.

7. *The bulletin board should allow a common set of file transfer protocols.* File transfer protocols are messages and characters that computers send to each other to translate material from one system to another. Unfortunately, not all computers are able to talk to each other; not all programs can be used by all machines. Be sure to choose a program in a computer language that is in common use. Your SYSOP should be able to make an informed decision.

What to Put on the Bulletin Board

The kinds of information you can include on the bulletin or text files section of your system are limited only by your imagination—and the time and staff available to enter the material. Here are some of the options we offer to our users:

• A list of jobs available at our institution. This list, which is updated three times a week, is probably the most popular item on the bulletin board. Just about everyone who calls checks it.

- The homecoming schedule of events and a campus calendar of events.
- A section of classified ads taken electronically from the on-campus employee newspaper.
- All of the articles that appear in the alumni publications. Users can read them there before the magazine arrives in their mailboxes. (The "class notes" section is particularly popular with our callers.)
- About 120 separate "bulletins" at any one time, ranging in size from a list of club presidents and addresses to fairly long articles and short stories submitted by users.

You can put any written material on your bulletin board. A brochure from your admissions office, for example, can be keyboarded in or, if it was written on a word processor, you can simply copy the computer disk to the bulletin board. In this way, you can share large amounts of information with very little work.

Your bulletin board will give a sense of belonging and participation even to those alumni who are not able to attend on-campus or club events.

OTHER FORMS OF ELECTRONIC COMMUNICATIONS

The price of video transmission via satellite is falling. Some alumni associations have held national meetings, live, on satellite TV; some alumni clubs are arranging live satellite transmissions of sporting events. Interactive training seminars are possible via satellite.

Tiny computer chips can carry a musical or verbal message in a card or letter, like the greeting card that sings, "Happy Birthday." Your card can play your institution's fight song or any message you wish to send.

The list of possibilities grows every day, but, before you select among the many exciting options now available, you must decide: What do you want to say, and why do you want to say it? How are you going to say it and to whom? Whether you are using pen and paper to write a thank-you to a treasured volunteer, or setting up a bulletin board system to carry your message to alumni throughout the nation, your goal is the same: communication.

PART 7

Alumni Education Programs and Services

CHAPTER
23

Alumni Continuing Education

STEVEN L. CALVERT

In 1863, the Xavier Alumni Sodality brought together the graduates of all Roman Catholic colleges "to promote the study of good books and to foster a taste for the sciences and arts."[1] The Association of Collegiate Alumnae was founded in 1882, also for the specific purpose of continuing education. . . . Today, after more than a century, fostered by continuing education and alumni relations, alumni continuing education stands ready to play an important role in enriching the future relationship between adults and their colleges and universities of all kinds—large and small, public and private, all around the country.[2]

Alumni continuing education is not, therefore, a new idea. In fact, its roots are so thoroughly intertwined with those of the alumni movement in general that the only unanswered question is how we lost track of alumni continuing education as we developed alumni relations along other lines.

As the advancement disciplines become more serious about themselves as professions, four strong arguments suggest that they will strengthen the ties to educational programming for which they have shown increasing interest in recent years. First, logic supports this movement of the advancement professions toward educational programming. Alumni, government and public relations, institutional publications, fund raising, and other advancement functions exist to support higher education's mission in American society. It only stands to reason that the closer their relationship with the educational enterprise at their host institutions the more effective they will be.

Second, history supports such a movement; since the nineteenth century, alumni continuing education has had strong support from some key higher education leaders. In his 1916 inaugural address as President of

Dartmouth College, Ernest Martin Hopkins called for significant educational offerings aimed at alumni:

> If the College, then, has conviction that its influence is worth seeking at the expense of four vital years in the formative period of life, is it not logically compelled to search for some method of giving access to this influence to its graduates in their subsequent years? . . .
>
> The College has no less an opportunity to be of service to its men in their old age than in their youth, if only it can establish the procedure by which it can periodically throughout their lives give them opportunity to replenish their intellectual reserves.[3]

Eight days later, Amherst's President Alexander Meiklejohn issued a similar statement.

Small but important programmatic experiments followed in a few of the nation's finest institutions, and then, in 1928–29, Lafayette College and the University of Michigan set examples that would carry alumni continuing education forward for the next 30 years. Lafayette opened a summer liberal arts alumni program and called it the "Alumni College"—the first time the phrase had been used. The University of Michigan, whose trustees had just committed $24,000 to start an alumni office based primarily upon the continuing intellectual relationship between alumni and the university, imitated Lafayette's summer program but called it the "Alumni University."

By 1956, college and university presidents and their alumni directors were ready for a serious discussion of the future of alumni continuing education. They met at the Shoreham Hotel in Washington, D.C., and the enthusiasm they generated launched the modern alumni college movement. Between 1958 and 1968, at least 10 new alumni colleges began around the country. Since then, the number of new programs has exploded—by the end of the 1970s, it was impossible to count them accurately.

During this period, Lowell Eklund, Dean of Continuing Education at the new Oakland University in Michigan, proposed what remains our best attempt at establishing a thorough alumni continuing education experiment. "The Oakland Plan," intended to prepare undergraduates for lifelong learning, required that each graduate file a continuing education plan with the university upon commencement. Eklund also intended that the Big Ten universities would engage in "alumni sharing" in order to provide graduates of each institution with educational services. This bold plan missed some crucial funding during a staff turnover at the sponsoring foundation, but Eklund's idea still provides us with worthy goals in alumni affairs and continuing education.

With logic and history on their sides, advancement professionals have also discovered two other compelling reasons to take educational programming more seriously for their alumni: the alumni wanted it, and the professionals themselves benefited. For example, when James Hopson, Executive Director of the Iowa State University Alumni Association, surveyed a large random sample of alumni in 1980, he found that nearly two-thirds wanted continuing education programs. Only one-quarter were interested in university athletic events.

Finally, it is important for those who develop support for colleges and universities to participate directly and professionally in the educational enterprise itself. This participation not only tunes them more closely to the mission of their institutions, but provides an adult relationship with higher education that can be rewarding and invigorating in and of itself.

WHAT *IS* ALUMNI CONTINUING EDUCATION?

Alumni continuing education is an overall program for continuing the relationship between alumni and the university. It is not one particular kind of alumni program, so much as a philosophy that at institutions like Yale and Brown Universities drives the entire alumni office's mission. This definition assumes that the relationship will be intellectual, cultural, social, and recreational, perhaps even in that order, almost as it was when the alumni were undergraduates. It also assumes that the relationship will be reciprocal, and that it will exhibit continuity from the acceptance of high school applications until the symbolic end in alumni magazine obituaries.[4]

The programs have not only attracted many graduates who have not been active alumni in the past, but also have generated measurable donations of time and money to the institution. Sallie K. Riggs, while at Brown University in the mid-1970s, found that 67 to 95 percent of seminar and Summer College participants were alumni who had not previously participated in alumni programs of any kind. Stanford University studied donor patterns in the early 1970s and again in 1987, and found a healthy correlation between any kind of participation in alumni affairs and increased giving to the university. This occurred especially among senior volunteers (trustees, overseers, presidents of alumni clubs and classes) and among participants in alumni colleges, seminars, and alumni travel programs.

Still, the goal of alumni continuing education programs has never been to generate either program revenues or eventual alumni giving. The purpose is to keep alumni attached to their alma mater in the one way that makes the most sense, so that they will be enriched and will understand the university's mission, strengths, and needs if asked later to help.

ADVANTAGES OF OFFERING ALUMNI LIFELONG "MEMBERSHIP" IN THE UNIVERSITY COMMUNITY

Philosophically, alumni continuing education provides a framework for alumni relations in which the university and the alumni can take one another seriously. Milton R. Stern, Dean of University Extension at the University of California–Berkeley, likes to call this relationship "membership" in the university for graduates and other adults looking for an intellectual home. Stern believes that eventually adults will consider their intellectual ties to a university as important as their religion or political party.

The importance of strengthening this relationship cannot be overemphasized, as Robert G. Forman reminds his audiences. Forman, Executive Director of the University of Michigan Alumni Association, believes that the purpose of alumni relations should be to keep America's educated adults so well informed about national and world problems that they can take an active role in working toward solutions. If we consider Stern's and Forman's views together, continuing education for an institution's alumni makes perfect sense from now on.

Clearly, the nation and the world would benefit from such educational programs for adults, if the programs were taken seriously by them and their universities. There are, in addition, many practical advantages to alumni continuing education programs. Trustees, regents, and presidents will be able to take advantage of adult members of the university who better understand its mission, practices, and programs, and who are in positions to help the university.

The faculty gains audiences of educated adults who can be more interesting (and more demanding) than adolescent students. Those adolescent students, on the other hand, can benefit from courses that originate in the less structured setting of alumni continuing education (few academic hurdles exist to restrict what is taught in these programs). Such courses often take advantage of a faculty member's special interests, even if those are no longer precisely in his or her area of official expertise.

The alumni office gains alumni knowledgeable about the institution today. The continuing education office gains a ready-made audience of adults who already have some affection for, and trust in, the institution. And the development office may be able to take advantage of a greater understanding and lively interest in various university enterprises with which alumni continuing education participants have become familiar. Alumni directors and their staffs can themselves benefit from their involvement in alumni colleges and seminars; many of the topics will be of direct personal interest; and most participants will be very favorably disposed toward the institution and willing to help.

Finally, of course, the alumni themselves benefit from continuing education provided by the institution they already know and trust, and which invites them into a nonthreatening environment to pursue adult inquiry in areas of interest.

PLANNING ALUMNI CONTINUING EDUCATION PROGRAMS

Before launching programs, a college or university will want to engage in self-assessment, focusing eventually on programs that showcase its strengths. An engineering school will not normally offer liberal arts seminars to alumni; nor will a small private institution always have the faculty for agricultural programs.

Organizing the Staff

Almost as many organizational arrangements exist as there are sponsoring institutions. The alumni office may take on the alumni continuing education programs alone or work cooperatively with the continuing education office in any number of ways. At Harvard, the summer Alumni College academic program has often been planned by the office of continuing education; the alumni office provides promotional expertise using a computerized alumni mailing list and also handles program administration before and during the actual program. Any organization that works is the right one.

Like any new product, alumni continuing education benefits mightily from the attention of a "champion," the individual who cares most about these programs, wherever he or she may be located within the institution. At Colgate in the mid-1970s, the champion was biology professor William Oostenink who invented Colgate's alumni college and ran it, with little administrative help, out of a passionate belief in its value. Other institutions have had great success by naming a faculty member the "academic director" of the alumni college or other alumni continuing education programs.

Choosing Faculty and Topics

Choosing the right faculty members and topics can make or break a program, but there are many ways in which successful programs develop. Ideas for topics can come from anyone in the alumni or continuing education office or from volunteer alumni directors or past program participants. Some of the most successful topics and faculty choices result from cooperative planning between a university office and the alumni themselves. This is never more true than with reunion seminars which, because they present audiences of uniform age, can tackle narrowly defined themes of special interest to young professionals starting work and families, or mid-life adults at their 25th reunion, or retirement-age alumni facing yet another major life change.

Like most short-term, noncredit continuing education programs, alumni continuing education programs depend less upon classroom activity than upon the self-directed learning habits of adult participants. For this reason, most programs should include advance reading packets of materials that registrants can study prior to the actual programs, follow-up reading, and a teaching style that late Dartmouth Professor of English James A. Epperson called the "depth charge principle." Epperson told his seminar and Alumni College participants that he did not mean to tell them what they wanted to know, but rather to drop intellectual depth charges into their minds that would explode with meaning for them at some time after the actual program ended.

Budgeting

Who will pay for alumni continuing education programs? There are several ways to look at an alumni continuing education budget. These programs have a value-added effect on institutional fund raising and can be thought of as an investment in alumni relations even if they do not pay for themselves. Outside funding may be available for some programs; in some cases the alumni themselves will guarantee the program budget for reunion or alumni club seminars. And, once a variety of alumni continuing education programs appears, some programs can subsidize others: alumni travel might help pay for long-distance alumni club seminars, for example.

The important points are these: (1) alumni continuing education, like most other forms of nonprofessional higher education, may not and perhaps even should not pay for itself, since its goal is alumni participation, not break-even budgets; and (2) some formats are more likely to require institutional investment than others. The summer alumni college is the most likely of all to need institutional investment and probably should be the last program format attempted.

Marketing

A new alumni continuing education program may require considerable marketing to sell it to alumni. Adults may initially be reluctant to jump back into a classroom setting after as many as 40 or more years away from university life. Promotion and marketing must be very attractive, and programs must be properly designed with the audience (sometimes a very specific audience, like a reunion class) in mind. Even so, it may take a couple of years before the programs take off; real success comes in numbers of participants and reasonable bottom-line budgets. But, once alumni have experienced the joy of participating in continuing education programs, they tend to return again and again. A two-thirds repeat rate is not uncommon.

TYPES OF ALUMNI CONTINUING EDUCATION PROGRAMS

Hundreds of program formats have been used successfully by all kinds of colleges and universities around the country. For a longer list than can be provided here, see Chapters 4 to 7 in my *Alumni Continuing Education* and Chapter 8 for 20 pages of successful topics, divided according to the length of the program in which they worked well. In general, alumni continuing education has come in the shape of on-campus summer alumni colleges (including computer and language programs); shorter seminars of one to three days' duration both on and off the campus; alumni colleges abroad (alumni travel with members of the faculty); and a variety of very specialized and still rather experimental media programs using videotape and other electronic advances.

The term "alumni college" can be reserved for the longest program an institution offers its alumni on the campus. Alumni colleges may offer a single theme or many theme choices; keep the same faculty throughout or invite individual lecturers; and may or may not provide afternoon or evening workshops or access to the campus theater, concert hall, or other major educational events. The shorter seminars tend to stick to a single topic. Many very successful seminars take place in conjunction with a cultural event such as a major traveling art exhibition or a theater performance that provides its own expensive promotion.

Alumni colleges abroad offer tremendous advantages to a sponsoring alumni association or university, but also bring pitfalls. While these programs offer alumni around-the-clock access to the faculty lecturers and may some day be used to their full potential as cultural exchanges among educated adults of different cultures, they have also attracted the attention of the Internal Revenue Service and the U.S. Postal Service. Sponsoring institutions must operate carefully within the laws applying to both areas. CASE, *Alumni Continuing Education* (see especially "Legal Risks," pp. 189–194), and college or university counsel can provide information on how to protect yourself and your institution from unpleasant experiences.

THE INTELLECTUAL RESIDENCE
OF ALUMNI

Alumni continuing education can help to define the future of adults and universities in a relationship that clearly and powerfully benefits both. The goal is a lifelong relationship filled with refreshing challenge and change, surprising and timely benefits. It should have balance and strength. It should be as good at all points for the adult as for the university.

As we approach the next century, knowledge continues to explode, and the world we live in changes several times in a human lifespan; thus, this relationship between adults and universities must be strong and healthy, for it will encounter pressures that we can only begin to imagine today. The average age of college students is rising well beyond the traditional 18 to 22 years so that educational institutions will need to continually adjust their views of, and services for, the adult learner.

In this context, the first place adult learners turn will be to their undergraduate alma mater, and we must be prepared to respond. We may need to begin teaching undergraduates how to design adult education packages for themselves to meet future learning needs. While we are at it, we should organize programs that teach these same lifelong learning skills to adults who have already passed through our portals at commencement. We may want lifelong learning centers on our best campuses, so that adults have an intellectual home with services designed specifically to fit the shape of their lives and learning needs.

As we work toward this goal, it will be important to organize a coherent plan—where we now have a host of separately operating professions and services—to encourage and utilize the attachment of adults to our universities. Adults now relate to universities in many different roles: part-time or full-time students and faculty members, public event participants, patrons through the fund-raising programs, advisers (trustees, regents, overseers, departmental visiting committee members), admissions or annual fund volunteers, and so on. Age or stage of life often determines what services an adult requires from, or can give to, the institution. In the present system of separate departments handling the different adult relationships to the university, there is great risk that a volunteer will "burn out" or that university resources will be wasted on the attempt to involve an adult who is not ready for the kind of involvement offered.

As we prepare for lifelong membership by adults in the university community, we must begin by drawing a coherent map of these involvements and then working out a plan for a better match between the needs of our alumni and those of the university.

In that process, it will be important to agree that adults and universities owe one another a lifetime of service. The profession that currently holds the greatest potential to define and facilitate that service is alumni administration. Taking on these greater challenges, however, will put great pressure on future alumni directors—those who are just now considering or entering the profession. For this reason, alumni administration must become more clearly a profession, and right away. We must establish the body of knowledge that defines it and press ahead with more research and writing to expand knowledge that is at present almost always orally transmitted. Then we must make a concerted effort to market our profession until Bob Forman's dream comes true and an undergraduate admits that his or her lifelong desire is to grow up to be an alumni director.

Ernest E. McMahon may be right that, in the future, the alumni administrator will be called the "dean of alumni college" in recognition of the crucial role as educator or educational broker that these leaders of the future will play. (As brokers, we will almost certainly find ourselves referring distant alumni to sister institutions for the educational services they need.)

But no matter what we are called, we do not want to lose to the continuing education office our role of linking adults and universities at a time when demographic shifts and advancing technology send greater and greater numbers of adults back to the university for education. When that happens, who will need alumni directors to keep them in touch with alma mater unless alumni directors are themselves the educators responsible for the lifelong education of graduates?

Because alumni continuing education is a philosophy of alumni relations, not merely a type of alumni program, it provides one perspective from which we can see into the brightest future for the profession of alumni administration. This is a future in which alumni directors see themselves, and are seen as, working at the heart of their colleges' and universities' educational missions.

Notes

Note: For a book-length study of this subject, see Steven L. Calvert, *Alumni Continuing Education* (New York: American Council on Education/Macmillan, 1987).

1. Malcolm S. Knowles, *The Adult Education Movement in the United States* (New York: Holt, Rinehart & Winston, 1962), 23.

2. Steven L. Calvert, *Alumni Continuing Education* (New York: American Council on Education/Macmillan, 1987), 3–4.

3. *Dartmouth Alumni Magazine*, 1916–17:16.

4. For a more detailed definition, see Calvert, *Alumni Continuing Education*, 4–7.

CHAPTER
24

Merchandising and Member Services

WILLIAM J. ROTHWELL

One description of salesmanship is "transferring a conviction by a seller to a buyer." This concept is extremely important to an understanding of merchandising and member services. This chapter describes the natural relationship between merchandising products that publicize the university and promoting member services as they relate to alumni administration.

Institutions of higher learning are always looking for ways to create a spirit of involvement among alumni. Alumni professionals and advancement officers of all kinds are constantly trying to create or maintain a love affair between the university and its graduates. Alumni should be reminded regularly that they are the caretakers and guardians of the institution and that they have a continuing responsibility to help make it a better college or university. This requires ongoing efforts to develop and instill pride in the individuals for their university.

Successful merchandising programs involving such products as articles of clothing, furniture, or watches will clearly establish symbols of individual pride for all to see. What better way than to display such a symbol across your chest or on your auto bumper sticker? Member services such as educational tours, special publications, and local club affiliation also help in creating this special feeling for the university.

All decisions concerning merchandising and member services should be guided by a philosophy that has been developed through consultation with the many people involved with an alumni association. This philosophy should clearly state the goals of the programs, the range of activities to be undertaken, and easily identifiable evaluation processes.

211

There should be a standing marketing committee to oversee merchandising and marketing programs. That committee should establish guidelines for dealing with outside providers such as:

- the product sold or the service offered must in some way provide visibility for the institution;

- the product or service should be exclusive, at least initially, to the association or institution and not something that the customer can buy elsewhere;

- only quality suppliers and merchandise should be used—satisfaction must be guaranteed;

- the association should try to use a third-party supplier to do all the work;

- products and services should use the institution's name or logotype in a recognizable form; and

- the number of products and services that are offered in any one year should be limited so as not to oversaturate the alumni market.

Ideally, there should be an opportunity for some small or reasonable gain for the association and no cost or liability to the alumni association.

MERCHANDISING

Merchandising is a method of establishing symbols of alumni pride in the institution. Merchandising enables alumni to show the world how happy and proud they are to be an integral part of a great institution. It can give the institution free advertising, develop pride and commitment, and take the first step toward involving someone with the institution.

Any item offered should be of the highest quality. You must ensure that you make a friend for the institution through the transaction. Thus, a product should be returnable for full value if it is not what the buyer had expected or if it is unacceptable for any reason. Be clear on arrangements for promotion and know who is going to pay for delivery.

The benefits of a merchandising program include the following.

Free advertising.   Merchandising can provide free advertising for your institution in two ways. First, when people buy your product and wear it or display it in their homes or on their cars, they create an identity or image for your institution. This helps prospective students and other potential supporters of the university throughout the nation to see the kind of pride that has been instilled in the alumni of your institution. Second, the companies with which you are working bear the cost of advertising the institution's or the association's logo or name in your publications, through individual flyers, and through other advertising media in various locations.

Your institution's alumni magazine can regularly advertise a variety of goods and services. With the fairly recent phenomenon of licensing university marks and logos, institutions and associations are beginning to realize substantial licensing revenues. Manufacturers or wholesalers can be required to provide 5 to 10 percent royalties on all goods and services sold with your logo. These royalties are providing millions of dollars to institutions for scholarship aid, student programming, alumni programming, and so on.

Pride and commitment.   Pride in the institution can lead to commitment when the alumnus buys an item sponsored by the institution. Once this first step has been taken, it is easier to sell the buyer future items. People who buy silk ties bearing the institution's mascot or seal are much more likely to attend alumni club meetings, donate money to the institution, and send their children there.

In the best of all possible worlds, every alumnus would display some symbol of the university in a positive manner. And the close working relationship among the institution's public relations office, bookstore, outside merchandising outlets, athletic department, theater department, continuing education unit, specialty summer camps, and other operations would result in a unified merchandising concept for the whole institution.

Initial involvement.   The development of initial involvement is particularly important for younger alumni. When alumni can be convinced to purchase something of perceived value from the institution, it has two effects. First, it sets in their minds the idea of getting something *from* the university, and, second, it allows them to make the act of giving something *to* the university in the form of the check or the credit card purchase for the merchandise. This often has a long-lasting effect in breaking down barriers that may exist for participating in other programs and for ultimate support of the institution through the donation of time, money, expertise, and other volunteer service.

Thus, quality merchandising has a far greater result than the small profit the institution may make—it helps "spread the word" about the institution and breaks down participation barriers in the minds of its various constituents.

Marketing Segmentation

It is important to segment your markets whenever appropriate. When you are promoting international educational alumni tours, for example, remember that the people who have traveled with you once and liked it are much more likely to sign up a second time than those who have never taken an alumni tour. If your travelers went to a bowl game or a "final four" tournament to support their team, they are likely to be more responsive to a promotional brochure for the same or a similar activity.

Do not, however, restrict your marketing efforts to previous customers. It is always important to add new names to your markets, and you should always market to new alumni who have never responded, particularly to those who have expressed an interest in other alumni programs.

When you are segmenting your market, try to develop an array of activities to meet various interests and needs. Some of your merchandising efforts can be joint ventures with other organizations or departments of the institution and some can be exclusively the property of the alumni association. Joint ventures might include university watches, mantle clocks and grandfather clocks, lithographs of buildings on campus, statues of landmarks, bookends, and university chairs. Chairs are always a popular item and come in three varieties—captain's chairs, rocking chairs, and ornate chairs with a campus scene painted on the backrest.

Other merchandising possibilities include:

Vanity license plates.   An unusual program that has brought visibility to several institutions is the marketing of vanity license plates bearing the institution's name and logo. Member organizations in Pennsylvania can receive permission to have their logos and names on the actual license plate that registers a vehicle. And now the states of Florida, Maryland, Virginia, and New Jersey are issuing organization license plates as well.

Publications.   Selling alumni directories or alumni registers not only makes money for the association but also helps you maintain accurate records by updating alumni occupations, phone numbers, and other demographic information. The directory creates renewed interest among purchasers for news about classmates, friends, Greek affiliates, and so on.

Two other publications show great potential. Marketing a cookbook, a fairly new concept, can bring real benefits to the alumni association. Motivated by loyalty, many alumni will submit a recipe to the alumni association that they would never submit to anyone else. This brings alumni closer to the university.

Dozens of institutions sell a picture book or viewbook, a "coffee-table book" of high-quality pictures of the institution. Championship season books for football, basketball, and wrestling are also popular with alumni.

Travel programs.   It is important to offer enough variety so that alumni can choose the programs that meet their interests. Many middle-aged and older alumni are in a position to travel around the world, for example. International educational tours are very successful with this market segment, especially when the guide is a faculty member with expertise in some aspect of the countries to be visited.

Football bowl-game programs and other collegiate athletic championship events receive a great deal of support from alumni who want to travel with friends and fellow alumni rather than attend the game on their own. Because of the short "window of opportunity" available to prepare and market these programs, it is extremely important to organize and plan during the athletic season. In all kinds of travel programs, bowl games included, be sure to investigate carefully items such as liability, the kind of transportation equipment to be used, the types of hotels being booked, and so on.

Insurance.   Many institutions have developed insurance programs of varying types. Most common is group life insurance. Major medical insurance is also very popular, including short-term or interim major medical policies for graduating students. This is particularly useful for students during the period between graduation and their first job when they are no longer covered by their parents' insurance.

Credit cards.   Affinity or group credit card programs through alumni associations, begun in 1985, are now affording some colleges and universities hundreds of thousands of dollars a year through rebate programs. Some institutions receive a percentage of the annual fees, others a percentage of the volume of the card, and still others a percentage of interest received on each account. Some institutions are doing a combination of two or possibly three of these alternatives.

The students of your institution need to establish a financial history. Develop a credit card program for your students and you will find this previously untapped resource to be almost limitless. And the students will perceive the credit card as assistance from the alumni association.

In-state banking is probably appropriate if you are a state-related school and might also be politically advantageous in that most of your alumni will be living in the state in which your college or association is located.

Car rentals.   Auto rental discount programs have existed since the 1970s. However, there are now new auto rental programs that give a percentage of volume to the university, not just a rental discount for the user.

Membership cards.   Engraved membership cards, engraved metal luggage tags, and paperweights identifying a person as an alumnus of an institution are becoming popular with travelers around the country.

Telephone service.   One of the most successful and innovative programs of recent years has been the "900" telephone service that broadcasts athletic contests all over the world to touch-tone phones. The phone is tied into a university radio broadcast which is carried over the telephone line. Although you have to pay a set-up cost for this activity, there is also a rebate that will offset initial costs if usage is substantial.

Educational vacations.   The number of participants in continuing education/vacationing events, such as alumni vacation colleges and family camping, has grown by leaps and bounds in recent years. These activities are not merely camping or attending lectures, but a combination of both in an educational vacation. Some universities take in large amounts of money in their alumni family camp ventures.

University clubs.   University clubs are eating and meeting clubs in major cities such as New York, Washington, and Los Angeles, where there are major concentrations of alumni. They offer a physical presence that promotes the institution and develops interaction among alumni. In addition, they serve as a great gathering place where alumni know they can get together with other graduates of their institution.

Potpourri of identity symbols.   Many alumni like to buy, wear, and give as gifts lapel pins, tie tacks, neckties, scarves, booster buttons, and so on, that display their institution's logo.

Your institution probably has programs adapted to its own particular identity, its geographic region, or its particular type of alumni body. For example, an engineering institution may be able to obtain computers or engineering equipment to offer to alumni at a discount.

Payoff

What does your institution get from all this merchandising? What is the real value of your merchandising efforts? Are you achieving your goals?

First, merchandising programs across the country have been a tremendous public relations success. We see university T-shirts, baseball caps, jogging suits, and other identifiers all over the landscape. When someone wears a hat with an institutional logo, it makes a statement of loyalty to his or her alma mater; it also makes a positive impression on the public and creates goodwill for the institution. Those people who take advantage of your merchandising programs are, in fact, your best volunteers, your best attenders, your best donors, your best recruiters, and, consequently, your best alumni.

In addition to the public relations benefits, the financial returns of merchandising can be substantial, giving the association the freedom to be creative and innovative with these additional revenues as it expands and improves its program. This payoff takes several forms:

- advertising the merchandise provides support to alumni and university publications;
- sales of merchandise result in cash payments to the alumni association; and
- purchasing the merchandise breaks down any barriers that may be keeping alumni from further participation and commitment.

Thus, monetary compensation, while important to the overall operation, is not the only reason for merchandising.

In many cases, merchandising programs are a response to alumni who want to buy T-shirts and chairs, or who need to solve a particular problem of what to give somebody for a graduation, Christmas, or birthday gift. Merchandising, then, satisfies alumni needs and builds a closer relationship between the institution and its graduates.

MEMBER SERVICES

The selection of services you offer to alumni should be based on a clear understanding of their needs and expectations. Alumni associations with dues programs offer services to attract and to retain members. People will not join and pay dues unless they perceive value for their membership dollar. And that value must be all-encompassing. In other words, alumni must also have an image of the institution as being of great value. You can, to some extent, shape their image of the institution through communications—alumni magazines, videotapes, sports-related newsletters, constituent society fliers, and academic messages—that help alumni appreciate the academic and other strengths of their alma mater and its place in society.

For the nondues alumni association, services to alumni are important to increase their identification with the institution and thus make it more likely that they will be active in the association and supportive of the institution.

Selection Criteria

Only your entrepreneurial creativity need limit the range of member services you offer. Limiting the overall number of services should not be a major consideration. In fact, the more different kinds of services you offer, the more likely your alumni are to find what they need at their particular stage in life. On the other hand, you don't want to develop programs for which there is little need. The following criteria can help you select programs.

1. What are the needs of your alumni? You can find out through a needs assessment, either done informally through word-of-mouth investigation or formally through a survey that goes to a representative sample of the membership.

2. How much of your resources must you invest to develop and offer the service? The ideal is to offer a service made available by an outside provider and for which there is little investment on the part of the association. This is possible, for example, when you offer group membership discounts for such things as rental cars, hotels, cultural events, and insurance.

   Often the providers will pay promotional expenses in order to get their message to the affinity group. The affinity factor is the very foundation of a membership service program, particularly from the provider's perspective. A strong affinity factor is based on three things: trust in the university, trust in the quality of any merchandise bearing the university name, and trust that any product the university endorses will be backed by the alumni association if the product is not what the alumnus anticipated.

   Many outside parties will be glad to provide services to your alumni. Organizations want to do business with a college-educated clientele. The fact that people join or participate in an alumni association indicates a degree of commitment to the services "endorsed" by the association.

3. Which segment of your constituency will be interested in the particular service? For example, career development services are most valuable to graduates of 10 years or fewer, whereas international travel is much more popular with older alumni who have established themselves in their careers and have more time and capital.

Segmenting Your Market for Services

You can segment the services you offer into those that appeal to all alumni, younger alumni, middle-aged alumni, and older alumni.

All alumni.   Publications and other methods of communication are usually of interest to the entire alumni body. The alumni magazine, whether monthly, bimonthly, or quarterly, should have a wide range of articles and features to meet the interests of the total alumni group. For example, all alumni like to find out when classmates marry, have children, or get promoted. They like to hear about the accomplishments of faculty members and fellow alumni.

To capitalize on the interest in athletic events, many institutions have a major sports-related newsletter that covers football, basketball, wrestling, soccer, and other major sports. Some have a secondary newsletter that covers all the other sports of the institution. These publications are very important to the fans who live far from campus and cannot find out about the teams through regular news media.

At some institutions, alumni who join the alumni association get "bonus points" (for example, 10 points for being a life member; 5 points for being an annual member; 2 points for every $100 donated) toward obtaining preferred seating for football or basketball games. Some colleges or universities offer members major athletic tickets at a discount.

Additionally, AT&T has instituted a "900" telephone number program that has been used successfully by several institutions to broadcast football games over phone lines to anyone with a touch-tone phone who accesses the 900 number. The fee is 50 cents for the first minute and 35 cents for each additional minute. It is also being tried with basketball events and could be used for such nonathletic events as the inauguration of a new president.

Using the alumni database, the association serves all alumni by providing information on their friends. Many institutions receive thousands of calls each year from alumni seeking up-to-date addresses and telephone numbers for former roommates, team members, lab partners, and others. While the database needs to be protected from wholesale use for private gain, providing such information in response to legitimate requests from alumni is a well-received service.

The affinity group credit card program, which can be considered either a merchandising effort or a service (depending upon how the alumnus looks at it), is also a useful tool in developing a sense of university spirit among alumni. When the card is used, the organizational logo it bears often starts a conversation about the institution, giving alumni an opportunity to express their pride in their alma mater and spread its name far and wide. By making the credit card available under special credit criteria to students as well, the association provides a much-needed service for these future alumni and begins to create their commitment to the association.

Younger alumni and future alumni.   The alumni association has many ways to woo new graduates. Dues-paying associations can entice new members to join by offering a free one-year introductory membership for the first year after graduation. Giving them the full array of membership benefits and merchandising opportunities makes new alumni aware of the kinds of opportunities available to them.

Alumni associations also can take advantage of the opportunity at commencement time to induct graduating students into their ranks and to have inserted in the diploma folder a laminated, miniaturized version of the actual diploma. These minidiplomas are a great source of pride for younger graduates; institutions that provide minidiplomas receive many calls from older alumni who want them, too. A congratulatory card in the diploma folder is another nice touch. Several institutions offer graduating students a free $ 5,000 life insurance policy for nine months to a year; this is a way of giving something to the new graduates before the university asks for their contributions.

Career development services are becoming very important because of the number of changes people expect to make throughout their professional careers. Some alumni associations arrange with offices of career development and placement to give currently graduating students and young alumni free access to resume reviews, career development seminars, and printed material about the job search. Then, on a fee basis, they offer placement services and placement newsletters that list job opportunities or possible opportunities and seek candidates with particular experience, knowledge, talent, or expertise.

Many alumni associations are expanding career opportunities by developing career centers in various cities throughout the country, usually in conjunction with the alumni club program. This enables alumni to network or contact one or more individuals in a particular region who will provide employment advice and assistance in that location.

The various kinds of insurance now available through alumni associations are particularly important to the young graduate. Parents appreciate short-term medical insurance that covers the son or daughter who is no longer eligible for the parental medical insurance upon graduation and who hasn't found or started a job that provides insurance. The free life insurance program mentioned above as a graduation gift introduces the concept of life insurance to graduating seniors as a way of preparing for the future. When these programs are available on a broad basis with large group potential, the rates can be kept at a reasonable level. Many other kinds of insurance can be offered to large affinity groups, and the ones you choose should depend upon the needs of your alumni.

Middle-aged alumni.   These people have begun to establish themselves in their careers or are already well established and have the time for activities with other alumni. Educational travel programs are a major attraction for this group. International travel or tourist travel to enticing locations develops institutional pride and creates a "family" feeling among alumni. A faculty member with particular expertise in a certain area of the world can serve as a host or guide on such a trip and at the same time provide special educational enrichment. There are also travel discount programs that offer members of an association reduced rates for travel or renting a car or vacation condominium.

Middle-aged alumni also participate in continuing education programs, both those that are professionally oriented and those that are geared to particular interests. Professionally oriented activities are "true" continuing education when they provide professional certification. Many alumni associations run programs on their campuses in the summer and at other times to provide professional accreditation. They also plan other events at the same time to make it fun to return to campus. In fact, from this idea grew the concept of the alumni vacation college where families stay on campus for a week or so to hear faculty lectures; tour laboratories, museums, and other sites on campus and in the community; and participate in such recreational activities as picnics and swimming.

One recent phenomenon in alumni association circles is the family camp. Many institutions have bought or received as donations camps with swimming and lodging facilities in wooded or mountain areas. Again, the whole family can enjoy camp activities.

Children of alumni.   Some institutions give special consideration to the children of alumni. Often, this means they will get special consideration not only for enrollment but also for acceptance to certain programs such as an honors group or a special academic discipline. At some institutions, children of alumni get special consideration for alumni scholarships. Create a space in your database for the names and birthdates of children of alumni; then you can send them birthday cards for their thirteenth through sixteenth birthdays when they are beginning to think about college. This special treatment can mean a lot to both the alumni parents and their children.

Older alumni.   As the "graying of America" progresses, alumni associations are becoming more sensitive to older graduates and their needs. Many institutions recognize alumni who have graduated 50 or more years ago through "honor" or pioneer classes and hold special reunions for these groups. Most institutions have reunions for older alumni, even if they don't have them for other classes. But there are many other services alumni associations can provide. For example, you might videotape older alumni giving oral histories of the institution and the times through which they have lived. The alumni will be flattered at your interest, and the tapes will be an invaluable resource for researchers and historians.

Many older alumni consider their alma mater to be a "senior citizens' resource," which, through their alumni association membership, provides access to athletic facilities, the swimming pool, the library, the institution's various museums, and more. In this way, the institution continues to be a very real part of their lives, and their commitment to it is strengthened.

Payoff

As with merchandising programs, membership services have many results, both tangible and intangible.

You cannot overestimate the public relations benefits when an attractive alumni publication is displayed in a graduate's living room and perhaps shared with prospective students, when an alumnus gets the address of a long-lost roommate, or when a graduate gets his or her first job through the institution's placement office. These services produce goodwill. Young alumni will carry that minidiploma in their wallets for years. And when you ask them to join the association, they will remember the benefits of the free one-year introductory membership you gave them when they could not afford to join.

Membership services also bring the association monetary returns, either directly, such as rebates from use of the "900" telephone number, or indirectly, from the increase in dues-paying members that results from the free introductory memberships and other services. For the nondues-paying association, it brings increased participation in events.

But the greatest return of all, and the ultimate goal of merchandising and member services, is the commitment of the alumni.

The alumni connection should be a lifelong experience. By working with children of alumni, prospective students, current students, young and older alumni, you develop a true family feeling that results in the commitment of the entire alumni body—and their families—to the institution.

This commitment need not be expressed in the same way the fan displays his or her enthusiasm for the winning football team; rather, it should be an underlying spirit of loyalty manifested in the myriad transactions of the daily lives of alumni. The committed alumnus supports the institution by demonstrated advocacy. He or she speaks highly of the institution when a business colleague's son or daughter is looking at colleges, contributes equipment or service the institution needs, encourages support of the institution and of higher education through the state legislature or at the federal level, maintains membership in the alumni association, and supports its merchandising and service programs. When all is said and done, these merchandising and member services are put in place to enhance the devotion and loyalty of our alumni and to allow them to display their special enthusiasm and spirit.

CHAPTER
25

Alumni Travel Programs

COMPILED BY CHARLES F. LENNON, JR.

WHY SPONSOR ALUMNI TRAVEL PROGRAMS?[1]

There are many good reasons to sponsor an alumni travel program. They include the following.

Providing Continuing Educational Involvement with the Institution

Some alumni directors believe that continuing education is the best—and possibly the only—reason for an alumni tour program. Among American adults, there is a growing demand for continuing education, and an alumni tour can be a valuable addition to a well-rounded program. It can also serve to recruit students for other continuing education offerings.

Since the writings of Jean Jacques Rousseau (and probably before), travel has been considered one of the finest types of education by experience. And educational institutions are in an advantageous position to use travel as an educational technique. Most schools, colleges, and universities have on the faculty—or among their alumni—people with a background of travel and the educational credentials to develop marketable credit and noncredit travel study programs. These resources, *not readily available to the many commercial agents who book tours*, enable the institution's alumni association to offer a unique experience and put the institution/alumni association in a noncompetitive position with the tax-paying travel business.

223

Identifying and Cultivating Prospective Donors and Volunteers

Good pre-tour planning and research, in-tour involvement, and post-tour activities provide identification and motivation. Although fund raising should never be the reason for alumni travel, it does provide a great opportunity—not for overt appeals for funds, but for becoming acquainted with tour participants. Many volunteers serving as board members, presidents of local clubs, and fund-raising chairs got their first taste of alumni involvement from a well-operated tour and follow-up activities.

Providing Outreach to Foreign Alumni

Your travel program may be the only contact your institution has with foreign alumni who are often potential high-level supporters of the institution. You can involve these alumni in the travel operation in several ways:

- they can speak to tour groups on their areas of expertise;
- they can arrange and guide tours through industrial plants, government offices, embassies, and so on;
- they can invite tour participants into their homes or host social events;
- they can arrange special activities with local governments, private agencies, businesses, and the like.

When your tour visits a city where you have several alumni, you can sponsor a formal event and invite all alumni, parents, friends, local media, and government officials. The foreign alumni will be flattered by the attention.

Developing Friendships among Tour Participants

Frequently relationships between tour participants develop into business associations, lifelong friendships, and possibly even marriages. When university officials accompany the tour, they, too, can develop personal relationships with participants. Ideas for new programs and other changes to foster better university–alumni cooperation often result.

Building Goodwill for the Institution

Receiving the announcement of the tour can help alleviate the prevalent feeling among alumni that "all they ever do is hit me up for money." Even those who don't go on the trip will be reminded that the opportunity for travel is a benefit provided by the alumni association.

Self-sufficiency

Tour programs can be totally self-supporting and even make a financial contribution to the alumni budget, as well as reimbursing it for staff time and expenses. But be careful not to price the tour so high that it looks like just another fund-raising technique. Also, you may incur tax liability for nonrelated income, so consult your accountant or other experts first.

Providing Fringe Benefits to Qualified Staff

You can reward good employees for their efforts by involving them in the travel program—and the trip itself. This helps you with retention and helps the staff member add to his or her experience and professionalism.

Travel programs make sense for most institutions. If you have a small alumni body, it may be harder to organize a tour, but even a small tour can bring good results.

DESIGNING THE TOUR[2]

Assessing the Market

Almost any organized alumni association has enough market potential to operate some kind of a tour program—even if as few as 10 to 15 people participate. But, before you plan your tour, you need to know the basics of your potential alumni market—age, geographical location, sex, approximate income level, and so on. Also determine the travel desires of the group.

You may already have some of this information in your files. If not, you can do a survey through a random sample questionnaire or other means. For example, in a 1980 random sample of alumni of a large private western university, respondents said they would like to visit the following places (top five in order of preference): eastern Mediterranean area, eastern United States, Mexico/Latin America, Europe, and the South Seas.

Although it is risky to generalize, you can probably use the following guidelines with some degree of confidence:

- Older alumni are in a better position regarding time and money to travel. We have had the most success with soliciting the 15th to 50th class year groups.
- Young alumni enjoy tours designed as family experiences.
- It helps to stratify the potential market by income levels. You may also be able to stratify your market by other factors such as social club membership as students, donor level, occupation, and so on.

Who Should Arrange the Tour? Who Should Go?

If you are not an expert in travel arrangements—and you probably are not—you will have to use a tour agent to set up your program. Institutions that have had a lot of experience with tours usually deal directly with wholesalers or even suppliers of hotels or air service rather than dealing with retail agents. This can save money, but it does take a lot of time and experience. If you're just beginning your tour program, talk to colleagues who have used travel agents to find a reputable one. Usually you can expect the travel agent to provide the following services:

- assisting in the development of an itinerary or even the general location if you haven't made that decision;
- making all arrangements for transportation to the location (air, sea, etc.), local transportation (bus, train, donkey, etc.), and schedules related to such travel;
- making hotel reservations;
- making local touring arrangements;
- paying bills;
- giving an accurate accounting of funds expended and people served;
- providing promotional material for tours; and
- putting up the "front money" to get the tour promotion started.

The tour agent will usually ask the alumni association to do the following:

- provide academic leadership and arrange for lectures, classes, and so on, if applicable, as well as course credit if offered;
- provide at least one staff member to direct the tour; and
- provide mailing lists (and possibly mailing services).

Involving Institutional Officials and Staff

To ensure long-term internal support of the travel program, involve institutional officials on some or all of the tours. They can be guest lecturers or academic leaders if applicable. Inviting a member of the development staff can provide many positive contact opportunities for low-key cultivation with good follow-up after the tour. An alumni staff member included in the tour can "make points" for the association and deal with any difficulties that occur.

Most tours should have a strong academic flavor. You can achieve this by inviting one or more professors to provide a series of lectures/classes/workshops as part of the tour.

If a volunteer has enough expertise to serve as an alumni staff person, academic lecturer, or bus host, by all means use that person. Sometimes you may only have to offer him or her a discount on the cost of the tour. In return, you have a loyal and helpful person who can add a lot to the success of the tour. It is also a good way to say thanks for volunteer service.

What to Do

What you plan to do on the tour determines more than anything else whether you will be able to sell it, what sort of problems you will have on the tour, and whether it will be successful. First, you should put together a specific mission statement for the tour program in general and the specific tour you are designing; for example: "to cultivate alumni and friends with a financially self-supporting tour program that highlights the best education experience we have to offer." Then ask yourself these six questions:

1. *What type of tour will it be?*   Alumni travel programs should provide a variety of good offerings to meet the various interests, time constraints, and financial resources of your alumni constituency. Most alumni tours will fall into one of three categories:

- The alumni travel/study tour: designed with a strong emphasis on the educational offering by qualified academic personnel. These are usually major tour offerings such as a museum tour of Europe.
- The alumni expedition: short-term travel programs that are usually low-cost and can be designed for families and/or young alumni. A family camping caravan, for example, combines a rich educational experience with many recreational activities.
- Alumni support travel: usually in conjunction with an athletic or other group that is traveling (to a bowl game, for example).

Tour agents will approach you with proposals, and this may determine the type of tour you offer. You usually use a part of the tour package for your alumni, taking a specified number of places out of the total available (usually in increments of 15). You may get a pretty good price for the packaged tour, although it pays to shop around, and the basic arrangements are already made and usually run smoothly. However, you may have to work hard to keep your identity as an alumni group. If your group is mixed in with other people, you will have to follow the program schedule whether you want to or not. If you want to do something extra for your alumni, you have to work it out with the rest of the group. On the other hand, if another group on the tour does something special, your alumni may feel cheated.

The basic travel styles of tours may dictate where, when, and how you go. They include:

- Fly/cruise: a convenient and popular way to travel but usually the most expensive.

- Fly/bus/train touring: although participants have to use many airplanes, buses, hotels, and so on, sometimes this is the only way they can see the many sights on your tour.

- Bus touring: when kept fairly short and involving good overnight accommodations, this tour provides many opportunities for education and fellowship.

- Recreational vehicle travel: an attractive way to provide a family outing at little extra cost for those alumni with their own equipment.

2. *Where should you go?*   Where you go often depends on what you want to accomplish. Fads play an important part in selecting a destination. Sometimes you can't sell a trip to Europe and sometimes that is all you can sell. By all means, talk to your alumni but don't put all your eggs on a random sample. Make the best decision you can on the facts you have and then try to sell the tour. Design the tour with enough flexibility in time and arrangements to make changes if necessary.

As a general rule, it takes at least six months to promote and sell a tour and four to six months to plan from scratch. So you should allow a year lead time. If the tour is prepackaged by a tour agent, you won't need as much time to plan. But you should still count on six months to promote and sell it. If you can, advertise your general tour destinations up to 18 months to 2 years in advance.

On the other hand, a simple (if you can call it that) trip to a bowl game can be put together in 30 days or so—and sometimes that's all the time you have. But, if there is a chance of a bowl bid for your institution, you should make tentative arrangements months in advance. Most hotels and airlines will work with you on that basis if they feel they will get your business.

3. *When should you go?*   You can run an alumni tour any time of the year, depending on where you go. But here are a few guidelines:

- For family travel, stick with June, July, and August.

- For longer or expensive tours (appealing to older, affluent alumni), go to a warm place in the coldest part of the participants' winter. If your tour coincides with the biggest snowstorm of the year, your alumni will love you for getting them away from it all.

- Check out the normal weather conditions in your tour location; several publications (e.g. Rand-McNally maps and Pan Am publications) have this information.

- Check out dates for special events in your tour location and see if you can work them into your itinerary—for example, major sporting events, or the passion play in Oberammergau every 10 years.

- Check off-season rates to see if you can schedule a tour that takes advantage of these discounts.

4. *How much will it cost?* Alumni travel programs should pay for themselves with perhaps a modest return to the alumni association to cover potential losses in the future. But be careful: an alumni tour program designed to make money for the association or the institution could raise warning flags at the IRS and probably will not sell anyway; participants usually shop around for the best deal they can get. Don't set the price until you have considered all the factors, such as the type of tour and all the points discussed above.

Most alumni tours should be first class in the deluxe category—at least as far as hotel and ground accommodations are concerned. Your participants are not students and don't want to "rough it." American tourists base their opinion of the tour on the quality of their accommodations. They may visit the seven wonders of the world and attend lectures by Nobel prize-winning professors, but what they will tell their friends is how well the toilet facilities worked—or didn't.

Especially if your tour is an educational one, include the cost of side trips in the total package. These are often sold separately to keep the published cost to a minimum, but travelers may feel they are being "nickeled and dimed" to death if there are too many extras to pay for. In particular, don't make the best side trips cost extra.

After a tour agent has quoted you a figure, call another agent and ask how much a similar tour would cost for a single person.

Everything you add to the tour will cost money, whether the association or the traveler pays. Therefore, consider each item before including it. The following, however, are "musts":

- A quality educational package: a top professor can be a great draw for your program.

- Alumni staff leadership: a staff leader usually handles all logistics and relations with the tour agent and/or representative.

- Something to identify participants and the tour with the alumni association and the institution, such as a special name for the group, name-tags, luggage tags, flight bags, banners, hats, whistles, and so on.

- Welcome-aboard letters, brochures, log books, and other printed material distributed before, during, and after the tour.
- Verbal communications while on tour: everything should be done in the name of the alumni association.

Often the tour agent or carrier or hotel will provide one free space per a certain number of tour members (15 in the past but that changes frequently). Be sure to check this with your tour agent.

5. *How long should the trip be?*   At present, the 8- to 14-day tours are the most popular, but price and destination seem to be the most important factors. Many people now have long vacations, but remember that you want them to wish the tour were longer, not shorter.

6. *Who will lead the tour?*   You have at least three choices: the academic type (or the top institutional official on the board), the tour agent, or the alumni staff person. The alumni staff person who has become as well informed as possible about all aspects of the tour is often the best leader.

First, only one person should deal with agents and their representatives to avoid confusion and misunderstanding in the arrangements. Second, the alumni staff person will probably handle pre-tour contact with the participants and tour agent; in their minds, he or she *is* the tour director. Third, you want to be sure that the tour is conducted as you planned it. The alumni staff person is most likely to have the ability and the motivation to make sure this happens.

While the academic leader who provides the educational component should be involved in the final itinerary selection in order to plan the lectures, he or she does not want to deal with the details of lost luggage or poor accommodations.

Educational Elements of Alumni Travel

The educational component of an alumni tour program should consist of as much material as the participants can handle. Give them too much rather than too little. The educational input to the program sets your tour apart from one operated by the local travel agent and makes it a unique experience for your alumni. This is what they will remember, and this is what shows them that your institution is changing their lives for the better.

For example, on a two-week fly/cruise tour of the Mediterranean sponsored by the BYU Alumni Association, there were five pre-trip lectures (also used as promotion nights for the tour) by five professors (only two of whom went on the trip). There were 14 lectures during the cruise, some given on board the ship and some on site in Egypt, Israel, Turkey, and Greece. This trip has been a popular alumni event for seven years so something is being done right.

In short, get good advice from other colleges and tour agents, price the tour right, lead with enthusiasm, and have a great time.

THE CARE AND FEEDING OF TOUR PARTICIPANTS[3]

To make a tour successful, there must be official hosts with clearly defined responsibilities. A tour host can be an institutional officer, a member of the faculty, an alumni association leader, or a well-known alumnus. In addition to the host, there should be a staff member assigned to every tour involving more than 60 people. The director of alumni travel should meet with the tour host before and after every trip to go over a checklist of responsibilities.

Responsibilities of the Tour Host

The tour host has six main responsibilities:

1. The host should understand that the general purpose of the tour is to build alumni support both for the institution and for the alumni association.

2. The host should help tour members continue to learn about the institution and be aware that the travel program is an educational program.

3. The host should help tour members broaden their acquaintance with other tour members and with alumni living overseas. He or she should be prepared to meet foreign alumni who are invited to socialize with the tour members, and he or she should take along badges, souvenirs, decals, pictures, certificates, and other materials of interest to alumni living abroad.

4. The host should be alert to sickness and accidents among tour members. Travelers often do not know how to deal with sickness overseas; they are reluctant to call the travel agent about their sickness, and sometimes retire to their rooms to suffer in silence.

5. The host should serve as a link between the tour agent and the members of the tour. Many travelers do not realize the services available to them through proper use of the travel agent's professional knowledge.

6. Immediately after the trip, the tour host should prepare a written evaluation; he or she should also send a friendly letter and evaluation questionnaire to each participant.

Hosting a tour group is hard work and requires 24-hour-a-day availability. The alumni know that the tour host did not pay his or her own way and is traveling on money paid by the group. Therefore, they expect the tour host to perform in a professional way. Being aloof or spending too much time with a few special friends among the group will lead to resentment among the others.

Special Events

Get-acquainted parties at the beginning of the tour and a reception on the final night are important parts of any travel program. And pre-tour lectures on the geography and languages of the areas to be visited are especially important for tours involving historical sites. Three to five weeks after the tour, a reunion of participants will enable them to share pictures, slides, and memories, and to cement new friendships. And it will also give you a good opportunity to evaluate the success of the tour.

Alumni associations can offer a group traveling abroad a unique advantage: contact with graduates living in the countries the group will visit. Conducting an overseas tour without providing contacts with these alumni is unthinkable. This involves planning several months in advance as international mail can be very slow. If there are alumni clubs in the countries you plan to visit, give these groups advance notice so that they can schedule a meeting or an event for tour members. In many cases, when local alumni meet the travelers, they will invite them to visit their homes or take special tours of the area.

Taking Care of Problems

The tour host should be prepared to deal with problems common to traveling with groups. The tour host can work with the tour agent to solve problems such as incompatible roommates or unacceptable hotel rooms. The most common problem however, is that of dealing with travelers who have just learned their plane will not leave on schedule. The tour host should make sure the tour members are told the reason for the delay and how long it will be.

The worst thing that can happen on a tour is a serious injury or death of one of the tour members. While the legal details of such a sad event are the responsibility of the tour agent, the tour host must communicate with the family at home and with the rest of the tour members. If a physician is traveling with the group, he or she can be a great help in time of accident, illness, or death of a tour member.

Experience indicates that "misfits" appear on tours no matter what you do to try to prevent them from signing up. The presence of someone who refuses to board the tour bus on time or who can't get along with anybody can be harmful to a tour. Usually, the best approach is to be honest; tell the person that he or she is spoiling the tour for the others. You might even offer to pay for a ticket home.

Keeping the Tour Host Informed

A master file on the tour can be invaluable to the tour host. It should contain the following:

- all mailings and personal correspondence regarding the tour;
- names of alumni who indicated interest in the tour as well as those who eventually signed up;
- special requests such as diabetic diets, special room arrangements, and so on; and
- a list of tour members' first names, nicknames, degrees received, birthdays, wedding anniversaries, and any other special occasion that might occur during the tour.

It is essential that the tour host read through this folder *before* the tour begins. During the tour, he or she should keep a log that includes observations on hotel accommodations, local sight-seeing tours, guides, agents, and individual participants. After the tour is completed, the folder should include financial statements of cost and income for the tour and the evaluation forms returned by the participants. You can then use the folder to plan future tours to the same area. When you have three or four years of tour experience, you realize that repeat tours are sometimes more successful than tours to new places.

Notes

Note: This chapter is adapted from *Passport to Successful Alumni Travel Programs*, edited by Stephen L. Barrett, Executive Director of the Brigham Young University Alumni Association, and published by the Council for Advancement and Support of Education (CASE). The material was the result of a 1975 CASE Conference on Alumni Travel Programs and was updated in 1983. The book contains an extensive appendix including a glossary, sample tour host checklist, and articles and success stories from several institutions.

1. The following people contributed to this section: Dick Wintermote, Frank B. Jones, Jack R. Maguire, Stanley R. McAnally, Harold M. Wilson, and Stephen L. Barrett.
2. Written by Jack R. Maguire and Stephen L. Barrett.
3. Written by Frank B. Jones.

CHAPTER
26

Alumni Athletic Events

Donald V. Dotts

Alumni interest in athletics has been evident ever since the first intercollegiate athletic event, a crew race between Harvard and Yale held in 1852. This rowing contest was actually a promotion gimmick by the Boston & Maine Railroad to develop and sell land around a lake in New Hampshire, and it must also have been the first alumni travel program to an athletic contest. The railroad provided free transportation for the contestants, the crew's shells, and "interested spectators."

According to Penn State Alumni Association Director William Rothwell, who cited this event in a speech at a recent conference, "It seems ironic that the alumni of the two schools were the target of this first intercollegiate athletic promotion, and the commercial aspects of alumni interest in athletics have been prevalent ever since."[1]

Anyone who has served on an alumni association staff at a university with a major football program knows that alumni are interested in athletics. Alumni professionals at smaller institutions with any kind of athletic program also realize that, to some degree or other, their graduates have an interest in the sports program.

To what degree do alumni want to be involved in the athletic program? If you believe present-day folklore, our graduates have an overwhelming interest in hiring and firing coaches, in recruiting student athletes (the National Collegiate Athletic Association now prohibits alumni involvement in recruiting), and in serving as "groupies" for coaches and athletes who are the real "stars" in collegiate life.

But hold on: A sociologist says that alumni interest in athletics has been overrated. James Frey, Associate Professor of Sociology at the University of Nevada, Las Vegas, even goes so far as to say deemphasizing athletics would not elicit the adverse reaction that the myths have led us to expect. And a 1972 survey by Washington State University, to which 90

235

percent of 800 randomly selected alumni responded, found similar opinions:

> Alumni leaders and the general alumni body agree that traditional academic programs should receive the highest priority. Funding extracurricular activities . . . received the lowest priorities. . . . Few alumni have any significant input into athletic policy. Most of them, in fact, think athletics are not all that important, particularly when compared to the need for other programs of higher education.[2]

ALUMNI AND ATHLETIC POLICY

While Professor Frey is correct that few alumni have any significant input into athletic policy, at some institutions the alumni executive director and sometimes an alumnus volunteer serve as voting members on the intercollegiate athletic boards. This gives alumni professionals some important input into the athletic policies and philosophies of their institutions. In addition, the alumni administrator who has, over the years, built up a trusting relationship with the president and athletic administrators at his or her institution may also have input through these channels.

While athletic support should not be the major interest or activity of an alumni program, as my friends in the athletic department like to remind me, "Nothing else brings 70,000 people to the campus six or seven Saturdays each fall!"

So it is important to have a place in our programs for athletics. A well-run, ethical athletic program that has the right academic values (and it helps to win some games!) can give the alumni association an excellent opportunity to relate to large numbers of interested alumni.

OTHER ATHLETIC SUPPORT GROUPS

Alumni associations should not be the only "booster" groups. Most larger institutions have athletic support foundations or clubs. The alumni office should be supportive of athletics but leave the role of major sports supporter to the group that has that as its major purpose. In many cases, the alumni office is better off co-sponsoring an event with the athletic support group than trying to do it alone.

While the following discussion of events that you can sponsor often refers to football, you can apply many of these ideas to support any size athletic program and any sport.

HOME GAME EVENTS

Pre-game Events

At many institutions, the tradition of "tailgating" is a well-established ritual, and there is no need to organize a parking area of picnics and parties before a game. This tradition, however, can be a successful organized event if the alumni association reserves a special area and provides decorations, entertainment, and food or drinks. Such an event is even more fun if the institution's marching band can come through the area to entertain on its way to the stadium.

Halftime Opportunities

If there is a special reception area within the stadium, you could arrange to offer refreshments during halftime. Some basketball arenas have such a room especially suited to entertain groups of VIP alumni who attend games there. You can offer more than refreshments at halftime. You can communicate the institution's educational message to the fans in various ways, such as making presentations of awards to faculty, alumni, or students who have distinguished themselves in some way. Halftime ceremonies at homecoming could highlight the alumni association and its goals and accomplishments.

Post-game Events

"The danger in having a post-game event," says a colleague, "is that you *might* lose the game—then you have a wake instead of a celebration!" While this is a valid concern, certain events are more appropriate after a game. Members of the coaching staff are usually not available to come to pre-game events to meet your alumni, but are happy to drop in after the game. Reunion groups or others who wish to "make an evening of it" often enjoy post-game dinners or dances. These events can be successful even if the team loses.

EVENTS AT AWAY GAMES

An athletic contest at the opponent's campus is an ideal opportunity to involve your alumni who live in that area. If you have an alumni club there, that group can host a pre-game event. If you offer travel opportunities to alumni and boosters, these travelers should be involved in any pre-game festivities. An away-game event can be fairly informal, such as a tailgate party, (a designated area where your fans gather to consume their own food), or it can be a fancy meal in a banquet room. Be sure to send invitations to attend the event—and to purchase tickets to the game—to alumni in the area. The reservations and order forms should be returned to your office or to the local host club.

Invite campus dignitaries to attend. If the local club or chapter co-sponsors the event, make sure you have final say on any contract with a restaurant or hotel. You may also wish to allow the local chapter or club to add a small amount to the ticket price to help its treasury.

If cheerleaders are traveling with the team, invite them to attend and add a pep rally atmosphere to the pre-game festivities. Or you may wish to involve the marching band if it is attending the game. While you probably can't offer to feed the entire band, an appearance by the group will add color and interest to your event.

Consider including bus transportation from the pre-game site to the game and back. Alumni will gladly pay a few more dollars for this convenience.

WORKING WITH YOUR
ATHLETIC ALUMNI

One of the best ways that the alumni association can be involved with athletics is by providing awards and recognition to athletes for their achievements in the field or in the classroom. An award to the team member who has earned the highest grades during the year is a good way to do this.

Some associations carry academic recognition further by sponsoring a banquet each year for all athletes who have achieved a certain grade index (often a B average). Try a luncheon on campus during a class day so that the largest number of honorees can attend.

With large, successful athletic programs, the alumni association has an opportunity to honor student-athletes who are members of a champion-ship team. The association can present special plaques to all members of a team that wins its conference or division championship or that is na-tionally ranked in the top 10 (or top 20) at season's end. An ideal time to make these presentations is during halftime ceremonies at a game later in the season. For example, if the football team earns such honors, the presentation could be made at a basketball halftime a month or so later. For institutions that have several championship teams, this can be expen-sive, but the goodwill earned and the publicity the association receives at the presentation make it worthwhile.

A WORD ABOUT BOWL GAMES

A bowl invitation for the football team can present both opportunity and difficulty for the alumni association. A bowl appearance can be "the best of times and the worst of times"! For the avid football fan, going to a bowl game can be the ultimate experience; for the alumni association administrator, it can be a nightmare of overtime for staff members (often during the holidays), coordination of endless details, handling gripes from alumni who can't get tickets or think those they got aren't good enough, and the pressure of trying to get too much done in too short a time. Here are some ideas that may help if there is a bowl game in your future:

1. Make sure that a quality travel program is available for alumni. If your office is equipped to handle large numbers of boosters with travel plans, put it together yourself. You can include a number of escort spaces for your staff to fill. Of course, the staff members must do a professional job of escorting the group, and this can provide you with some net income to help your budget. Or you may prefer to hire an experienced group travel company and let it handle all details—even moving personnel from the travel agency into the alumni office to handle calls, reservations, and so on.

2. If your institution is participating in a New Year's Day bowl game, you have a great opportunity to sponsor a New Year's Eve party. It can be a formal dinner-dance with party favors and a well-known band, or it can be an informal get-together the night before the game. This is a big event for a New Year's Day bowl. Sponsoring such a party is a service to the institution, providing a large gathering where all its fans can be in one place. It takes a lot of planning and preparation, attention to detail, and expert marketing and promotion, but it can be the highlight of any bowl game week.

3. Pre-game or post-game parties are naturals for a bowl game, and they should be held near the stadium. If you don't plan to charge admission to this event, ask the athletic department or the athletic booster group to co-sponsor it. Because a good pre-game celebration benefits the entire institution, it can be a legitimate expense in the institution's bowl budget. Some of the costs might include rental of a meeting room or a big tent, security personnel costs, entertainment, decorations, public address system and lighting rental, and even rental of portable toilets if you're planning an outdoor event for a large crowd.

4. Costs can sneak up on you, and you should work out a detailed budget with other university administrators before you make your plans to support a major bowl appearance. Find out if some of your costs can be covered by the institution's overall budget for the bowl appearance (which comes from bowl revenues). Be sure to consider the expense of any extra personnel whom you might need to handle the workload. For example, an

appearance in the Rose Bowl can mean the sale of 45,000 game tickets, payments by 1,000 to 2,000 travelers (just for your alumni travel plans alone), and so many details for your staff that you may not be able to survive without extra clerical or accounting help.

5. Yes, you can make money from such a major undertaking. In fact, you *should* build in revenues for the alumni association to compensate for the great amount of time you and your staff will have to devote to the endeavor. Add enough to your charge for travel programs and to any admission charges to bowl events that you sponsor to cover all expenses *and* to give you some additional income. If you do not get any backing from the institution's bowl budget and consequently must stick your neck out to make travel or bowl events happen, you should be especially careful to make sure your own budget can benefit in some way.

SOME CLOSING THOUGHTS

In few major institutions is the relationship between the athletic department and the alumni office always a love affair. Too often the athletic department sees the alumni association only as its support group, and the alumni association hopes for unlimited 50-yard-line seats for all dues-paying alumni, and everyone is disappointed. The challenge, then, is to make sure that these two highly charged departments are mutually supportive.

Coaches and athletic administrators should be willing speakers at alumni events. The alumni office should make its alumni lists available for athletic promotional mailings. The athletic department should consult with alumni leaders before making major changes in ticket pricing or seating arrangements. The alumni office should provide such input and be aware of its role in interpreting alumni viewpoints to the institution as a whole and also to the athletic administrators.

Above all, you as an alumni administrator should provide your graduates with many opportunities to enjoy a good athletic program. Your institution's athletic events should be fun for them—and for you, too.

Notes

1. William Rothwell, "Alumni Relations/Intercollegiate Athletics Achieving a Successful Symbiosis" (Speech delivered at Council for Advancement and Support of Education Conference, Washington, D.C., October 1987).
2. James H. Frey, "Alumni Love Athletics: Myth or Reality?" *CASE Currents*, December 1981:46.

Type of Institution

CHAPTER
27

100 Ways to Lose the Battle of Managing the Small College Alumni Office

MARALYN ORBISON GILLESPIE

You've found your perfect mate and it's been love from the start,
He whispers, "You're the one to who I give my heart,"
Don't say, "I love you too, my dear, let's never, never part."
Just say, "I'm afraid you've made a grammatical error. . . ."
That's a fine way to lose a man.

(Wonderful Town*)

Comedian Rosalind Russell enumerated 100 ways to lose a man in the 1953 Broadway musical *Wonderful Town*. With apologies to her and to librettists Betty Comden and Adolph Green, we alter the song to consider 100 ways to lose the battle of managing a small college alumni office. By accentuating the negative, we may illuminate, in the process, some solid truths about effective office management.

Here we go!

100. *Know it all.* You're the boss; somebody put you in charge because of your ability and track record. Your staff exists to follow. If you remain true to this style of leadership, you are guaranteed to run out of your own

good ideas within six months. And since you have a small staff and can't possibly take on any more programs, you save yourself the mental anguish of choosing between old (and possibly tired) and experimental (and possibly risky) programs.

99. *Do not expect more from your secretary and clerical help than is standard for these nonprofessional jobs.*   Do not take them away from their assigned tasks for staff meetings either. This practice will ensure that your established routines for office procedure and all aspects of your tried-and-true programs continue undisrupted by change. (I know of one secretary who, during a staff meeting, suggested substituting a beach towel for a T-shirt as a giveaway to student participants in the traditional Crum Regatta. That's trouble.)

98. *Make your lists of things to do every morning in approved managerial fashion, with an A list for the must-dos, a B list for the next highest priorities, and a C list for those jobs that are not crucial.*   (The latter may indeed go undone—the C list should include thank-you notes to volunteers and congratulatory notes to alumni who have received a nice honor, had a baby, gotten a promotion.)

Swerve not from those lists regardless of the temptation, such as alumni who appear out of the blue in your doorway. If they didn't have the courtesy or foresight to phone ahead that they were bringing a son to the admissions office and wanted to drop in for a cup of coffee and conversation, you owe them nothing. Jump up from your chair, meet the alumnus at the doorway (blocking entrance into your office), and with a few deft phrases about how busy you are, you can send the intruder packing in three minutes, thus keeping intact your schedule.

97. *Hold fast to your conviction that friend raising and fund raising don't mix.*   Better yet, proclaim that fund raising is definitely inimical to friend raising. Make sure there is no guilt by association. Keep your program plans from the ears of development types; do not travel with them. Don't confuse the president by putting him or her on the road for alumni meetings and sharing his or her time for corporation calls and capital campaign cultivation in the same cities. For an A-plus in this category, manage regularly to make a few disdainful remarks about the dirty business of money grubbing.

96. *Remember, you are the spokesperson on campus for your institution's biggest constituency; maintain your dignity.*   When meetings are scheduled among the heads of several offices on matters of mutual concern, insist they always be held at the seat of power—your office. (In

Chapter 9, Ray Willemain recommends "foot diplomacy"; this tactic displays a decided unwillingness to stand up and be counted.)

95. *Don't be a wimp.* If some colleague in the dean's office down the hall or upstairs in the career office moves a little more slowly than you'd like on a mutual project or seems to stonewall it, be aggressive. Save face (yours). Fire off a memo and let the offender know just how you feel. (This danger of close association is acute at a small college where the administrative offices are likely to be in one building. Hence it is particularly necessary to guard one's territory unflaggingly.)

94. *When credit is due, grab it.* Some alumni directors claim you can't put yourself up front in this business; volunteers must get the credit. Wrong. Alumni association officers and key volunteers must be aware of who's really running the show or they will have little respect for the staff member in charge.

93. *B&G is there is to serve you.* When you're expecting a thousand guests on Alumni Weekend, you've got to inform the head of Buildings & Grounds in no uncertain terms that he or she and staff have to perform— or else. If you tell the person who answers the phone in B&G that you need podiums in Du Pont and Martin Halls at 11 a.m. and 3 p.m. respectively, and 36 round tables and chairs in the Field House Friday night, 12 in the quad behind Hicks, and 18 in the social center for lunch, by golly you expect those orders to get through. And if one doesn't and you lose your temper with B&G when you are trying to correct the situation, you are within your constitutional rights.

Ditto for college food service.

92. *Do not share your good programs with your colleagues at other institutions.* They are competitors. Corollary: do not phone an alumni director at a similar institution to ask how he or she handles insurance for a travel program or whether this year's continuing education programs on campus are succeeding (your numbers are unaccountably down). Such a phone call will be perceived as a sign of your inadequacy to do your job.

91. *Do it yourself if you want it done right.* You've done it before; you have no time to explain to a volunteer how to do it. By following this advice, you will get the job done (you may not get as many jobs done), and it will be done the way you want it.

Corollary: another not-to-be-underestimated benefit is that, by discounting the value of volunteers, you avoid having to train them, a costly and time-consuming process. Some well-intentioned alumni directors claim that volunteer training workshops on campus are worth the effort, even considering the dollars it takes to house and feed them (some even pay transportation); the hours of planning an agenda; and the effort of bringing faculty, students, and other administrators into the program.

90. *Go by the numbers.*   Here's a tough one, a two-sided coin under the heading of accountability. The experts say it's a wise manager who evaluates a program at the end of the year. To mismanage effectively, we're in murky waters here. Accountability is not necessarily a bad practice, but we can set up some helpful guidelines to make it so. We can go by the numbers. How many alumni, spouses, friends, and parents showed up at the museum tour in Chicago? How many alumni registered for the Alumni College on campus? Do not include in this tough evaluation any brownie points for goodwill engendered by the reminder to your Chicago area alumni and parents that there is a Swarthmore presence in Chicago in the form of a regional alumni organization; no pluses either for the invitation to all alumni from the institution to sit once more in a classroom and have their minds stretched by a brilliant faculty member. As a hard-headed executive, when evaluating your events, certainly forget about asking whether alumni had a good time. How can you measure that intangible?

89. *Goodwill never paid the heat bill.*   By now you've probably gotten the hang of this exercise—how to lose the battle of managing the small college alumni office—so you can continue through the eighties and into the seventies on your own. But to make sure you get off in the right frame of mind and at the risk of saying the obvious, the last trick of the trade enumerated here is one of those high-minded philosophic admonitions that cuts to the heart of our business. For heaven's sake, don't take your mission too seriously. The real business of the institution is carried on by faculty and students. The alumni are a kind of interesting side show, useful at times but also a darned nuisance. Few of them, if any, paid the full freight for their education at your private institution; they *owe* it their dollars and loyalty.

And don't ever forget that it is the bottom line—and translate dollars—that is the key phrase when you are talking about good alumni. All that lip service about alumni contributions to admissions, career counseling, legislative relations, and just plain putting in a good word for the old alma mater with friends, relations, and fellow members of the local school board amounts to just that, so much lip service.

88. It's your turn to create your own ways to lose the battle of managing the small college alumni office.

Alumni Relations at Two-Year Institutions

James D. Van Houten

Alumni programming at two-year, nonresidential campuses has great potential, but successful community college alumni efforts are a rarity. It is not easy to establish and sustain an alumni program on this type of campus. It can be done, however, and this chapter considers some of the obstacles and suggests realistic approaches to implementing a successful program. My observations are based on the experiences of the 30 community colleges of the State University of New York (SUNY) over a 10-year period. During this time, I visited campuses and organized workshops and conferences with the goal of helping SUNY's community colleges develop alumni programs.

ALUMNI PROGRAM GOALS

Asa Knowles, Editor-in-Chief of the *Handbook of College and University Administration*, suggests that, within higher education generally,

> the role of the alumnus has the least obvious function in the life of the institution and therefore is the most difficult role to define in the formulation of policy and the governance of the institution.[1]

Knowles suggests that "masses of alumni traditionally represented an enigma to educational theorists and administrators who have been at a loss to deal with them." As Knowles observes, it is in the area of alumni involvement where most colleges, both two-year and four-year, fall short.[2]

Educational administrators neglect the basic step of goal setting for alumni programs; too often, they look back to their own collegiate and alumni experience, thus perpetuating the stereotyped alumni program: "Yes, I remember my first contact from college when I graduated—a request for money!"

If the alumni program does not have a positive effect on teaching, learning, and research, if it is not personally rewarding to the alumni volunteer, then the program is extraneous to the institutional mission. Presidents are inclined to want results by today—or at least by tomorrow. The short-term goals of more students and more dollars are attractive ones and can be implemented at relatively low cost during the president's tenure. A solid, sustained alumni relations program, however, is not a short-term effort. The benefits of beginning such a program might not appear for several years.

The SUNY experience indicates that long-term objectives for the alumni program are the only objectives that are successful. At some SUNY campuses, it has taken 10 to 15 years for an alumni program to become a sustained and contributing force.

David Moore, Coordinator of Jefferson Community College's Placement and Alumni Office, describes the approach to alumni programming this way:

> At an old tradition-rich, four-year college, the role of the alumni is often chiefly that of boosters for enrollment and contributors to one fund or another. There is often the clear expectation that alumni who do well financially will make substantial contributions during their lifetimes or as legacies. As a consequence, programming for alumni at these institutions is geared to stimulate nostalgia and good will as well as to provide services to former students.
>
> Jefferson Community College, by contrast, has no traditions that evoke nostalgia automatically on the part of alumni. Most of our graduates are in the early or middle stages of their careers, and few, if any, are in a position to remember JCC in their wills. Clearly, the emphasis in cultivating JCC's alumni lies in other areas.
>
> The goals for alumni programming at JCC stress primarily service and, secondarily, fund raising and public relations. They are:
>
> 1. to offer programs that perpetuate the ideal of lifelong learning for alumni and members of the local community in general;
>
> 2. to involve alumni and friends in the placement and career preparation efforts of the college;
>
> 3. to create and maintain a sense of cooperation among alumni, students, faculty, and administration;
>
> 4. to acquaint alumni and friends with the progress and needs of the institution; and
>
> 5. to ensure the continued confidence and support of the alumni and friends who may contribute to the institution's financial and other material needs.

Furtherance of these goals requires that the college maintain a positive and realistic image in the eyes of its alumni and other constituencies. Consequently, JCC does not try to compete directly with more traditional colleges; it succeeds by being a good community college, period. As a result, most graduates have memories of JCC as a place where they received personal attention and a sound education.[3]

Moore uses the word "personal"—a good word that is too often overlooked by community college faculty and administrators when they think about alumni programming. Perhaps it would be wise for them to forget the word "alumni" and to focus on the word "people." The alumni program ought to provide the opportunity for people who are presently sharing the same educational experience to be helped by those who have preceded them.

For example, any alumnus would be flattered by a request to return to campus to talk to students about why he or she is successful; what to look for in profession "X"; or what institution to transfer to for major "Y."

The myth that community college graduates transfer their allegiance to their four-year colleges isn't true. "We are only a simple two-year college," say a number of community college leaders and faculty, but this is wrong. As Moore indicates, a two-year college should concentrate on being a good community college where most students receive "personal attention and a sound education." Community colleges are not second-rate high schools, but many community college staff seem to think they are. Both faculty and staff would be in for a pleasant surprise if they were to ask the graduates what they thought of their alma mater.

At SUNY, most of the community college alumni boards are comprised of graduates of four-year colleges who believe they got their start at their community college alma mater. These alumni volunteers feel a strong commitment to the personal educational environment of the community college. Community colleges are in a better position to reach out to alumni as individuals than are the typical four-year colleges.

George Angell, a former President of the State University College at Plattsburgh, observes:

> [Alumni] association programs are means, not ends. Unless we systematically evaluate associations in terms of goals rather than programs, we will fall into the trap of congratulating ourselves about well-attended banquets, boisterous reunions, and receipt of friendly, newsy letters. Such associations will suffer defeat after defeat in budget hearings and legislative decisions.[4]

Goals are important. Don't get caught in the trap of thinking that just because you have alumni activities, you have an alumni program—a situation that happens all too often at community colleges.

MOVING BEYOND THE MYTH: THE
NUTS AND BOLTS OF ALUMNI
PROGRAMMING AT THE
COMMUNITY COLLEGE

SUNY seminars on alumni programming at the community college identified several needs:

- the need to educate the campus president about the value of alumni
  programming;
- the need to participate in image building in order to solve any identity problem the institution might have;
- the need to do research on who the alumni are: adequate information
  about the college's alumni must be at the heart of alumni programming;
- the need to develop long-range and short-range planning;
- the need to have budget support—some colleges have successfully
  implemented an undergraduate/alumni association that charges an
  optional/voluntary fee of $10 per semester to underwrite programs
  that link alumni and present students, usually through career
  orientation/job placement activities. Other campuses allocate a portion of the graduate fee to alumni activities;
- the need to have volunteer continuity:
- the need to provide frequent communications to the alumni and to
  the faculty about alumni accomplishments;
- the need to generate recognition and visibility for the alumni program on campus and in the county;
- the need to promote loyalty to the major or curriculum (perhaps
  through a market segmentation approach and minireunions);
- the need to sustain the initiative once the alumni program is begun—
  by providing, for example, for alumni membership on the college
  board of trustees and having alumni curriculum advisory committees; and
- perhaps most important, the need to enable alumni volunteers to
  assist the college in meaningful ways.

We then surveyed SUNY community college presidents about how best
to initiate alumni programs. One president responded as follows:

> Our first problem was establishing a database. We did not know who our
> alumni were or where they were. We started trying the easy approaches of
> getting names from faculty and staff. Finally, we decided we had to do it the
> hard and thorough way so we developed a questionnaire and are now sys-

tematically contacting all graduates, following up with second and third mailings, and then developing a database on an IBM PC.

The second obstacle we confronted was determining which alumni were interested in being associated with the association.

Initially, we made an assumption that once we had a list of a number of alumni, we could plan events and they would come. Not true. An invitation to 1,500 did not generate much of a response. So, again, the hard approach of getting the questionnaire that indicates interest. At this point, we are getting about 15 percent return from that questionnaire mailing.

A third obstacle we have faced relates to developing an interest on the part of alumni for an alumni association and alumni programs/events. We are attacking that problem by asking our academic departments to recruit graduates for the association. Additionally, the association is beginning to work with the academic departments in planning departmental alumni events.

It is our feeling that rather than the broad-based alumni associations that we find at other institutions, we are having somewhat more success with discipline-related alumni groups. The nurses who spent two years together, or the medical laboratory technologists who did likewise, feel more of a kinship to each other and their curriculum than they do to the college as a whole. Accordingly, they have retained friendship and loyalty for one another, and we should capitalize on that.

Major stumbling blocks at our college are: finding an interested volunteer who is willing to put in the time and effort needed for an alumni association. Finding a funding area where seed money could be obtained for supplies and postage. Maintaining an up-to-date address file since most of our students move in rapid succession following their graduation. A truly viable alumni association requires a full-time person with support staff. Creating and funding this area is extremely difficult in a limited college budget. There has been a lack of enthusiasm by a majority of our alumni to recognize their association with a two-year college following their graduation from a four-year institution.[5]

Here is that myth again; it is such a convenient "cop-out" that the respondent couldn't resist.

The most perceptive response began with the importance of good records:

Records are the key. Must be computerized and allow for searches and sorts on a variety of information items. There must be hardware and software *dedicated* to this activity. Adequate staff time must be allowed for research as well as keyboarding. The job will never be done.

We used to think that the key to programming success was department/program loyalty. It still seems to be greater than institutional loyalty for a non-residential campus, but it's not strong enough on its own to support programming. . . . Geography (distance) and age (length of time since graduation) are a help; absence does seem to make the heart grow fonder, but not without a push from us.

I'm convinced that current students/clubs have to be brought into the picture, to strengthen the departmental/institutional loyalty *now* to the point where it will survive after graduation. My next suggestion is likely to be a student/alumni council within departments, although that does pose a risk of alumni opposition when an administrative decision goes against a particular department or favored faculty member.

The discordant relationship between alumni and development appears to be universal [money is easier to obtain and considered to be more important than alumni volunteered time and talent] and is only worse in the community college where the per capita giving potential is lower than in other kinds of schools and where the development staff are more likely to look to local business and industry for the "quick" payback to ensure survival. Must be creative in bridging the gap and at the same time be sure to look to alumni for other types of assistance, probably well before any broad development efforts are undertaken.

I strongly recommend "cross-pollination" between the alumni association and the foundation, although we haven't gotten the right people involved here; neither is a believer in the other—indeed hostility remains even though it's denied. Must convince the foundation to *invite* representation from the alumni association, as a start, on the foundation board of directors. Recruiting individual alumni who are not involved with the association does not have the desired effect. Indeed, it can seem to undercut and downplay the official association.[6]

If at first you don't succeed, try, try again—persistence is the bedrock of alumni programming. It takes three or four years to establish new alumni programs at Ivy League institutions, and it's certainly no easier at a two-year college.

We have to apply great amounts of patience, resources, and commitment if the alumni effort is to reach critical mass and mature. Dues income will almost never be enough. Operating support, over and above the alumni director's salary, the records system, and production/postage for mailings, may be required.

A foundation grant tied to alumni support for development probably needs to be explored. It will take time though; that has to be emphasized. Not an excuse, but reality.[7]

This president provides insights into some of the problems confronting the community college that wants to establish an alumni program. He also offers a number of observations that apply to most alumni programming and the special relationship that should exist between fund raising and alumni volunteer programming.

The common denominators that the SUNY experience has identified as essential elements of a new alumni program are:

- budget support,
- staff support,
- records,
- communications to alumni,
- departmental programming,
- president's support, and
- willing and able volunteers.

WHERE TO START? HOW TO BEGIN— THE FIRST STEPS

If your goal is to develop an alumni program for your two-year college, begin with these five steps:

1. Develop a funding source.
2. Appoint a secretary (part-time if full-time funding is not possible) who will maintain records and process correspondence for the budding volunteer board.
3. Assign the public relations/communications office the responsibility of establishing an alumni newsletter.
4. Identify a handful of able, willing, and (preferably) leading alumni to form the genesis of an alumni board.
5. Last, meet with trustees, deans, and important faculty to identify goals and objectives that truly further institutional goals.

Never lose sight of the fact that an alumni organization is a service group: first, the college sets the goals; then it seeks alumni who can accomplish them.

Several of the SUNY community colleges developed realistic approaches to gaining alumni support, and their experiences can help you.

Campus A

Campus A began as a two-year technical college, which the county converted to a community college. In 1962, the campus president decided to begin an alumni program that would not be a traditional program but merely a means to keep former students informed about the college. To fund the program, he established a mandatory alumni fee of $5. The fee was in effect for 15 years and then became a voluntary/optional assessment. During that time, the money was used to generate a newsletter, fund an alumni office secretary, and maintain basic alumni mailing labels.

College direction and leadership for this effort came from the student affairs office and was a minimal, part-time support position. An alumni board of a few dedicated graduates held meetings, planned an annual social event, and served as the administrator of the revenue given to the alumni association through the undergraduate alumni fee paid by students. The board made grants to various departments, student clubs, and scholarship aid. The program functioned in this matter until four years ago when a full-time foundation director was hired to manage the campus-related foundation that had served as the solicitor and repository for private gifts received from the community and some alumni.

The new foundation director sensed that more could be accomplished through alumni volunteers working with the foundation and not simply as an aid to private gift-getting efforts. With the support of the campus president, he decided that it was time to approach the county for direct funding for an alumni director position.

After two years of proposals and meetings with the county education committee, the college prevailed. It did so by virtue of the fact that an alumni program, albeit a minimal one, had continued over a 20-year period. The college maintained an accurate mailing list of graduates, which showed evidence of the impact graduates had on the sponsoring area (the county) in terms of numbers of alumni residing in the area after graduation.

After the position was approved, a full-time professional alumni director was hired, and the alumni association was able to fund a full-time alumni office secretary through the accumulation of funds from the student fees.

The initial focus for the fully staffed alumni office had four components:

1. to upgrade alumni records with occupational information;
2. to identify top alumni to serve on the alumni board of directors;
3. to develop an annual alumni fund; and
4. to increase contact between the alumni and present students as well as to involve more alumni in on-campus events.

Several key factors were instrumental in making Campus A's alumni program a success:

-   presidential support;
-   a source of funding;
-   the presence of dedicated alumni volunteers over a long period of time;
-   an alumni newsletter;
-   departments that maintained contact with their graduates;
-   sustained campus support over the long term prior to county support for an alumni professional; and
-   an established foundation which was a solid base for funded alumni programs.

Campus B

Campus B began its alumni program by hiring a full-time alumni professional with the provision that the program be self-sufficient within two years (a worthy goal but unfortunately one that no institution of higher education has yet accomplished). A person with prior professional experience was hired. His first goal was to develop a newsletter. The college relations office helped produce it, and it was sent to all alumni.

Developing alumni records and, from these records, a network of dues-paying alumni was the next priority. To accomplish this goal, the college offered dues-paying alumni a number of campus services, such as library privileges and the use of the gymnasium. Many community residents who wanted to continue their education took advantage of this offer, as did those who were aware of the high cost of nearby athletic clubs and were happy to have access to the campus gym.

The program was a success. Alumni *did* care about their two-year alma mater! The county appointed an alumnus to the board of trustees. Euphoria set in.

However, the program did not become self-sufficient at the end of two years. To justify salary support, the alumni director's position was split, and he took on additional duties. The annual fund competed with the alumni dues program, and alumni became confused. Alumni programming goals became murky, and some initially zealous alumni volunteers began to drop out of sight. The short-term goal of self-sufficiency evaporated, and there were no long-term goals that had the support of the campus. The former alumni director became a full-time professional in a student support area.

Campus B's program faltered, but it did not die. A new president came on the scene who linked the foundation and alumni offices in a separate but equal configuration.

An aggressive and ambitious annual fund drive is now in place, and a development/marketing staffer devotes part-time direction to the alumni programming. This person is careful to maintain the balance between alumni programming and alumni fund raising. The alumni board has been upgraded to include alumni who are community leaders and leaders in business and education; several on-campus departmental alumni reunions have been held; a major theatrical production was sponsored for alumni; and plans are underway to have alumni participate in a faculty appreciation week celebration and to organize reunions at local companies that have a significant roster of alumni employees.

The college is sensitive to the need for harmony between programming and gift getting. It follows the axiom, "Identify, interest, and involve," to produce long-term relationships and significant gifts.

Key factors for Campus B's success include:

- presidential support;
- a source of funding;
- departmental support and involvement; and
- office and staff support from the campus-related foundation.

Campus C

Campus C's alumni program grew out of the efforts of a well-intentioned admissions person and a few dedicated alumni volunteers. There was little support from the president's office or from the deans and department chairs. This was the classical case of an alumni program being forced upon a college in spite of the almost total lack of interest of the college leadership.

For seven years, a hardy band of determined alumni volunteers, with part-time staff assistance from the admissions office, met monthly to plan socials and organize the sale of soft drinks and hot dogs at home football games. But eventually the program died on the vine. Nothing much has happened in the intervening years. The college administration has yet to set meaningful goals for an alumni program. The principal focus of college leadership appears to be on "today" and "now," on programs that serve immediate campus needs, rather than those that reap the long-range benefits of an alumni support program.

The more the alumni volunteers did for the college, the less attention the college paid to their efforts. In fact, the alumni were not serving important college objectives. With little support and encouragement, they began to feel defensive about their program and finally "formed their wagons in a circle"; few other alumni were allowed into the inner hierarchy. Prospective new volunteers felt rejected by, rather than attracted to, the group.

While Campus C did have two positive factors—dedicated staff and dedicated alumni volunteers—these were outweighed by significant negative factors:

- no presidential support;
- no budget support;
- no support from the departmental chairs;
- no clear-cut goals set forth by the administration; and
- limited opportunities for "new alumni blood" to replace the seasoned alumni veterans.

In a proposal for "The Development of an Alumni Association at Nassau Community College," Hughie Mills, the first full-time alumni director at Nassau, which has over 48,000 graduates, said:

> In conversations with directors of active alumni programs and with members of the college community who have been involved with previous attempts to establish an alumni program here, two important elements for success emerged . . .
> 1. The president of the college must be committed to the need for an alumni association. He should appoint the director and give him full freedom to administer the program. The board of directors, once established, should

formulate policy and programs for approval by the president. The director should be constantly responsible to the board of directors for the success of programs he administers and for carrying out the policies promulgated by the board and the president. The association and the president must establish specific goals upon which the effectiveness of the association will be evaluated. These goals must be communicated to the director. The president must maintain a close working relationship with the board to see that policies and programs are established in accordance with college needs and are permissible within the rules and regulations of the college.

2. If the president believes in the need for an association, it should be reflected in his budget. Even if the association is to be self-supporting, the president should provide adequate funds for start-up expenses. Until the association can generate operating income from dues and other related fund-raising activities, financial support from the president is of primary importance.[8]

The message is loud and clear—presidential support (more than just lip service) fuels the engine of any successful alumni program.

CONCLUDING OBSERVATIONS

As we have seen, certain fundamental elements must be in place if an alumni program at a community college is to succeed. Rushing headlong into an alumni fund-raising program does not yield long term benefits and should be avoided. While most community colleges cannot sustain a dues-supported alumni program, those in an urban environment with significant alumni numbers may have better luck in launching a dues effort that could involve 1 to 2 percent of the alumni.

If you are undertaking an alumni program at a two-year college, I recommend:

1. that the college make at least a five-year budgetary commitment to the program, with annual and five-year goals set forth by the president, the deans, and the alumni board of directors;

2. that there be a full-time director with at least half-time secretarial/clerical support;

3. that there be a commitment to establishing an alumni records base that includes occupational information for graduates; and that a newsletter to the alumni, parents, and friends of the college be initiated;

4. that the county and state be pressed to support funding the alumni program and staff support as a legitimate function of the college;

5. that the president, with the assistance of the deans and a full-time alumni office staff person, select the alumni to serve on the board of directors;

6. that qualified, informed alumni be appointed to serve on the board of directors;

7. that the college nominate qualified, informed alumni for appointment to the college board of trustees by state and/or county governments;

8. that departmental advisory committees include "the best and the brightest" from their alumni ranks;

9. that the college work diligently to promote, in the community and among its alumni, a sense of pride in the college—willingness to identify with a deserving cause will attract talented volunteer leaders;

10. that if fund-raising efforts are begun among the alumni, they be dedicated to student scholars; and

11. that alumni serve as enlightened advocates for the college in county and statewide legislative relations (an activity almost completely ignored by most community colleges).

In your efforts to begin an alumni program, don't forget that often ignored constituency—your students. They seek help in dealing with the real world which they must face in two short years. Who is a better source of practical advice than alumni who had the same major? Establish an undergraduate/alumni association immediately, funded by an optional $5 or $10 fee, and follow it up with direct involvement of key alumni with students, and the program is launched.

Notes

1. Asa S. Knowles, editor-in-chief, *Handbook of College and University Administration* (New York: McGraw-Hill, 1970), Section 5-205.
2. Ibid.
3. Internal SUNY survey.
4. Internal SUNY alumni paper.
5. Internal SUNY document.
6. Ibid.
7. Ibid.
8. Internal SUNY document.

CHAPTER
29 ═══

Urban Universities

Dorothy C. DiIorio

Building a strong alumni program for the urban university requires an innovative approach and special creativity. If you plan and execute your program skillfully and if you give it time to work, you will see your alumni develop deep and lasting relationships with your institution.

WHAT IS AN URBAN UNIVERSITY?

Urban universities are frequently thought of as offering a nontraditional college experience. A study conducted several years ago by the Council for Advancement and Support of Education (CASE) indicated that the predominant characteristics of a nontraditional institution include:

1. It awards degrees other than the standard bachelor's degree.
2. It offers part-time and evening classes.
3. Students are older than the average college student.
4. Class structure or class identity is virtually nonexistent.
5. It offers fewer extracurricular activities.
6. Student body primarily commutes to campus.
7. It has no football team or nationally ranked athletic program.
8. A high percentage of alumni live in the area.
9. It has few long-standing college traditions.
10. It has a reputation as a regional institution.[1]

By definition and by geographic placement and mission, the urban university plays a unique role in higher education and in urban society. A special relationship often develops between the university and its immediate surrounding neighborhood that can result in strong business and community ties.

Urban Students and Alumni

Alumni from urban universities tend to represent a significant part of the area work force, and consequently they can have a strong influence on the city and help reinforce the institution's positive image.

If you hope to have active alumni, you should get to know them while they are still students. Their unique educational experience will affect how you involve them in your association.

Most urban university students are older than their traditional university counterparts; it is not uncommon to find 26- and 27-year-old freshmen on an urban campus. Often, they are the first members of their families to attend college, and they take their education more seriously than traditional college-age students. They schedule classes around their jobs and, in some cases, take off a semester or several quarters to work to earn money for tuition. Some have already raised families and are returning for an advanced degree, while others still have children at home and are seeking to better their lives through education.

Most, if not all, students at urban universities live in the metropolitan area and commute to campus. Because of work and family commitments, they tend to leave campus immediately after class. One clever observer calls the urban university the gas station of higher education—students drive in, fill up, and pull out—and that makes your job as an alumni programmer that much tougher.

Urban alumni typically do not form the strong emotional ties or loyalties that you find among alumni from more traditional campuses. As students they did not have a lot of free time to make new friends or to participate in extracurricular activities. They did not develop strong class affiliations because their education was frequently interrupted by part-time jobs, cooperative exchanges, internships, or clinical programs.

And it is true of students today, whether at urban or traditional institutions, that they often must incur large debts while in school. Thus, their top priority after graduation is getting established in a career and repaying their debts. You will have to accept the fact that alumni involvement may not be among their highest priorities.

The Urban Setting

When you are planning your alumni relations program, you should consider the advantages and disadvantages of the urban setting. Because your alumni are concentrated in a relatively small geographic area, you can serve more alumni with each program and make more efficient use of your resources. You can also offer short, informal programs where alumni can come and go without taking a full day out of their busy schedules.

If you can find unique and interesting ways to use the vast cultural, musical, ethnic, and athletic resources available in the city, they will work for you. On the other hand, these resources can be a disadvantage by competing for the time, attention, and disposable income of your alumni. Your events must be especially attractive to draw alumni away from these other activities.

PLANNING AN ALUMNI RELATIONS PROGRAM

A comprehensive urban alumni relations program should reflect the mission of the institution and create an atmosphere that encourages a lifetime commitment to the university. It should be dedicated to cultivating and serving alumni and friends of the institution by providing an extensive variety of educational and social programs and activities.

The alumni periodical and publications have great meaning for urban alumni. They may not be able to attend—or even want to attend—all the programmed events, but they do want to keep up on what is happening at their university. Use your publications, which are the primary communication link between alumni and the institution, to give them news of the university, its faculty, and its alumni.

Traditional alumni programs put on with a special twist or inventive new nontraditional activities can play a big part in the success of your program. Remember to keep your volunteer alumni involved through all the planning stages; communicating with your alumni is essential.

Here are some important guidelines for planning your programs:

- identify special-interest groups and plan special events for them;
- hold events on campus or in locations close to your alumni;
- plan activities for, and with, students, young alumni, emeritus groups, and, when appropriate, parents of current students;
- offer continuing education courses and seminars;
- establish an awards/recognition program (distinguished alumnus, volunteer leaders service/achievement, loyalty);
- plan events well in advance and at similar times each year; and
- use faculty and outstanding alumni as centerpieces for alumni events.

Two primary areas for programming at urban institutions are collegiate units and special-interest groups in areas such as theater, music, athletics, minorities, and vocations. Although class years are not significant for most urban alumni, if they are for yours, you may want to plan reunions.

Substantive and effective programs for your alumni can focus around the college or school unit. Many alumni spent most of their student time in this smaller academic unit, sharing experiences with fellow students of the same unit. They identify with this group rather than with the university as a whole. Encourage the development of a board of alumni volunteers to work with the administration of the unit to plan appropriate social and educational programs—it is a good volunteer involvement tool. The success of such programs depends on the commitment of the head of the college unit. The faculty, alumni, and students must be integrated into the overall plan for academic unit-based programs. [Editor's note: see also Chapter 16, "Professional School Organizations and Other Constituent Associations," by Mary Ruth Snyder.]

You can present alumni programs in several different ways to encourage your audience of diverse alumni, who have tremendous competing demands for their time, to become involved with your institution. Choose a variety of approaches. Since traditional activities often don't exist for the nontraditional university, try creating your own.

Program Ideas

You can develop general-interest programs that center around events at local art museums, observatories, architectural centers, science museums, concerts, cultural centers, major league sporting events, libraries, and special research institutions. These facilities and their programs are most effective if you use your faculty, staff, or alumni as lecturers. For example:

- Have an art professor lecture and guide your alumni through the latest exhibit at the art museum in your city.
- Combine an alumni event with a local sports activity as New York University does at the time of the New York Marathon.
- Offer alumni the chance to attend a campus theater performance preceded by a dinner with the director of the theater.
- Arrange a bus tour through a special architectural area with the art professor as guide and lecturer; the tour could stop for lunch at an ethnic restaurant.

Educational and informational programs on timely subjects such as tax planning, health and nutrition, retirement planning, real estate and financial planning, time management, and managing stress can all be big draws for your alumni.

For young alumni, you can offer a brown bag series featuring faculty or alumni as speakers on timely topics. These low-cost programs can tie into commuting and workday schedules if you schedule them close to, or in, the workplace of alumni. Supper seminars are also attractive.

Even if you do not have a strong athletic program to rally around, plan social get-togethers on campus or at a popular nearby restaurant before or after an athletic event. These are good student/alumni events that can also support the teams.

Informal get-togethers after work in popular meeting places or private clubs can be extremely successful, especially with younger graduates.

Coordinate alumni programs with existing educational programs, conferences, and seminars sponsored and planned by the academic units, both on and off campus. Use your faculty, current and emeritus, to attract alumni.

Try a class reunion, even if yours is a young institution, and bring the alumni back to campus. Plan a continuing education program, or ask a panel of top administrators or faculty to give an update on the campus. Include time for campus tours and for reminiscing and socializing.

You may have great success with a campus open house for alumni and their families, faculty, staff, friends, and the neighboring community. The alumni office should plan this cooperatively with the administration, academic units, and student organizations.

Programs gaining in popularity are events and activities for corporations and businesses where there are large concentrations of alumni employed and for special-interest groups in finance, business, tax, law, advertising, and so on. Look at the accounting, law, architectural, and manufacturing firms and the hospitals in your city or wherever you have large concentrations of alumni. See if it is possible to form groups within those organizations. The University of Houston organized a group of 300 dues-paying members within Houston Industries, Inc., and held four major functions. Programs can be monthly or quarterly. Breakfasts, luncheons, and gatherings right after work seem to be most convenient for alumni.

Don't forget alumni who have left the area. Invite them back for reunions and special campus programs or plan programs wherever they live or work—if there are enough alumni to make it feasible. When the president, chancellor, faculty, student musical group, or athletic team travels, plan an event to coincide. If your alumni get together at professional association meetings around the country, take or send slide shows or videotapes of the campus. Where you have larger concentrations of alumni, you may want to form clubs that will plan social and educational programs.

If you are part of a multicampus system, your regional programs will very likely include graduates of all campuses. In programming for these regional groups, be sure to include faculty from all campuses.

Marketing your programs in a timely manner is extremely important. There are several effective ways to let your alumni know about programs without doing a first-class mailing to everyone. They can be done through:

- your alumni periodicals and newsletters;
- monthly or quarterly calendar of events sent to members or those who have expressed interest or attended events in the past;
- special segment mailings by class year, academic unit, business, ZIP code, special interest; and
- local newspapers, radio, television, and magazines.

Planning programs well in advance is imperative.

Alumni Involvement

Equally important to developing alumni loyalties is involving alumni with the university. Some ways alumni can serve are:

- career advising and networking;
- arranging opportunities for student interns, externs, cooperative programs;
- sitting on advisory boards for academic units;
- identifying and recruiting qualified students; and
- hosting foreign students and visitors.

At the University of Illinois, we developed an Alumni Service Program that provides 10 ways that alumni can help:

- as admissions/prospective student contacts;
- through legislative relations;
- as alumni information resources;
- as service club/civic club contacts;
- as a host for alumni who are relocating;
- through foundation activities;
- as foreign representatives;
- through participation in an alumni network;
- as contacts for random assistance (occasional help as needed); and
- as university hospital volunteers.

Alumni can provide meaningful service to the institution—and they like to be asked to help.

Student Involvement

Students at a urban university do not automatically develop a strong loyalty to the institution, as do students at traditional institutions. For this reason, it is most important that your office and alumni be involved with students while they are on campus.

You should serve as an adviser to the honorary societies, committees, and organized student activity groups. Award scholarships or establish short-term loan funds. Form a student/alumni association or recruit student ambassadors to help with alumni events and activities and to represent the university at alumni programs. Welcome students to campus and assist with their orientation. Present student leadership awards. Have students serve as representatives on college alumni boards. Actively develop and co-sponsor alumni/student programs. Assist with career decisions.

Continuing contact from the day students start until they graduate is important—they are the alumni of tomorrow.

CONCLUSION

According to standards established in the long-range plan developed by the CASE Committee on Alumni Administration, all alumni relations programs should meet at least one of the following criteria:

- enhance communication with alumni;
- help generate voluntary financial support;
- help generate new volunteer supporters for the institution; and
- provide the vehicle for input by alumni into the conduct of the institution.

Experiment with your programming. Urban alumni deserve your careful attention. They provide a special challenge, but if you can meet that challenge by developing their loyalty and helping them establish a lifelong relationship with your institution, you will find the rewards well worth the effort.

Notes

I would like to thank Frank R. Holmes of the University of Houston Alumni Organization and Gavin Ross of the Graduates Society of McGill University for responding to my questions.

1. Laurence M. Lerner, "Traditions with a Twist," CASE *Currents*, May 1986:28.

CHAPTER
30

Large Alumni Associations

JACK KINNEY

The large alumni associations in the United States and Canada, although they operate differently in many ways, share a number of common characteristics:

1. They represent large alumni bodies ranging in size from 75,000 to 400,000 graduates.
2. Their annual operating budgets exceed $500,000 with some going as high as $12 million.
3. They are involved in a wide range of program and entrepreneurial activities to serve members and obtain income for operations.
4. In addition, many are nonprofit corporations of the state with policy determined by a governing board elected by the members. Also, many are dues-paying organizations with membership ranging from 20,000 to over 100,000 members.

Currently, some 75 alumni associations in the United States and Canada might be classified in the "large" category outlined above. While this number may appear small considering the hundreds of colleges and universities that exist, these 75 institutions represent approximately 10 million alumni—a significant percentage of all graduates of institutions of higher learning today.

The breadth and diversity of the programs and activities sponsored by the large alumni associations generally have major impact on all alumni programming. Furthermore, the large alumni associations are expected to play a major leadership role in new programming, governmental relations issues, staff training, research, professional advancement, and critiquing the profession.

ORGANIZATIONAL STRUCTURE

Large alumni associations are generally organized in one of three ways:

1. The independent alumni association is usually a nonprofit corporation of the state, with policy determined by a governing board of directors elected by the membership. Normally, under this structure, the association will hire an executive director to manage its affairs and to work directly with the administration of the institution.

Alumni associations organized in this manner include Ohio State University, the University of Michigan, Stanford University, the University of California–Berkeley, Kansas State University, the University of Texas, Virginia Tech, and New York University. Usually, there is a dotted line relationship between the executive director of the association and a university officer. Also, a representative of the university administration is likely to sit as an ex-officio member of the association's board of directors to help provide coordination between the two. Often the executive director and certain staff members are paid through university channels, and the university provides some monetary support to the association.

The independent (some like to use the words "interdependent" or "autonomous") alumni association endeavors to serve as a partner of the university in attaining broad goals and objectives. The association usually publishes an alumni magazine or periodical for its members, which emphasizes association and university news and often reflects strong editorial opinions. Membership dues are the major source of operating income for the organization.

Many of the independent or autonomous alumni associations were formed early in the twentieth century with an alumni secretary as the chief staff officer. Ohio State University, the University of Michigan, and the University of Minnesota were the early leaders in the independent alumni movement.

2. The dual alumni organization structure is characterized by a department of alumni relations of the university and an alumni association similar to the independent one. Under this structure, the director of alumni relations wears two hats. As director of alumni relations, he or she reports to a university officer, but as executive director of the alumni association, he or she reports to a board of directors of a corporation.

The director must make sure the goals and objectives of the university and the association are compatible. Normally, the alumni relations department is responsible for certain assigned areas, such as alumni records and governmental relations; while the alumni association sponsors a variety of alumni programs to serve the university and alumni.

Generally, the university officer responsible for alumni relations (usually a vice president for university relations or advancement) represents the institution as an ex-officio member of the alumni association board of directors, providing coordination between the two groups.

The dual alumni organization structure appears to be the most popular in large alumni associations. Brigham Young University, Duke University, the University of Washington, Pennsylvania State University, the University of North Carolina, McGill University in Montreal, and the University of California–Santa Barbara have this type of organizational structure. It seems to satisfy those university presidents and governing boards who are concerned that independent alumni associations may become self-serving or out of concert with university goals and objectives. At the same time, it gives alumni the autonomy they seek and the ability to serve as a conscience of the institution.

3. The office of alumni relations is a department of the university and all alumni relations activities are generally sponsored and paid for by the institution. The director of alumni relations reports to a vice president for university relations or advancement, and all alumni personnel are employees of the university. An alumni council or advisory board typically provides alumni input and involvement for alumni programs. (While they are not policy-making bodies, recommendations made by these alumni councils or advisory boards are likely to be followed by university administrators seeking support in developing an alumni relations program.) In many cases, there is no membership dues program, and the university is responsible for publishing a magazine or periodical for alumni and the university community.

Institutions with large university-directed alumni associations include the University of Cincinnati, Florida State University, Northwestern University, and Syracuse University.

PUBLIC VS. PRIVATE

There appears to be no significant difference between the large alumni associations at private universities and those at public institutions. Large associations at private institutions tend not to be incorporated and generally do not have a membership dues program. However, the Stanford Alumni Association is a corporation and has an extensive membership dues program. But the associations at Northwestern, Notre Dame, and Southern Methodist are unincorporated and are not dues-paying.

More of the associations from public universities tend to be incorporated and have dues-paying members. This is evident in most of the Big Ten universities and at other institutions such as Penn State, the University of California–Berkeley, UCLA, the University of North Carolina, the University of Washington, Arizona State, and the University of Connecticut. Also, the large associations at private universities are apt to be responsible for—or at least more involved in—fund raising, particularly the annual fund. Most of the associations at the large public universities no longer have much contact with fund raising, which is now the responsibility of the development office or foundation.

Whether they are public or private, the large alumni associations appear to have more in common in personnel and programming than they have differences. At professional conferences, workshops, and seminars, alumni directors from institutions in both sectors meet to share information and discuss common problems.

PROGRAMS

Alumni programs at the large alumni associations are broad and diverse. A majority of the associations publish an alumni magazine or other periodical to keep alumni and friends informed about the institution. A heavy emphasis on regional alumni clubs is also evident. Many of the associations have developed constituent associations representing colleges and departments of the university as a method of decentralizing alumni programs. To supplement these efforts, special alumni clubs have been formed to represent constituencies such as ethnic groups and athletic teams.

The large alumni associations also sponsor traditional events—homecoming, class reunions, alumni awards—and special events such as a Women's Day. Most of them sponsor extensive travel programs, many with a continuing education format. Several, such as the University of Michigan, Stanford University, Indiana University, UCLA, and the University of California–Berkeley and –Santa Barbara, have family camps or vacation centers. These provide educational and recreational programs and are attended by hundreds of alumni in the summer. Dartmouth sponsors an outstanding continuing education program for alumni, and many other associations are following suit.

Many associations at public universities conduct legislative relations programs that organize alumni to advocate on behalf of the university. For example, UCLA has an excellent program in governmental relations that involves large numbers of alumni.

Student alumni associations have also become very popular within various alumni associations. They are a primary means of involving the students of today so they will be the active alumni of tomorrow.

Most of the associations provide a wide range of member services such as group insurance, credit cards, loan programs, library and recreational privileges, and merchandise discounts. (These are discussed in greater detail under "Sources of Income" below.)

Programs and projects to serve the university and alumni are the heart of alumni association work, and every means possible is used to relate alumni to the campus in support of their alma mater. Each campus offers unique programs to serve pluralistic alumni bodies, and alumni associations are constantly developing new ways to retain alumni interest and involvement.

SOURCES OF INCOME

The large alumni associations generally rely on three main avenues of support:

- university allocation,
- income from the foundation, and
- association income.

Most of the alumni associations receive appropriations from the institution for personnel and alumni programs. The amount varies. For example, Penn State, the University of California–Berkeley, and the University of Michigan receive minor support from the university, while Northwestern, Harvard, and Syracuse are heavily dependent upon the institution for dollars to operate.

Many campus foundations support alumni organizations because they believe it is a good long-range investment: alumni programs help create a positive atmosphere for fund raising. Duke University, the University of Kansas, and the University of Florida are prime examples of this commitment to synergism.

A main source of association income continues to be membership dues. Some associations, such as Ohio State and Penn State, raise more than $1 million each year from annual and life memberships. Normally, the associations invest a high percentage of the life membership dues income to provide for future life member services. Income from the investment portfolio of the association is often used for the annual operating budget.

Other sources of association income include the sale of merchandise, alumni travel programs, group insurance dividends, credit card royalties, loan program remuneration, magazine advertising, family camps, continuing education programs, and gifts to the association.

PERSONNEL

Staff support for the large alumni association varies from 10 to 12 people to more than 60, with an average of 18 to 20. In addition to an executive director, most associations have an associate or assistant director. They also have several professional staff people assigned to specific areas such as alumni clubs, constituent associations, student relations, marketing, publications, and financial administration. These individuals need additional support staff.

Staff training and development have received a great deal of attention in recent years. The Council for Advancement and Support of Education (CASE) provides specific job-related training through district conferences and special workshops. The large associations often employ specialized staff such as an editor, marketing director, and financial officer, in contrast to the smaller office where the director and assistants must wear several hats.

Recent years have seen a great deal of discussion about the discrepancy in alumni staff salaries compared with those of personnel in other departments on campus, particularly the development office. This discrepancy is often not as great at the large alumni associations, which have achieved status as one of the more important offices on campus. In many cases, alumni are represented at the highest levels of university governance. For the most part, however, the executive directors of alumni associations are still placed in secondary management roles in the institutions.

Universities generally support alumni associations because they provide services that the university would otherwise be responsible for. Some alumni professionals fear that alumni organizations are becoming too commercial and that entrepreneurial activities are thriving at the expense of basic alumni programming. However, university administrations continue to encourage associations to become more self-sufficient to relieve the institutions from the need to devote badly needed dollars to alumni programs. Thus, many associations find that they must generate outside sources of income if they are to continue to offer many of their programs.

Ideally, this dilemma will be resolved and some sort of balance will be achieved. Institutions and foundations should tangibly support alumni relations programs to the best of their ability. It has been amply demonstrated that, in the long run, this will prove to be a wise investment.

PHYSICAL FACILITIES

For years, the alumni office was often found in the union building or the university center, and that practice is still popular. But many associations have a headquarters adjacent to the campus. The University of California–Berkeley was one of the first associations to build an alumni center on campus. Several years ago, Ohio State built an alumni house that holds both the alumni and development offices in a wing of its Center for Tomorrow.

FIGURE 30.1.
Exterior and interior views of University of Utah Alumni House, built with funds raised by the alumni association.

272

In recent years, the alumni associations at the Universities of Michigan, Nebraska, Kansas, Arkansas, Utah, and California–Irvine have conducted capital campaigns and built alumni centers (see Figure 30.1). These serve as a base for alumni operations as well as providing facilities for faculty, staff, and student use. Several other associations are contemplating building alumni facilities, either as a separate entity or in conjunction with another building or department on campus. Others are in the midst of renovating an existing building to serve association needs.

The underlying motive for these building programs is to provide the alumni association with an identity on campus. Alumni need a home they can return to, that can be easily found and has convenient parking, and where they can receive information and assistance. The association must be able to host a number of functions—board meetings, reunions, alumni receptions, and committee meetings—and still be able to encourage the faculty, staff, students, and administration to use the alumni center for a variety of events.

For most of the large alumni associations, the university provides maintenance and utilities. However, the association often must provide equipment and any refurbishing that is needed.

At professional meetings and conferences, physical facilities are a hot topic. The expansion of staff and the increase in alumni programming have left many associations in dire straits with regard to office space. Therefore, the renovation of existing facilities and the building of new ones are likely to continue to be a top priority.

CONCLUSION

Large alumni associations as an integral part of higher education are unique to the United States and Canada. Although some in the alumni world fear that the large independent alumni associations might become a thing of the past because of increased costs of operations and the desire of university administration to have more control, associations continue to flourish. Perhaps, after all, increased interdependence will satisfy the university's need for control.

For a time, alumni associations were abandoning membership dues programs lest they compete with the annual fund. But with increased costs and the need for more financial self-sufficiency on the part of the alumni organization, more associations are launching dues programs, not only to obtain income but also to determine alumni interest and involvement.

As alumni bodies grow, the large associations of the future must look to more innovative methods to retain alumni support. By the year 2000, many universities will have 300,000 to 500,000 alumni—staggering numbers of people for whom to provide services and keep records. Electronic information processing will be essential. Keeping up-to-date with the latest developments in this field will be a challenge that may necessitate significant changes in personnel, office equipment, education, and training.

Finally, and most important, alumni associations and senior alumni administrators must continue to provide leadership for alumni relations. Through its volunteer president and its executive director, the alumni association must represent the views, concerns, and needs of the institution's alumni to the university administration. And only a strong, viable alumni association, with a proven record of service to the institution and to its alumni, will have the credibility to play that role.

CHAPTER
31

Less Is More: Paradoxes of Small College Alumni Administration

NENA THAMES WHITTEMORE

As Alexis de Tocqueville observed in *Democracy in America*, "If men [and women] arc to remain civilized or become civilized, the art of association must develop and improve among them. . . ."[1] In alumni associations, the basic principles of building a reciprocal relationship between the institution and its graduates apply whether the institution serves 100,000 or 10,000 graduates, but implementation and emphasis may vary. Lack of size prevents small colleges from benefiting from what economists call "economies of scale." But small colleges have compensations, perhaps best summarized by the phrase, "Less is more." If you work for a small college and have a small staff (usually fewer than five), a limited budget (under $200,000), and a small alumni body (fewer than 30,000), there are creative ways to turn these limitations into opportunities. That is the challenge for the alumni director at a small institution: doing more with less.

While you can't dismiss the cramping caused by staff limitations or budget strictures, you can work creatively within the parameters set by the size and wealth of your institution. Small college alumni programs excel because the directors have found innovative ways to solve problems, use skimpy resources creatively, rely on well-trained volunteers, and in-

275

volve the entire college community in the alumni program. The dialogue among alumni, students, faculty, and staff in shaping the program can lead to a stronger institution with greater alumni support in every arena. This is not to say programs, budgets, or staff size *should* be small or stagnate, but that, even with realistic limitations, you can still create an exciting and magnetic alumni program.

LESS STAFF, MORE VOLUNTEERS

Where there is less staff, there must be more volunteers. In other words, staff must use their time not just to do but to train others to do, thereby increasing the effectiveness of the program. The efforts of an alumni director working with different types of volunteers—club leaders, faculty, student groups, and other staff—are like a pebble thrown into a pond to create ripples in ever-widening circles. For your volunteers to function effectively, each must be recruited for a specific task and given a clear job description and a definite time-frame in which the work must be accomplished. Each volunteer takes special handling and a different approach, but all will respond to clear direction and an understanding of how their work will contribute to the college. While the rewards may be intangible, they must include recognition, praise, and the volunteers' own feeling of accomplishment.

Here are some principles to follow in training all types of volunteers:

1. Train volunteers having the same function in a group.
2. Show how each task fits into the mission of the college.
3. Expose volunteers to institutional leaders.
4. Have a job description, an outline of tasks, a handbook, and a time limit for the job.
5. Provide adequate staff support.
6. Show interest in volunteers' suggestions and follow up on their ideas.
7. Celebrate the completion of the task and reward the volunteer with praise and recognition.

These guidelines apply to working with volunteers in any institution. However, they are particularly important to the alumni director in a small college who must rely on dependable volunteers to find a location for a club meeting, drive prospective students to campus, squire the president around when he or she visits another city, arrange for career internships, prepare a regional newsletter, set up phonathons, and so forth. All of your volunteers—even the students who carry bags for alumni during reunions—need to understand their roles and responsibilities.

And don't forget those important volunteers who serve on the board of directors of the alumni association. The board should have several meetings a year that include briefings on the state of the college, instruction on how tasks can be performed, reports on programs and events, well-planned committee meetings with action as well as discussion, and outside speakers to provide inspiration and objectivity.

A growing trend among alumni associations is to set aside time for a board retreat and strategic planning session. Carleton College (Minnesota) undertook such a program modeled on the mentor system constructed by the Association of Governing Boards of Universities and Colleges. Grinnell College (Iowa) and the University of Puget Sound (Washington) arranged low-cost programs by asking other small college alumni directors to act as mentors during the retreat weekend. The Council for Advancement and Support of Education (CASE) assists in matching colleges with mentors, and similar ACM (Associated Colleges of the Midwest) institutions do their own matching.

Because alumni association boards turn over every few years (or should!), these retreats should be held every five years or at important junctures in the history of the college, such as the advent of a new president or the launching of a capital campaign.

LESS MONEY, MORE INGENUITY

No one would ever suggest that tightening a budget creates a better program, but, when money is scarce, an alumni director must look carefully at which programs to mount and how much money these programs will need. Some small institutions simply allocate a lump sum to the alumni office or use the same budget categories as other offices, but subdividing costs for events and functions and allocating sums to each event in some detail are important steps in tracking and cutting costs. Getting a clear handle on exact costs is essential both to cost cutting and to budget justification.

You may need to ask the controller or treasurer to help you set up special categories in keeping with the needs of your office. Before you can plan your budget, you need to know the cost of reunion, homecoming, the alumni board weekend, and whatever other programs you are proposing, as well as the cost for duplicating materials for these events.

The advent of computer-assisted record keeping makes these tasks easier. A course in Lotus 1–2–3 or the help of an accountant will enable you to set up a system that suits your needs. Good record keeping provides a sound basis for requesting budget increases.

Once you know exactly what various programs cost, then you can begin to examine the cost-effectiveness of each. You can divide your office's activities into "essential" and "enriching" and allocate funds accordingly. Choices must be made. Jules Trapp, Assistant Director at Wheaton College (Illinois), notes:

> Tried and true programs are less costly than experimentation, especially on a smaller budget. If a budget is established that can absorb the cost of an experimental failure, then some experiments can be built into the planning.[2]

Often, on-campus programs like reunions and homecoming are the least expensive and the most basic, but off-campus clubs or chapters are essential unless the college is entirely local or regional. In addition, volunteer training and communication are necessary for all programs, on or off campus. Finally, funds must be allocated for necessities such as balloons, banners, and name-tags.

You can make the simplest, bare-bones reunion or homecoming festive and exciting by providing a helium tank, some yellow balloons, and a parade. The Princeton P-rade may be famous, but Carleton graduates made humorous banners out of sheets, and Hollins College (Virginia) alumnae competed to create colorful felt banners with class mottoes. My favorite was stitched by the white-haired ladies in the 1936 50th reunion class whose banner proclaimed, "A Perfect 36."

Talent enriches programs and makes them exciting, but it is often the cheapest item in the budget. At Carleton, when the grant ran out that had provided a music festival during reunions, necessity was the mother of invention. We put on an alumni recital which was such a success that it has been a tradition now for over a decade. Alumni concert pianists, opera singers, modern dancers, and singing groups have shared the stage with faculty performers and an occasional student. No one asked for payment, but the payoff in pride and entertainment enriched the college community. Showcase talent, and everybody wins.

Students often provide the least expensive labor for reunions, homecoming, or alumni board weekends. And using student labor is not only cost-effective, it is also good business. Students embody what the college stands for, and they can be eloquent spokespersons for the needs and accomplishments of the institution. For example, one year Laurence McKinley Gould, a former President of Carleton, returned to the college for a reunion. Dr. Gould always wore a red tie, so we gave our student helpers red ties or red carnations to wear. We found that they dressed up to the tie or the flower and matched their manners to their clothes. We didn't have to instruct them on the proper dress or behavior for working with alumni. This investment in ties and carnations gave students pride in their work and an identity; alumni loved the students and their "uniforms," and a tradition was born.

Humor rarely costs anything, yet it adds immeasurably to a program. By using clip art for invitations and newsletters or cartoons for handbook or class letters, you can substitute humor for expensive paper or design. Student interns may welcome the opportunity to design or produce newsletters, create invitations, or design letterhead. While quality and taste should always guide the program, the inventiveness of a student often adds ginger to a publication.

You can use humor in sports events as well. In the days when "Ironman" triathalons were gaining prominence, the Carleton reunion included a "Tin Person" contest of considerably shorter duration for both men and women. In the late 1960s, softball games became "Rotblatt games," named after a long-forgotten pitcher for the Chicago Cubs, and contests between classes or decades became *de rigueur* at all Carleton reunions. Bryant College (Rhode Island) loves "oozeball," a messy form of volleyball played in the mud. The humor and mythology of a college cost nothing, but they can unite alumni in loyalty to their alma mater.

Some touches cost little and add much. Pictures from the year of graduation on the name-tags of special classes at reunions; hats, ribbons in different colors, or buttons for the various reunion classes; welcoming banners; and songsheets all add to the fun and festivities. Balloons make any event a celebration. A few pennies for fun and creativity can add more than expensive, custom-made materials.

REUNIONS ARE THE FIRST PRIORITY

The budget limitations of a small college alumni office often restrict programs to the basic and essential services to the college and its alumni. Small college alumni directors seem to agree that reunions are the number one priority. James Hackney, Director of Alumni Programs and the Annual Fund at Wofford College (South Carolina), says that reunions, which occur during homecoming, are "the center of our universe."[3] He points out that, rather than making extensive and expensive road trips, alumni directors could better use resources in getting more alumni to campus.

Gilbert Swift, Alumni Director at Lawrence University (Wisconsin), points to a paradox in reunion programming: while reunions are not focused on money, the best programs yield financial returns. Swift says, "The key to having a successful alumni relations program is to focus attention . . . on the nonfundraising aspect of alumni support for their alma mater and leave the fundraising efforts to the development office staff. This is critical to a successful reunion program."[4]

Whether reunions occur every five years, by cluster, or according to a combination known as the Dartmouth Plan (clusters for most classes but individual reunions for key reunions, such as the 10th, 25th, and 50th), they all have the purpose of encouraging alumni to return to campus. Many institutions offer a cost-free weekend to the 50th reunion class or to the 50th and older classes. Cecil Eckhoff at Gustavus Adolphus College (Minnesota) offers free housing to all returning alumni. These incentives repay the college through increased giving.

The principle behind every successful alumni reunion is that it recreates, or expresses the essence of, what is unique about the institution. The key is to match reunion activities to the character of the college. One way to ensure that a wide range of interests and festivities is included is to begin early and to work with committees and staff that represent all the constituencies of the institution and all the alumni constituencies.

Alumni directors may find it useful to read the annuals of the appropriate years to gain perspective on the classes involved. Reading history is important too. For example, entertaining the classes of 1929 and 1939 is very different from entertaining the class of 1945. During the war years, a number of coeducational institutions became almost single sex, and reunions for these years may benefit from a special format.

Whatever the format of the reunion program, it should meet the needs of all age groups; build pride in the institution; educate the alumni and their families; include programs appropriate for spouses and children; offer substantive programs, entertainment, and recreation; and involve the entire college. Alumni should leave with an understanding of what the college has been in the past and what it aspires to be in the future.

Constituent alumni programs are not as prevalent at small colleges as they are at large universities, but they should not be overlooked. If time and space permit, you can plan reunions of special groups during class reunions, or you can schedule them during homecoming or other special events. Wofford holds reunions for several constituent groups—presidents of the campus union, black alumni, alumni who are presidents or owners of their own company or organization, lawyers, former glee club members, and former members of the theater workshop. Wofford's Alumni Director James Hackney says that, after a year-long recognition program, the reunion of alumni presidents of companies "was the most interesting and most productive. . . . Giving from these 700 increased 28 percent."[5]

Midge Brittingham, Executive Director of the Alumni Association at Oberlin College, does one reunion a year for a special constituency such as the Gilbert and Sullivan Players, the student newspaper, the radio station, athletic teams, and dormitories. A special reunion of the Oberlin 250-voice oratorio choir, the Musical Union, generated coverage on National Public Radio. Hollins College hosted a highly successful creative writing reunion that drew students, graduate students, and alumni, including two Pulitzer prize-winners. Statewide publicity followed. Such special reunions attract public attention while also bringing back alumni who probably would not attend the usual gathering. By-products of the event are updating of alumni records, publicity that helps admissions, and increased giving.

LIMITED STAFF,
BETTER ORGANIZATION

Your limited staff and budget need not prevent your institution from having a national network of alumni programs, but these chapters and clubs may not have a special person to handle their needs, as they would at a university or wealthier college. Paradoxically, while the small college may need to delegate more to volunteers because of staff limitations, it must also have greater centralization and coordination of activities. The piggybacking principle must go into play—that is, every function and every trip must serve multiple purposes. This requires coordination both at the college and in the field. For instance, a presidential trip to visit alumni may include receptions for prospective students, dinners with major donors, and talks with corporate or foundation officers.

On the campus, all offices need to cooperate in planning and sharing time. Likewise, volunteers in various cities must understand that a trip cannot be cancelled or rescheduled to suit a change in their plans. Such piggybacking takes more work on the part of both staff and volunteers, but the college benefits. Tight organization is essential to success.

Some 11 years ago, Carleton reorganized its outmoded club system to reflect a more coordinated, functional view of alumni programming. As we moved from clubs to steering committees, alumni in cities or in larger regions replaced nonfunctioning officers with committees representing the needs of the college and the alumni: events, admissions, careers, fund raising, and sometimes continuing education and a newsletter. Volunteers coordinating these activities for the college met regularly to plan and communicate.

Somewhat tongue-in-cheek, the alumni office called these regional groups by the acronym SCHOLA—Steering Committee Heads of Local Areas, but also the Latin word for "schoolhouse" and for a group of Roman generals. The alumni represented our "schoolhouse" and often marched like generals for Carleton.

Similarly, Oberlin College's new ACTION program (A Campaign to Involve Oberlinians Now) involves alumni in regional groups in four main areas: recruiting, fund raising, public relations, and summer jobs for students. A number of small colleges have moved to this functional model, which focuses alumni efforts on these essential services.

In serving clubs or steering committees, the alumni director acts like an old-time circuit rider traveling from one geographic region to another—usually on a predetermined schedule—to inspire volunteers, bring news from the college, and recruit new volunteers. Periodically, depending on budget, most colleges have the alumni equivalent of a revival: a training weekend for volunteers. Wellesley, Hollins, Oberlin, and Carleton, among others, offer comprehensive training weekends annually or biennially for their volunteers. Some colleges pay the expenses of volunteers on campus; others have the budget to pay travel as well.

These meetings revitalize the regional organizations, reward the volunteers, and help the alumni director evaluate present volunteers and recruit new ones. The meetings also facilitate coordinated planning so that goals and objectives are clear in all areas of the alumni program. Lee Harlan, veteran Director of Alumni Relations at Pomona College (California), now asks his volunteers to do a three-year plan, as even five-year planning is too quickly out-of-date. Having all the volunteers—reunion planners, class agents, admissions representatives, career networkers, and local chairs or club presidents—on the campus together creates a shared understanding of the college's needs.

STUDENTS ARE
ALUMNI-IN-RESIDENCE

At more and more institutions—both small colleges and large universities—student and young alumni programs are growing. While a few small colleges insist that they have neither staff nor time for these groups, others believe that these programs are a crucial investment in the future of the college and the alumni association.

These colleges include prospective or accepted students in alumni functions before they ever set foot on campus by inviting them to alumni holiday parties or summer ice-cream socials. This increases what admissions directors call the "yield" from an area by binding future students to the college.

When the newcomers arrive on campus, they may be greeted with inexpensive gifts from the alumni association—car decals or coffee mugs, for example—as a welcome from present alumni to future alumni. Often the association provides an activity or event for each year of the students' college career: a welcoming party for freshmen; a sophomore symposium on how to choose a major; and a senior/alumni banquet or a senior information night (SIN)—advice for seniors on how to get by in the real world.

As these events mark the rites of passage from freshman to alumnus, they convey the message that the alumni association is there to offer support and help, and they also provide the alumni director with opportunities to meet and recruit campus leaders for future alumni work.

Whether the alumni office puts extensive time or budget into a special program for young alumni, it should take the opportunity to work with students while they are "alumni-in-residence."

CONTINUING EDUCATION: NOT SEPARATE BUT ALWAYS

As John Hall, former Vice President for Alumni Administration at CASE, recently noted, continuing education is growing considerably.[6] In some alumni offices, especially at large universities, continuing education is the responsibility of a separate staff member who plans only alumni colleges, special alumni weekends, and faculty visits. Steven Calvert (see Chapter 23) and Linda Carl (see Bibliography) have been advocates and creators of extensive programs.

But every office—no matter how small—can use faculty and alumni to create learning opportunities and workshops, whether they be day-long or weekend programs or those lasting a week or longer. Faculty seminars renew ties with a favorite professor, stimulate an exchange on political issues, or provide insight into new scientific theories. They can be held in glamorous spots like the Greenbrier (a resort hotel in West Virginia) or facilities at a state park like Asilomar in Monterey, California.

All alumni events—reunions, homecomings, club meetings—should nurture the intellectual life of graduates. If each meeting of your alumni has the learning dimension that only the college can offer—such as a faculty member, alumni expert, parent speaker, or student panel—each will demonstrate the strength of your institution. For alumni who cannot return to campus, you can offer a "course" by providing a syllabus of resources that can be ordered through the bookstore. (Ask the bookstore to give the alumni association a percentage of the profits from sales of this self-taught course.) Continuing education programs can be directed to all the passages that alumni face: from young adults to lively older learners.

A travel program can be part of your continuing education program if it includes a teacher or host from the college who will endeavor to see that participants get more from the trip than entertainment. Lawrence University, for example, is offering a tour to New Zealand and Australia with a professor of biology as leader; Carleton offers a rafting trip in Colorado with a geology professor as lecturer and an alumni couple as guides. While travel programs can be costly and take a lot of staff time to nurture, development offices may be willing to support the tours because they are a good way to identify donor prospects. However, the time and risks involved suggest that you should begin a travel program only when your other programs are running smoothly.

MORE TRADITION,
GREATER RESPONSIBILITY

The alumni office has always been the guardian of tradition and the purveyor of nostalgia. But it also connects the college's past with its present every time a student becomes a graduate. Alumni, while they naturally wish to savor and celebrate the past, must see themselves as guardians of the future—the future of the institution. Rather than looking backward, they must work toward a vision for the future. No doubt you've already discovered the phenomenon of "instant tradition." Add a new event to the alumni calendar and you have created a tradition. With this power comes responsibility; you—and your alumni—must consider carefully what traditions should shape your institution's future.

Being an alumni director in a small college requires attention to detail, many talents, great patience, tremendous energy, and enormous creativity. Most of the time you are a one-armed paperhanger, but you soon discover the many arms of volunteers that help in this satisfying task. Together, you do it. Together, less is more.

Notes

I would like to thank the following people who responded to my questions: Midge Brittingham, Cecil Eckhoff, James Hackney, John Hall, Lee Harlan, Gilbert Swift, Jules Trapp, Caroline Wanstall, and John Wu.

1. Alexis de Tocqueville, *Democracy in America*, ed. J. P. Mayer and Max Lerner (New York: Harper & Row, 1966), 488.
2. Personal communication.
3. Personal communication.
4. Gilbert Swift, "Reunion Programs to Enhance Friend and Fundraising" (Presentation at CASE V District Conference, Chicago, December 1986).
5. Personal communication.
6. Telephone conversation.

CHAPTER
32 ═══

Alumni Administration at Independent Schools

EDWARD B. AYRES

Two or three decades ago, few of us in independent school alumni and development offices would have predicted that total voluntary support to independent elementary and secondary schools would reach $386,700,000 in 1985–86, a 27 percent increase over 1984–85. The Council for Aid to Education (CFAE) had not published the 1986–87 figure at the time of this writing, but my estimate is that it may be close to half a billion. We've come a long way since our humble beginnings.

THE GROWTH OF
ALUMNI ADMINISTRATION

The Beginnings

Formal alumni fund raising began in 1899 when the Yale Alumni Fund first flexed its muscles. For those independent schools in existence at the time, alumni programs and, indeed, any fund raising—and alumni administration and fund raising are *very* closely linked in independent schools—were almost exclusively the domain of the headmaster or headmistress, the original alumni and development officer. Heads in those days were men and women of incredible vision who were able to concoct dreams on a shoestring because that was often all they had. Any fund raising they did caused no problem with the IRS; taxes were inconsequential until 1913 when the income tax became law, and the benefit of tax deductibility did not really become a factor in fund raising until after World War II.

School alumni associations usually had a modest dues structure and some volunteerism, a special gift of a building or other facility, and the occasional windfall bequest. But for most schools, tuition provided 100 percent of the annual operating budget. And, if there was a shortfall, the faculty received no raises. During the hard times of the 1930s, many schools cut faculty salaries and some schools disappeared altogether.

World War II

World War II was a stressful period of doing without for independent schools as it was for everyone. Our institutions tried to maintain the status quo in spite of the reduced numbers of students and faculty. Students were taking accelerated programs and graduating in midsummer or midwinter, and faculty were joining up or being drafted. This era saw the development of a basic concept essential to any alumni effort—communicating with alumni. "V-letters," battlefield notes, and touching letters of nostalgia came back in droves, and they had to be answered. The volume was too much for the head, and the alumni office came into being to help him or her with this important task.

By the end of World War II, when construction materials were again freely available to shore up existing buildings and construct needed facilities that had been placed on "hold" for the duration of the war, the concept of the alumni office was firmly established. While these early alumni directors were not institutional advancement professionals—they were history or math teachers, alumni veterans, or junior administrators from other departments—they were all in the "people" business; they believed in their schools.

The 1950s and 1960s: The Greening of the Alumni Office

During these two decades, "development" became part of our language. Since World War II, alumni class agents had been in place, seeking modest annual gifts to their class funds, but it quickly became evident that larger funds were needed for buildings, endowment, scholarships, and faculty salaries. The capital campaign arrived on campus simultaneously with a development director and even a publications director for those schools that had the budget. At many schools, however, the alumni director simply became director of development and director of publications as well, and thus the birth of the one-person shop took place.

With the accumulation of many more graduates, the "old boy (and old girl) network" began to explode, with one person doing much more than he or she could comfortably handle. In addition, because of mounting costs in every area of a school's budget, tuition income no longer covered the school's expenses, and the quest for annual gifts took on an added importance.

The 1970s: Crises and Change

The 1970s were tough times for most schools as changes in rules and philosophy were forced upon them. Students began questioning the rules, challenging the administration, and petitioning for a new set of less stringent rules. In some schools, discipline took a holiday. The Vietnam War added to the uncertainty; many alumni returned from this unpopular war with bitter memories—and some did not return at all. But our schools survived. Voluntary support of independent schools in the 1970s began to produce million-dollar annual fund drives. In 1975, John ("Rusty") Chandler of the Hotchkiss School in Connecticut compiled the figures in the accompanying table.

Support for Seven Eastern Schools, 1974–75

	Enrollment[a]	*Alumni/ development budget*	*1975 giving for current operations*[a]	*1975 total support*[a]
Choate Rosemary Hall (CT)	886	$320,000	$801,738	$1,435,184
Deerfield Academy (MA)	548	234,232	590,850	2,424,890
The Hotchkiss School (CT)	489	214,163	657,466	1,870,103
Phillips Academy Andover (MA)	1,124	250,000[b]	557,578	1,495,519
Phillips Exeter Academy (NH)	956	335,183	597,561	1,399,668
St. Paul's School (NH)	499	222,500	481,892	1,111,021
The Taft School (CT)	525	141,800	415,725	815,042

[a]Figures taken from *Voluntary Support of Education 1974–75* prepared by the Council for Financial Aid to Education (CFAE).

[b]Andover's budget does not include expenses for its $50 million capital campaign. The school estimated expenses for this over the next four years would be between 6 and 8 percent of the total to be raised, or approximately $3,500,000.

In 1975 the seven schools listed in the table tallied a total of $10.5 million in voluntary support. But in 1987, only a dozen years later, according to 1986–87 annual reports from these seven schools, the total for the seven was over $41 million. And two of the schools reported amounts that passed the 1975 total for all seven.

The 1980s: Computers, Sophistication, and Proliferating Programs

Now, in the 1980s, the computer has expanded our horizons until there seem to be no limits to what we can do in identifying and segmenting our constituency. With the arrival of the mainframe for alumni and development use along with desktop hook-ups, many schools now realize the importance and the value of a research operation—a long-standing and critical part of fund-raising success at the college level. All sorts of useful data are now at our fingertips, from stock ownership and directorships to a listing of roommates and sports and clubs the alumni were involved in while at school.

ALUMNI ADMINISTRATION TODAY

The over 900 independent elementary and secondary schools that are members of CASE run the gamut: old-line eastern "preppies"; country day schools; Catholic, Episcopal, and Lutheran schools; a strong Canadian contingent; and schools in Europe, Asia, and Australia. Despite the wide variety of schools represented in CASE, we all dwell under the umbrella of independent education, and we all have alumni whose support—through both money and volunteer service—is vital to the well-being of our institutions.

Although there was a declining birth rate in the seventies, today our independent schools are full, and most of us are turning away many more applicants than we can handle. Meanwhile, our tuitions inexorably rise year after year—even beyond the rate of inflation. We're still playing "catch-up ball," and this has enabled many of our schools to add personnel in the alumni office or, as it is more appropriately called these days, the development office.

The one-person shop has been consigned to antiquity at most schools. If you still wear too many hats—if you're the alumni, development, planned giving, and publications person and also teach English, coach lacrosse, run a dormitory, and sell pencils in your school store—your school is not in tune with the times. Working with alumni is a special and vital part of your school's operation. It should require 100 percent of your time. If that is not the case, your school may not see the year 2001.

Programs That Work

Whether your goal is to increase financial support or volunteer services from your alumni—or both—you must begin with this basic rule: know your constituency. And how do you get to know them? The answer is, as it has always been, research. But unfortunately, most of our schools cannot or will not put a full-time research clerk on the payroll. The returns of research are slow and hard to quantify. The expense is difficult to justify to a budget committee. But consider what Robert Duke, Vice Rector of St. Paul's School in New Hampshire, says about the purpose of research:

> Another pet peeve [of mine] is reading in our journals about how important [it is to do] research on prospective contributors. I have even seen it reported that research is the most important aspect of fund raising these days. It seems to leave the idea abroad that all this research is done to find the Achilles' heel of some poor unsuspecting fool. It never seems to come across that the real reason for research on projects is simply to try to find if the cause we are representing will in some way attend to the interest of the prospect. Most people believe in some things that are very important to them in life and very important to the society in which they live. They like to see these things perpetuated. If through our work we can help them fulfill and extend themselves in an important way, then we have done our job. That should be the purpose of research. I wish it always came across that way.[1]

Use research to get to know your constituency. Remember that the contributions to your school generally come from less than 20 percent of your constituency. So it is important to pay attention to your school's major donors. Evaluate every class. Do you know the top five donors by name? Do you know the top 100 donors to your school? You should. In fact, you should keep a list of these people in the left-hand drawer of your desk. (I keep mine on top of my desk—it's not even in a drawer. And I *use* it.)

But just knowing their names is not enough. Do you know their birth dates? David Fowler, head of Proctor Academy in New Hampshire, remembers birthdays by sending flowers to the women or wives or widows on the list. It shows that you care, and caring is your business.

Give these top 100 people special attention. Invite them to campus gatherings and give them advance information on future plans for the school. You could put together a newsletter from your school's head to provide "insiders' information" for these alumni.

Find ways to maintain contact with them and use ink to make it personal. In this age of the magic of the computer, the third finger on my right hand has a callus from writing so many "SLNs" (silly little notes). You can add a handwritten note on a gift acknowledgment to congratulate the donor on a job promotion, a wedding, the arrival of a new baby, or to express sympathy for a death in the family. It may take a little extra time, but these personal notes show the alumnus that he or she is more than just a name in your database.

Richard Odell, formerly Director of External Affairs at Northfield Mount Hermon School in Massachusetts, suggests several ways to personalize your alumni program:

> Take the programs to the people rather than relying on on-campus events. We now have 24 active area associations and will add 12 more. Each is serviced by us with programming for at least one meeting per year; some meet monthly. These area events use a slightly different approach. We invite alumni, parents, friends, and prospective parents to a two-hour cocktail party with a cash bar. Midway through the gathering we get everyone's attention and do a 15-minute presentation using faculty, administrators, or students. When the cocktail party concludes, we invite everyone to join us for a Dutch treat dinner at a local restaurant. This works well as it requires a minimal commitment on the part of our guests and is easy to organize.
>
> Some of our area associations are organizing volunteer projects in their towns—for example, helping churches or town governments rehabilitate run-down houses.
>
> We are hoping to create a life-care facility on our property which will give elderly people a place to live and earn some income by working part-time at the school. Our students can gain some special insight by teaching those in the facility things they are learning, such as a foreign language.[2]

Independent schools can use practically every technique used by postsecondary institutions in alumni efforts. We all do phonathons, and many schools use professional phone-mail campaigns. Auctions, although difficult to organize, work wonders for some schools. An open bar makes the bidding spirited. Alumni travel is also a lot of work to organize but can be great fun, especially if it involves a "freebie" that gets you to Tokyo, Hong Kong, Singapore, and Bangkok. In 1977 I accompanied the late Bob Crow of Deerfield on a tour of the Orient with Choate, Deerfield, and Hotchkiss alumni and parents.

While neatness and aptness of thought help, creativity can make your school—and your program—something special. Tom Mulligan, Executive Director of Development at Pembroke Hill School in Missouri, has had great success with an annual "Clothesline Sale" which is organized by parents. The goods are donated by alumni, parents, friends, and merchants of Kansas City, and many are purchased by alumni in the area of this merger of two local schools, Pembroke Day and Sunset Hill.

THE TWENTY-FIRST CENTURY

Our major hope for 2001: surviving and thriving with dignity and quality. The twenty-first century will be a different world; even my SLNs may not survive in the high-tech future. The personal touch, however, will still be essential. We have all received enough computer-generated letters to know when that personal touch is absent. My favorite was addressed to "Choate

Rosemary Ha" and began "Dear Mr. Ha." Times may have changed but the importance of people hasn't. Director of Development John Corkran of the Bush School in Seattle, Washington, comments:

> [Twenty years ago] I was privileged to listen as two of the "greats" looked back over their years of service—David McCord, alumni secretary at Harvard, and George Cooke, director of the Princeton Alumni Association. It was a humbling experience—not because they knew more than I, which they certainly did, but because of the way they devoted their knowledge, indeed their lives, to people and institutions rather than to themselves. And they did it with humor, kindness, imagination, grace.
>
> [Today] we have developed the capacity to amass and handle great amounts of data about people and institutions. Where does that put the alumni administrator of today, when the alumni "family" he or she is to nurture bears as little resemblance to that of even 20 years ago as today's nuclear families do to earlier families? Perhaps out of necessity, we now have the "professional," one who manages, rather than relates, who plans, budgets, and schedules, who transmits through staff (if he or she is lucky), or through volunteers, the goals and aspirations of the institution. [The professional's] level of knowledge regarding things mechanical, elements of human behavior, economics, and educational trends is extensive.
>
> Now an alumni office may offer or cooperate in a panoply of programs: alumni interviewing of applicants, homecoming, parents weekend, grandparents weekend, alumni and student phonathons for the annual fund, alumni gift prospect rating, screening and cultivation efforts, an alumni magazine, an alumni directory, an alumni newsletter, alumni holiday gatherings, alumni-undergraduate dialogues about college and what to prepare for, alumni career seminars (describing careers for the undergraduates), alumni job placement and referral services, alumni professional mentoring programs, alumni reunions, alumni summer programs, alumni tours.
>
> All of this is important, but more important is the attitude with which it is undertaken. Is it to get alumni to support my institution? Is it to design a program that supports my career? Or is it to extend the support we have given these young men and women when they were students, so that they still feel our concern, and sense our desire, to serve them?
>
> I believe that, unless the latter is our first and bedrock motivation, the others will hold sway and our alumni will end up feeling exploited and manipulated rather than loved and needed, and they will leave us.[3]

What does the future hold for our independent schools? Diversity must be one of our primary selling points. Dick Cadigan, Director of Development at Greenhill School in Texas, says, "Demographics indicate that this country will be more ethnically diverse in the year 2000 than anyone ever imagined in 1960 or 1970."[4] Statistics suggest that in the coming decades the largest group of surnames among our undergraduates will not be Jones, Johnson, or Smith but rather Lee and Li.

What sort of support can we expect in the future from our increasing—and very well qualified—Far Eastern contingent? Check your records—if you dare—to see how many of your foreign graduates are solid donors to your annual fund. Fund raising for education is still primarily a North

American phenomenon. This is something to consider as we face the future. As we seek and promote multinational diversity for our independent schools, we will have to develop special programs and methods for communicating with our foreign alumni.

Richard Odell offers three more thoughts for our future:

- Develop strong networking programs for alumni.
- Establish special summer job placement programs for students through alumni.
- Link off-campus alumni events with the campus through greater use of videos or satellites.[5]

In this chapter, I have mentioned many techniques for effective alumni administration at secondary schools. If you want more information on any of these ideas, feel free to contact the people quoted: this is the essence of our profession—people helping people.

CONCLUSION

It is important to emphasize that survival of our schools—or even of independent education—is not our goal. John Corkran comments:

> But notice—the more money that is raised, the more programs embarked upon, the lower our standing has become in the public's, and in the Congress's eyes. That is because we have become so interested in survival (like our nation) that we have forgotten that our role is not to exist, but to give some quality, some dignity, and some hope to life.[6]

Independent schools, responsible as they are for the education of children and youth, have a vitally important role in society. Dick Cadigan of Greenhill School says:

> If independent schools are to produce individuals who will become something more than smart "Watergate alumni," then we have an obligation to infuse, ignite, seed plant a sense of genuine concern for others in our graduates. I believe some recent studies have indicated that the adolescent years provide the most fertile ground for influencing the ethical dimension of individuals. Whether we like the label or not, independent schools do produce an "elite"—that is to say, highly able and intelligent and potentially influential graduates who have the opportunity and capacity to contribute to society way out of proportion to their numbers. As Plato said, "True education is moral, all other merely training."[7]

Elementary schools can put this even more strongly; they have the priceless opportunity to instill values in the very young student. No one could overestimate the importance of pre-college education, whether public or private. Two Roosevelts went to Harvard but Groton deserves some kudos too. It is easier to remember the school connection in the case of President Taft; most of his family went to the Taft School before going on to Yale. While Princeton and Harvard can claim John F. Kennedy as an alumnus, so can Choate Rosemary.

John Corkran asks the question: "Unless we realize we have a common calling—the preparation of young people to run the nation, the society, and its institutions, and not squander what has gone before—what right do we have to claim privilege?"[8]

The challenges ahead of us are as enormous as they are exciting. In the early 1970s, the New York Mets came up with the right slogan: "You gotta believe." Believe in your school; make it a very special place worthy of support, and then promote it to the best of your ability. If you find you have developed a callus on your middle finger from adding those handwritten SLNs, chances are you are on the right road. Hang in there, and you and your school will be on your way to greatness.

Notes

1. Personal communication.
2. Personal communication.
3. Personal communication.
4. Personal communication.
5. Personal communication.
6. Personal communication.
7. Personal communication.
8. Personal communication.

Managing the Future

CHAPTER
33

Alumni in the Twenty-First Century: The Planning Starts Now

DAN L. HEINLEN
LINDA S. CROSSLEY

WHO WE ARE

The formation of the Association of Alumni Secretaries in 1913 started the alumni movement on the long road to maturity. Over the years, demands for greater productivity to meet the increasing needs—and numbers—of alumni have forced those in the profession to develop sophisticated management abilities. While a "seat-of-the-pants" management style continues to be the rule at some institutions, it has steadily given way to the planned growth and development of effective alumni programs produced by skilled, well-trained, and competent staffs.

But for many administrators, planning is not a function that comes easily. To project future association operations accurately, we must know what our alumni and our universities will identify as their needs at that time. Too often "planning" consists of developing programs from the bright ideas of alumni staff or transplanting successful programs from other institutions. While this reactive approach may occasionally be effective, it is not very predictable nor is it efficient in building better, larger, and stronger programs for alma mater and its alumni.

The better long-range association plans have evolved from a thoughtful process incorporating staff and volunteers along with members of the faculty, student body, and administration. This is essential where those constituencies will be involved in making the plan work, since "the only plans which get carried out are the ones built by the people who will be responsible for their execution."[1]

More than 50 years ago, the *Manual of Alumni Work* attributed to the alumni association a role in supporting the university through its alumni—the same role played by that first alumni association founded at Williams College in 1821. Some things never change.[2]

WHAT WE DO—AND WHY

Alumni associations try to initiate programs and to involve alumni in order to bring alumni closer to their colleges and universities. Because individuals respond according to their personal interests, an alumni association must offer a variety of programs to attract a broad representation and large numbers of participants. But which programs work best? Those that have stood the test of time or show promise for alumni involvement may include reading an alumni magazine; making a gift to the institution; watching an athletic event; participating in continuing education; traveling with other alumni; using special credit cards; and attending alumni club meetings, class reunions, or other events.

It is up to association management to select, organize, promote, and energize these activities with enthusiasm so that both the institution and the participant benefit. Involvement is the name of the game—if alumni don't participate, there is no program.

But why is alumni involvement important? Is it only to raise funds from graduates or to keep the alumni office busy? There are four things alumni can give their alma mater: money, new students, advice, and advocacy. Name what you will, it will fit in one of those four categories. (A university administrator recently said there was a fifth—alumni could give the institution trouble! We won't go into that one in this chapter.) But involving alumni has a goal beyond these four objectives: ultimately it seeks to develop stronger institutions of higher education that will produce more disciplined and brighter graduates who will be better prepared to contribute to the quality of life and the well-being of humankind. And if these graduates are able to make progress toward finding cures for some of the physical, social, and spiritual ills of the world, our efforts will be well rewarded indeed.

WHAT DOES LONG-RANGE PLANNING
MEAN TO US?

In the assessment of your institution's future direction, you must look at its origin, its current position, and its probable destination, if neither its philosophy nor its operation changes. Envision a snowball rolling down a hill. You can predict fairly accurately where the snowball will go if you look at its path to see where it came from. Institutions, too, start out small, increase in size as they pick up speed, and then run into a more controlled growth. Or they may suffer an impact that shatters their structure, or sometimes melt away when things get too hot for them. And, like a snowball, if an institution changes direction, it may go down another slope and get even bigger.

Shifts in organizational direction often come when decision makers take a fresh view of their problems. If the New York Central had decided it was in the business of transportation rather than railroading, it might be an airline today. Oil companies that decided they were in the energy business made dramatic shifts by diversifying prior to the oil embargo of the early 1970s and thus improved their survival rates. Hospitals attempted to meet competition and reduce costs by developing aggressive programs to keep people well rather than concentrating solely on curing sickness and disease.

The authors of *Consumer Behavior* talk about lifestyle trends that drive marketing strategy. For instance, if there is a trend for the middle-aged to be concerned about appearance and health, what would the product implications for manufacturers and retailers be? They might point to "a potential market for health and exercise equipment that has good design and is like furniture so that it looks well [in the furnished areas of the home.]"[3]

The entrepreneur whose planning enables him or her to exploit a trend early may turn a handsome profit, but a late start could spell trouble. The entrepreneurial alumni association that identifies trends early may put together plans and strategies that give direction to successful activity.

As the personal computer craze was heating up a few years ago, a few associations established computer camps for children of alumni. Because they hit the trend on its upswing, the programs worked well until public interest waned as familiarity with PCs increased. Planning by the organizations allowed for built-in flexibility to respond to a unique opportunity and supplied financial incentives for such creative innovation.

What would the picture look like today had alumni associations implemented the principles of long-range planning years ago when, on many campuses, they were responsible for the full scope of what is now known as institutional advancement? Would those duties have been reassigned to a variety of separate specialized functional areas? Or might the associations have shifted their pattern of operation to incorporate superior institutional service functions outside the alumni audience? We will never know.

The downside to long-range planning is that many administrators are uncomfortable with it, do not understand it, and do not know how to do it; some make the process overly complicated. For many, "a plan represents a commitment that they suspect they may live to regret."[4]

Some managers feel that there is so much planning going on that it prevents them from getting any "real work" done. To avoid or overcome this situation, everyone concerned must understand the planning process; and it must be clear in its mission and workable by those who are to make it function. Also, it must be seen as useful—and necessary!

THE CONCEPT

What will alumni associations be like in the twenty-first century? And how will they get that way? Some will act; some will react; but all will change. Long-range planning is both a product and a process that can help manage the inevitable changes that lie ahead.

At its best, the long-range planning process allows an organization to anticipate change and then act to position itself for success; at its least, it is a productive management exercise that makes an organization stop, look around, and think. Long-range plans, the product of this process, are never final solutions. Rather, they are an evolving system for managing the change that is occurring at an increasingly accelerated pace in more areas of life than ever before. Now more than ever, failure to plan is planning to fail.

> The greater the rate by which change and complexity are taking place, the more difficult it becomes to plan—especially on a long-term basis. Yet, the more important it becomes to plan—lest the manager be ruled by the future.[5]

Many of the changes taking place right now will affect higher education and alumni—the institution and the audience that are the association's reason for being.

Good long-range planning is an ongoing process that continually watches for changes and helps produce plans to turn those changes into opportunities rather than problems. It is a must for every organization that wishes to survive, much less prosper, in the twenty-first century. It is also an antidote for institutional inertia and the unjustified, but no less intense, sense of invulnerability many associations have.

> We all tend to see our institutions as permanent, as lasting forever and as unchanged from the way we know them now. Indeed a view of the world from inside an institution is fatally flawed by confidence in the institution's invulnerability.[6]

Long-range planning is not, as some might suspect, the latest management fad. It is a basic behavior common to many everyday activities. Take, for example, some of the principles behind safely driving a car. One of the first things you were told during your first driving lesson (or, maybe, you had to find it out the hard way) was to look beyond the front edge of the car—far beyond. If you didn't, objects and changes in the roadway reached your field of vision (your very short field of vision) too quickly for you to respond safely. And the faster you went, the farther ahead you had to look. Long-range planning is simply an organized means of looking ahead, and there isn't an alumni association of any size or structure anywhere in the country that can do without it.

How do your long-range planning practices rate? Check yourself against these questions from "The Good Strategy Guide" by Brian Houlden.

1. Do you know the strategic issues facing your association?

2. Do you devote time to addressing these issues?

3. Do you have sufficient awareness and appropriate sensors of the environment to throw up the strategic issues and assist in considering them?

4. Are you prepared to face up to the issues and where necessary to decide how to change the business?[7]

If you answered "no" to any of these questions, read on to find out how to begin long-range planning at your association.

THE PROCESS

There are a number of people who can be called upon to perform long-range planning tasks—association staff, association volunteers, hired consultants, and so on. Each association should consider its needs and resources and then pick the group best suited to its circumstances.

Regardless of the way an association chooses to go about long-range planning, the basic process is pretty much the same. It involves five activities:

1. environmental scanning,

2. internal assessments,

3. impact statements,

4. "final" report, and

5. working the plan.

Environmental Scanning

Alumni associations function in such a way that a number of environments—conditions within which the associations must operate but that are outside their control—are critical to their success. These environments include, but are not necessarily limited to, higher education in general and the individual college or university in particular, business conditions (particularly nonprofit business), government regulations, society in general, and economic conditions. Changes in any of these environments will have consequences for alumni association operations.

For example, many institutions of higher learning now have student populations that are at least 50 percent female; what will that mean for alumni programming in 10 years? For-profit business is claiming unfair competition from nonprofit organizations and their revenue-generating projects; what will it mean if associations lose either their nonprofit status or their ability to merchandise programs? Congress may someday do away with the nonprofit postal rates; could alumni associations survive? Declining interest rates mean significant decreases in investment earnings; what other sources of revenue can be pursued? Younger members of society are proving to be more self-centered than previous generations; will they join the association? And so on.

Environmental scanning is the process of looking around to see what is happening now and what might be happening in the future—in any and every area affecting the association's operations. There are four ways your alumni association can do this without a significant investment of staff time or money:

1. Keep abreast of what other associations are thinking and doing; occasionally survey associations in comparable situations.
2. Keep abreast of any long-range planning the institution is doing.
3. Consult with key alumni in fields having access to demographic information about the alumni body and/or information on future trends in any of the environments critical to association operations.
4. Collect materials for a "Future File" that will accommodate articles, books, reports, notes, etc., on subjects of interest to the association's future.

The environmental scanning process is a continual one that is never complete. These four activities should become part of everyday management operations. At least once a year, at minimum, you should prepare a report on potential problems and opportunities or any major changes in areas that affect the association's activities. These reports are critical parts of the long-range plan and provide feedback to judge how well the plan continues to fit ever-changing reality.

Internal Assessments

In order to operate an automobile correctly, you must know not only what is going on outside the car but what is going on inside as well. It does you no good to know that your freeway exit is 10 miles away if your gas tank reads empty. Similarly, what is going on inside the association is just as important as what is going on outside.

Internal assessment involves rigorous and brutally honest self-examination to identify the association's strengths and weaknesses. You should ask senior staff as well as staff with direct responsibility for a particular program to assess the following points in their areas:

1. strengths;
2. weaknesses and problems;
3. external threats to the program;
4. external opportunities for the program;
5. the business or service the program really offers;
6. the real nature of the program's audience;
7. the basic alumni needs the program serves;
8. major changes that are anticipated:
   a. among the alumni served by this program,
   b. in the resources required for this program—especially the technology;
9. the association's aspirations for this program:
   a. for the next five years,
   b. for the next 10 years,
   c. for the next 15 years,
10. resources needed to accommodate these changes and aspirations, including:
    a. staff,
    b. facilities,
    c. equipment, and
    d. budget.

These assessments can be made annually, semiannually, or every five years, depending on the rate of change experienced by the association. The environmental scanning being done by the association is important to the success of internal assessments, especially when new opportunities, new threats, changes in alumni, and so on, are being analyzed.

Impact Statements

Study the overall picture presented by the environmental scanning and internal assessments. Now you are ready to develop several scenarios of what alumni might be like in the future and what the association could or should be doing for them. This is the time for aggressively creative, no-holds-barred, blue-sky thinking. Some combination of senior staff, junior staff, and volunteers may be used for this task. Formal brainstorming sessions or an informal afternoon of playing "what if?" can lead to great ideas. After you have explored all reasonable and—even more important—seemingly unreasonable possibilities, you can set priorities and prepare contingency plans to implement selected scenarios. Be sure to include in the contingency plans how you will obtain resources as well as how you will execute the program.

The impact statement covers what needs to be done and what resources are required to implement change. This "impact" on the association may be great (lots of money and more staff) or small. The impact statement indicates how the data developed in the internal assessments and environmental scanning may shape the alumni and the programs of the future.

Final Report

The top leadership of the association (some combination of board members, chief executive officer, and senior staff) should now review the environmental, internal, and impact assessments in order to answer one question: "What will the association do?" And sometimes, believe it or not, the answer will be, "Nothing." At other times, the answer will be some course of action. For each program or service proposed in the impact statement, association decision makers should review the following critical factors:

1. Does this program or service fit the association's mission?
2. What portion of the alumni will be served? Can they get this program or service elsewhere? Can the association do it in a unique way or better than other providers?
3. What are the start-up costs? The ongoing funding costs? Staff and technology needs?

When an idea passes favorably through this stage, it should be placed on a "Do List." When the list is completed, top leadership should set priorities and then decide which of the highest-priority items should be implemented and when.

WORKING THE PLAN

The final report serves two purposes. First, it is a base upon which to plan for the future; second, it is the starting point for the next round of planning. It must be reviewed periodically both informally and formally to judge whether or not it is still viable. In this review, you should ask:

1. Are the assumptions upon which the plan is based still true?
2. Are the priorities still correct?

3. What has happened environmentally and/or internally that should be noted for future decision making?

You should review and update the plan in this manner as often as circumstances dictate, but certainly annually, and it should probably be redone completely every five to seven years.

Long-range planning is an ongoing process and is never complete. The final reports are starting points as much as they are end points. This chapter sets forth a simple procedure that can be performed by small associations as well as large ones. It can be done simply by just a few people or in greater complexity by large numbers. But it must be done by somebody.

Notes

1. John N. Bailey, "Lead Your Association Today with a Plan for Tomorrow," *Leadership*, Spring 1981:27.

2. Committee of the Alumni Magazines Associated and the Association of Alumni Secretaries, *The Manual of Alumni Work* (Ithaca, N.Y.: 1924), 6.

3. James F. Engel, Roger D. Blackwell, and David P. Collet, *Consumer Behavior*, 3d ed. (Hinsdale, Ill.: Dryden Press, 1978), 192.

4. Jack Picou, Senior Vice President of Phillips-Ramsey (San Diego advertising and public relations firm), quoted by John N. Bailey in "Lead Your Association Today with a Plan for Tomorrow," *Leadership*, Spring 1981:28.

5. Dale D. McConkey, "If It's Not Broke, Fix It Anyway!!" *Business Quarterly*, Spring 1986:50–52.

6. Arnold Brown and Edith Weiner, *Supermanaging* (New York: McGraw-Hill, 1984), 7.

7. Brian Houlden, "The Good Strategy Guide," *Management Today*, November 1985:94–97.

Future Prospects for Alumni Administration

PAUL B. CHEWNING

From the first system for organizing alumni by class, which Yale University developed in 1792, to the establishment by Mount Holyoke College of an overseas club in 1891, and from the first organized alumni association at Williams College in 1821 to the formation of the Association of Alumnae Secretaries in 1919, there have been many important events in the field of alumni administration. Since 1913, organized alumni work has strengthened our institutions, involved alumni in traditional and non-traditional programs, and provided professionalism and ethical standards to the field. The direction alumni administration has taken during its past 75 years has prepared us to travel into the twenty-first century—a journey that will take us back to the future.

Charles W. Eliot, the visionary President of Harvard University, stated, "It is, of course, largely by the extent of support accorded to a college by its own graduates that the world judges the right of that college to seek cooperation of others in a planning of futures. . . . It is not merely what alumni give, it is the fact that they do give that is of supreme importance."[1] More than a century later, President Eliot's words have taken on new meaning with the expanding role of institutional advancement on our campuses.

Alumni professionals are still the driving force behind "the extent of support accorded to a college" and "what alumni give." They preserve the institutional mission, provide historical perspective and continuity, and develop and maintain relationships. Significant financial support is the result of long-term relationships with our institutions, rather than casual encounters with advancement officers. Alumni directors have been forging these ties longer than professionals in any other area of institutional advancement.

The Columbus II Colloquium, which recognized the 75th anniversary of organized alumni work, provided a clear message—there have been many accomplishments in alumni administration, and now it is time to be more effective and aggressive in stating those successes and articulating the alumni mission to our institutions. Those achievements include, among others, alumni admissions programs that enable institutions to attract outstanding students, career placement and relocation services, networking and mentoring programs for women and minorities, and active class reunion and class gift programs.

These programs, and many others, use the expertise and talents of our alumni; in return, our institutions receive the critical support and involvement of dedicated and informed volunteers. These "stockholders" invest in our institutions for a myriad of reasons; among them, belief in the mission of the institution, commitment to alma mater, or the repayment of a "debt." It is the alumni association that provides, preserves, and strengthens the vehicle for involvement.

Alumni administration has played an important part in the shaping of our institutions over the last two centuries. If there is a singular focus to alumni relations today, it is advocacy, particularly in the area of societal needs. Our alumni must play an increasing role in addressing such issues as adult illiteracy, drug and alcohol abuse, and the need for an educated and informed society. If our alumni associations become involved in the efforts to find solutions to today's problems, the impact will be immeasurable. What better way could we find to demonstrate to the general public the importance of, and the need for, education?

Note

1. Quoted in John A. Pollard, *Fund Raising for Higher Education* (New York: Harper and Brothers, 1958), 91.

Bibliography

Alberger, Patricia L., ed. *How to Involve Alumni in Student Recruitment.* Washington, D.C.: Council for Advancement and Support of Education, 1983.

Andrews, Paul. "Bring Nearby Alumni Nearer," in *Building Your Alumni Program,* Virginia L. Carter and Patricia Alberger, eds. Washington, D.C.: Council for Advancement and Support of Education, 1980, 70–71.

Apps, Jerold W. *Problems in Continuing Education.* New York: McGraw-Hill, 1979.

Ayres, Edward B. "Reunions: Many Splintered Things." *CASE Currents,* January 1981: 26–27.

Baggerly, Joyce. "The Great Alumni Trace: Out of the Files and Into the Computer." *CASE Currents,* September 1978: 33–34.

Bailey, Anne Lowrey. "The Case of the Class of '73: The Mystery of the Immense 10th Reunion Gift." CASE *Currents,* February 1984: 14–18.

Bailey, John N. "Lead Your Association Today With a Plan for Tomorrow." *Leadership,* Spring 1981: 27–28.

Barrett, Stephen L., ed. *Passport to Successful Alumni Travel Programs,* rev. ed. Washington, D.C.: Council for Advancement and Support of Education, 1983.

Bartkevicius, Jocelyn. "Surveying Your Alumni." *CASE Currents,* January 1977: 12–13.

Battillo, Kathryn, and Suzanne A. Villanti. "A Manager's Manual." CASE *Currents,* April 1986: 10–13.

Baumgarten, Leonard J. "Jobs On-line." *CASE Currents,* September 1978: 29.

Bennett, Sam. "A Touch of Class: 13 Ways to Make Your Reunions Sparkle." CASE *Currents,* February 1984: 10–12.

Berkowitz, Eric N., Roger A. Kerin, and William Rudelius. *Marketing.* St. Louis, Mo.: Times Mirror/Mosby College Publishing, 1986.

Caffrey, John, and Charles J. Mosmann. *Computers on Campus.* Washington, D.C.: American Council on Education, 1967.

Calvert, Steven L. *Alumni Continuing Education.* New York: American Council on Education/Macmillan, 1987.

_____. "Planning Meaningful Reunions," in *Handbook of Institutional Advancement,* 2d ed., A. Westley Rowland, gen. ed. San Francisco: Jossey-Bass, 1986, 450–459.

Carl, Linda. *The Alumni College Movement.* Washington, D.C.: Council for Advancement and Support of Education, 1977.

_____. "Arranging Alumni Education." CASE *Currents,* March 1986: 38–40.

Carter, Virginia L., and Patricia Alberger, eds. *Building Your Alumni Program.* Washington, D.C.: Council for Advancement and Support of Education, 1980.

Committee of the Alumni Magazines Associated and the Association of Alumni Secretaries. *The Manual of Alumni Work.* Ithaca, N.Y.: The Committee, 1924.

Council for Advancement and Support of Education. "Market Research." *CASE Currents,* May/June 1982 issue.

Council for Advancement and Support of Education Committee on Alumni Administration. "Long-range Plan." January 1985.

Cross, K. Patricia, *Adults as Learners.* San Francisco: Jossey-Bass, 1981.

Cunningham, Earl L. "Pizzazz for Pennies: Promoting Alumni Programs the Low-Cost Way." *CASE Currents,* October 1983: 26–28.

Dewey, Mary E. "Here Are 300,000 Reasons for a Flexible Data System." *CASE Currents,* October 1976: 20–21.

Diffily, Anne Hinman. "Human Interest," in *The New Guide to Student Recruitment Marketing,* Virginia Carter Smith and Susan Hunt, eds. Washington, D.C.: Council for Advancement and Support of Education, 1986, 62–63.

Duplass, James A. "Your Software System Needs You: Learn Everything About It, Control It, Define It, and Reorganize Your Office and Staff for It." *CASE Currents,* March 1983: 18–23.

Eklund, Lowell. "The Oakland Plan for the Continuing Education of Alumni." Reprinted from *Adult Leadership,* November 1966.

Fisher, James L. *Power of the Presidency.* New York: American Council on Education/Macmillan, 1984.

Forman, Robert G. "A-L-U-M-N-I Doesn't Just Spell M-O-N-E-Y: Thoughts of a Professional Alumni Administrator." CASE *Currents,* September 1984: 26.

Frey, James H. "Alumni Love Athletics: Myth or Reality?" *CASE Currents,* December 1981: 46.

———. "Make Your Survey Scientific." *CASE Currents,* December 1977: 18–19.

Gilbert, Heather Ricker. "Keep 'em Learning: Continuing the College Relationship Through Alumni Education." CASE *Currents,* June 1985: 42–43.

Goldman, Robin. "Trump Cards: How to Deal Your Alumni Clubs a Winning Hand." CASE *Currents,* February 1985: 10–13.

Gorman, Brian. *Finding Lost Alumni: Tracing Methods Used by 19 Institutions.* Washington, D.C.: Council for Advancement and Support of Education, 1981.

Green, Suzanne R. "The Wizardry of Computer Connections: Using Your Computer in PR." CASE *Currents,* September 1986: 14–22.

Halpern, Sheldon, and Jesse H. Rosenblum. "Computerizing the Crystal Ball: Using Spreadsheets in Recruitment." CASE *Currents,* September 1986: 54–57.

Harlan, Lee. "Add Color to Reunions." *CASE Currents,* May 1979: 34–35.

———. "To Club or Not to Club: Making a Decision on an Alumni Clubs Program," in *Building Your Alumni Program,* Virginia L. Carter and Patricia Alberger, eds. Washington, D.C.: Council for Advancement and Support of Education, 1980, 66–68.

Harper, Nancy, and Jocelyn Bartkevicius. "Reunion Ideas." *CASE Currents,* October 1977: 16–19.

Harrington, Fred Harvey. *The Future of Adult Education: New Responsibilities of Colleges and Universities.* San Francisco: Jossey-Bass, 1977.

Houle, Cyril O. *The Inquiring Mind.* Madison: University of Wisconsin Press, 1961.

Iaquinta, Len. "Good Vibrations: Surveys and Newsletters Improve Alumni Participation." *CASE Currents,* December 1981: 30–31.

Kaye, William G. "Haverfordian, I Presume? How One College Found 593 Lost Alumni." CASE *Currents,* April 1985: 32–36.

Kitsmiller, Gary. "You Are What You Program: Involve Users in Developing Your Computer System." *CASE Currents,* March 1983: 24–26.

Knowles, Asa S., editor-in-chief. *Handbook of College and University Administration.* New York: McGraw-Hill, 1970.

Knowles, Malcolm S. *The Adult Education Movement in the United States.* New York: Holt, Rinehart & Winston, 1962.

Knox, Alan B. *Adult Development and Learning: A Handbook on Individual Growth and Competence in the Adult Years for Education and the Helping Professions.* San Francisco: Jossey-Bass, 1977.

Kotler, Philip M. *Principles of Marketing.* Englewood Cliffs, N.J.: Prentice-Hall, 1980.

_____, and Bernard Dubois. *Marketing for Non-profit Organizations,* 2d ed. Englewood Cliffs, N.J.: Prentice-Hall, 1982.

Lerner, Laurence M. "Traditions with a Twist." CASE *Currents,* May 1986: 26–29.

Lineback, Donald J. "Keep Your Volunteers On-line." CASE *Currents,* September 1986: 58–60.

Lovelock, Christopher H., and Charles B. Weinberg. *Marketing for Public and Nonprofit Managers.* New York: John Wesley & Sons, 1984.

McKenna, Barbara, comp. *Surveying Your Alumni: Guidelines and 22 Sample Questionnaires.* Washington, D.C.: Council for Advancement and Support of Education, 1983.

McMahon, Ernest E. "New Directions for Alumni: Continuing Education for the College Graduate." Chicago: Center for the Study of Liberal Education for Adults, 1960. (Available from Steven L. Calvert, Dartmouth College, Hanover, N.H. 03755, $8.50.)

McWilliams, Peter A. *The Personal Computer Book.* Los Angeles: Prelude Press, 1983.

_____. *The Word Processing Book.* Los Angeles: Prelude Press, 1983.

Mills, Robert D. "Let Your Fingers Do the Walking: The Nine Steps of Surveying Alumni via Telephone." *CASE Currents,* May/June 1982: 38–40.

Moore, George M. "Good-by Addressograph, Hello Computer Records: Clemson Learns About Its Alumni." *CASE Currents,* October 1976: 18–19.

Moore, H. Martin. "The Postman Rings Thrice: How to Survey Your Alumni Through the Mail." *CASE Currents,* May/June 1982: 44–47.

Morris, Sharon. "Help Wanted: Alumni Relations: How to Start an Alumni Relations Program at a Community College." CASE *Currents,* March 1984: 36–38.

Myrinx, Elaina M. "On Target." CASE *Currents,* February 1985: 25.

Olson, Thomas L. "Can Do, Can Do: What a Computer Can Do for Independent Schools." *CASE Currents,* March 1983: 28–30.

O'Shea, Terri. "Cutting Across Class Lines: Raise Attendance and Spirits with a Cluster Reunion." CASE *Currents,* February 1984: 25.

Pattee, B. J. "Are Alumni Clubs Important? If So, How Do You Keep Them Lively?" in *Building Your Alumni Program*, Virginia L. Carter and Patricia Alberger, eds. Washington, D.C.: Council for Advancement and Support of Education, 1980, 65–66.

Pendel, Mary. "Beyond Gallup: Alumni Surveys Give You People, Not Just Numbers." CASE *Currents*, September 1985: 40–42.

Petranek, Jan G. "How to Polish Your Data Base." CASE *Currents*, February 1984: 33–34.

———. "Little Big Computers: How to Build an Alumni/Development System for Less Than $100,000." CASE *Currents*, February 1984: 30–33.

Pfizenmaier, Emily. "A Software Primer: What the Chief Development Officer Needs to Know." *CASE Currents*, March 1983: 12–16.

Prentice, Elaine, and Sally Rodgers. "A Cast of Thousands: Recruit Everybody— Volunteers, Staff, Students, Faculty—to Make an Alumni Program Produce." *CASE Currents*, June 1983: 44–46.

Reunions and Homecomings: How to Stage a Great Comeback. Washington, D.C.: Council for Advancement and Support of Education, 1986.

Rowland, A. Westley, gen. ed. *Handbook of Institutional Advancement*, 2d ed. San Francisco: Jossey-Bass, 1986.

Rudolph, Frederick. *The American College and University: A History.* New York: Vintage Books, 1962.

Rudolph, R. J., and Mary Ruth Snyder. "Gala Week at Purdue: Let's Hear It for Tradition." *CASE Currents*, January 1980: 16–17.

Sewell, Richard B. "A Backward Look." *CASE Currents*, June 1976: 4–5.

Shaw, Wilfred B. *Alumni and Adult Education.* New York: American Association for Adult Education, 1929.

———. *Hand Book of Alumni Work.* Ann Arbor, Mich.: Association of Alumni Secretaries, 1917.

Siddons, Anne Rivers. "Reunions Make Me Cry." CASE *Currents*, February 1984: 6–9.

Sommers, Edward. "Personalizing Direct Mail with the Computer." *CASE Currents*, September 1975: 16–18.

Stevenson, Scott C., and Kent McElvania. "Ambassadors with Portfolio," in *The New Guide to Student Recruitment Marketing*, Virginia Carter and Susan Hunt, eds. Washington, D.C.: Council for Advancement and Support of Education, 1986, 60–61.

Stilwell, Jean. "We Did It: How to Link Your Computer with Your Word Processor— Without Really Crying." *CASE Currents*, March 1983: 50–52.

Swift, Gilbert. "Reunion Programs to Enhance Friend and Fundraising." Presentation at CASE V District Conference, Chicago, December 1986.

Taylor, Karla. "Payment in Kindness." CASE *Currents*, February 1985: 14–18.

———. "Why We Need Better Marketing: An Interview with Philip Kotler." CASE *Currents*, July/August 1986: 44–50.

Titus, Charles. "Low-Cost Program Reaches Many Groups at One Time," in *Building Your Alumni Program*, Virginia L. Carter and Patricia Alberger, eds. Washington, D.C.: Council for Advancement and Support of Education, 1980, 71.

Tocqueville, Alexis de. *Democracy in America*. J. P. Mayer and Max Lerner, eds. New York: Harper & Row, 1966.

Topor, Robert S. "Marketing Higher Education." Newsletter available from Topor & Associates, 6737 Friars Rd., Suite 164, San Diego, Calif. 92108.

_____. *Your Personal Guide to Marketing a Nonprofit Organization*. Washington, D.C.: Council for Advancement and Support of Education, 1988.

Turner, Toni S. "Close Encounters of the Silicon Kind: How to Survive a Computer Conversion." *CASE Currents*, March 1983: 56–57.

Wanstall, Caroline. "How to Survive in the Alumni Office: From Balloons to Banquets." Carleton College publication, April 1980.

Whittemore, Nena Thames. "Mainstreaming Young Alumni." *CASE Currents*, January 1983: 24–26.

_____. "Roman Generals on the March: How Carleton Revamped Its Alumni Club System." *CASE Currents*, April 1980: 24–27.

Williams, Lisa B. "A Mine of Information: Using Databases for Your Prospect Research." CASE *Currents*, September 1986: 30–38.

Williamson, Jim. "Computerphobia: How to Conquer It Before It Conquers You." *CASE Currents*, March 1983: 6–8.

Contributors

EDWARD B. AYRES, Director of the Annual Fund at Choate Rosemary Hall in Wallingford, Connecticut, has served the school for 28 years. He has been active in independent schools programs, both for CASE and for CASE's predecessor organization, the American Alumni Council. In 1980, Ayres was the first recipient of CASE's Robert Bell Crow Memorial Award for continued outstanding service at an independent school.

STEPHEN L. BARRETT is Executive Director of the Alumni Association of Brigham Young University in Provo, Utah. He is the editor of *Passport to Successful Alumni Travel Programs*, originally published by the Council for Advancement and Support of Education in 1976 and revised in 1983.

ANDREW W. M. BEIERLE is Director of University Periodicals and Editor of *Emory Magazine* at Emory University in Atlanta, Georgia. Under his editorship, *Emory Magazine* has received more than 60 national awards, including a Grand Award and a Grand Gold Award from the Council for Advancement and Support of Education.

MERILYN H. BONNEY is Director of Alumni Relations at the University of Redlands in California. She has been active in CASE national and district affairs, chairing the 1988 Summer Institute in Alumni Administration, speaking at district conferences and the Annual Assembly, and contributing to CASE *Currents* and other CASE publications.

STEVEN L. CALVERT is Director of Continuing Education and Conferences at Dartmouth College in Hanover, New Hampshire. He is the author of *Alumni Continuing Education*, the first full-length book on the subject, published by Macmillan in 1987 in the ACE/Macmillan Series on Higher Education.

MARGARET SUGHRUE CARLSON joined the University of Minnesota Alumni Association as Executive Director in 1985. She has 22 years' experience in volunteer organizations as a professional manager and community activist.

JOHN B. CARTER, JR., is Vice President/Executive Director and Assistant to the President for Alumni Affairs at the Alumni Association of the Georgia Institute of Technology in Atlanta. He was previously a partner in an executive search firm that specialized in recruitment for high-tech industry in the Southeast.

RICHARD E. CARTER is Assistant Executive Director of the Alumni Association of the University of Michigan in Ann Arbor. In his 13 years with the Alumni Association, he has also directed the national clubs program and the constituent societies program.

PAUL B. CHEWNING is Vice President for Alumni Administration for the Council for Advancement and Support of Education, where he is responsible for working with CASE's 2,000 alumni professionals on a variety of issues and projects. He has served in both alumni and development positions at institutions ranging from the independent college to the major research university.

LINDA S. CROSSLEY, Assistant Director and Editor of *Ohio State Alumni Magazine* for the Ohio State University Alumni Association, has worked in the advancement field for more than 15 years. She has served CASE District V in a number of capacities, including 1988 Chair.

JAMES HARDWICK DAY, formerly Associate Director of the University of Minnesota Alumni Association, is an independent management consultant. He began his career in institutional relations as the Director of Public Relations at Cornell College in Iowa.

JOHN A. DIBIAGGIO is President of Michigan State University in East Lansing. He has served as Chair of the National Association of State Universities and Land-Grant Colleges, president of the University of Connecticut, and is on the board of directors of the American Council on Education.

DOROTHY C. DIIORIO, Director of the Alumni Association of the University of Illinois at Chicago, has served the university for 30 years. In 1987 she completed a two-year term as alumni administration trustee for the Council for Advancement and Support of Education, chairing the Committee on Alumni Administration.

DONALD V. DOTTS has been Executive Director of the Alumni Association at Arizona State University in Tempe for nearly 25 years and has spent 30 years in institutional advancement. He has been a member of ASU's Intercollegiate Athletic Board for 20 years.

NANCY MORSE DYSART is Director of Alumni Activities at the University of Maine in Orono. The winner of two CASE Recognition Award citations for excellence in student programs, she is also adviser to the Student Alumni Association/Student Foundation Network.

WILLIAM J. EVITTS is Director of Alumni Relations at Johns Hopkins University in Baltimore, Maryland. Previously, he was Assistant to the President and Chair of the History Department at Hollins College; he is the author of several articles, reviews, and books on history.

JAMES L. FISHER is President Emeritus of the Council for Advancement and Support of Education and President Emeritus of Towson State University.

He is the author or editor of *Power of the Presidency, Presidential Leadership in Advancement Activities, The Effective College President, The President's Role in Institutional Advancement, The President and Fund Raising, The Handbook of Academic Administration,* and *Leaders on Leadership.* He is now a consultant living in McLean, Virginia.

ROBERT FORMAN is Executive Director of the Alumni Association of the University of Michigan in Ann Arbor. He has served in that capacity for 22 years.

M. LANEY FUNDERBURK, JR., is currently Assistant Vice President for Alumni Affairs and Director of Alumni Affairs at Duke University in Durham, North Carolina. He first came to Duke as Assistant to the Director of Alumni Affairs in 1960 and also served several years as Administrative Assistant to the Governor of North Carolina.

ROBERT L. GALE has been President of the Association of Governing Boards of Universities and Colleges in Washington, D.C., since 1974. A former board member of the Council for Advancement and Support of Education, Gale has served on the alumni board of Carleton College for eight years and has been a trustee of Carleton for 18.

MARALYN ORBISON GILLESPIE, Associate Vice President of Swarthmore College in Pennsylvania, has been active in the Council for Advancement and Support of Education since its formation. She served on the organizing board and as a trustee for periodicals/publications, was a member of the faculty for summer institutes and other programs, and has won several CASE and American Alumni Council awards.

DAN L. HEINLEN has served 15 years as Director of Alumni Affairs for the Ohio State University Alumni Association during his 24 years on the staff. In 1988 he chaired the Columbus II Colloquium, which celebrated the seventy-fifth anniversary of organized alumni work. He was also the alumni track chair for the 1988 CASE Annual Assembly and served on the CASE board of trustees as an at-large member (1986–88). He is the author of "Managing the Alumni Program" in *Handbook of Institutional Advancement* (Jossey-Bass, 1986).

JAMES A. HOPSON, who began his career in alumni administration at Iowa State University in Ames in 1968, is currently Executive Director of the Alumni Association there. He was instrumental in developing and marketing the ISU on-line information system, which is now operational in over 30 institutions of higher learning.

FRANK B. JONES recently retired after 40 years at Indiana University in Bloomington, where a successful travel program has been in operation for many years. He was formerly Director of Alumni Affairs.

JACK KINNEY, Executive Director of the Alumni Association of the University of California at Santa Barbara, has spent 33 years in higher education administration, serving 19 years as Executive Director of the Michigan State University Alumni Association. He has also served on the board of trustees of the Council for Advancement and Support of Education and as District V chair.

MICHAEL J. KOLL, Executive Director of the California Alumni Association at the University of California–Berkeley, has been on the alumni association staff since 1949. Koll was a member of the organizational board of the Council for Advancement and Support of Education, served as CASE's first treasurer, and has participated in numerous CASE programs on volunteers and alumni administration.

GAYLE M. LANGER has served the University of Wisconsin–Madison Alumni Association for 30 years. She is currently Associate Executive Director and will assume the directorship in December 1989. A former Treasurer and trustee of the Council for Advancement and Support of Education, Langer has been active in both regional and national CASE programs.

CHARLES F. LENNON, JR., is Executive Director of the Alumni Association of the University of Notre Dame in Indiana. He was previously Coordinator of Research and Sponsored Programs at Notre Dame.

STANLEY R. MCANALLY has been in fund raising and development for 27 years at the University of Tennessee, the University of Missouri, and Southern Illinois University. He is now Vice President for Development at the Children's Hospital Foundation in Louisville, Kentucky.

JACK R. MAGUIRE, Executive Director of the University of Texas Ex-Students' Association for 20 years, and Director of UT's Institute of Texas Cultures at San Antonio for a decade, has authored or co-authored six books about Texas. His weekly column on Texas' past is syndicated to 22 state newspapers.

JACK MILLER is Vice President for University Advancement at Ball State University in Muncie, Indiana. He was previously Executive Vice President of the University of Nebraska Alumni Association for 15 years and Director of Alumni Administration at the American Alumni Council for two years.

GARY H. QUEHL has been President of the Council for Advancement and Support of Education since September 1986. Prior to that, he served for 12 years as President of the Council of Independent Colleges.

JAY M. ROCHLIN is Associate Director for Marketing and Communications for the University of Arizona Alumni Association in Tucson, and hosts "Arizona Magazine," a radio program broadcast statewide in Arizona. Before becoming Editor of the Arizona Alumni Association's magazine, he had a successful 15-year career in broadcast journalism and production.

KENT D. ROLLINS is Executive Director of the University of Arizona Alumni Association in Tucson, and hosts "Arizona Alumni Forum," a television program broadcast throughout Arizona. Rollins has been a higher education professional for 15 years and has participated in many CASE programs.

STEPHEN W. ROSZELL is Associate Vice President for Alumni Relations and Development at the University of Minnesota in Minneapolis. He also serves as Executive Director of the University of Minnesota Foundation.

WILLIAM J. ROTHWELL is Vice President for Development and Alumni at the University of Louisville in Kentucky. He was formerly Assistant Vice President of Pennsylvania State University and Executive Director of the Penn State Alumni Association, where he coordinated a $2 million budget with a $250,000 marketing income.

MARY RUTH SNYDER is Assistant Vice President for Alumni Relations at Rutgers, the State University of New Jersey, where she is responsible for 16 constituency alumni organizations serving 20 undergraduate and professional schools on three campuses. Snyder has served the Council for Advancement and Support of Education as alumni trustee, consultant, speaker, and magazine contributor.

WILLIAM E. STONE has been the Executive Director of the Stanford Alumni Association since 1977. At Stanford University since 1969, he has served as a faculty member for many CASE programs and has chaired the Summer Institute in Alumni Administration. Stone currently represents senior professionals on the CASE Board of Trustees.

JAMES D. VAN HOUTEN, Coordinator of Alumni Affairs at the State University of New York in Albany, serves as an in-house consultant on alumni administration and development for SUNY's 64 campuses, including its 30 community colleges. He has spent 13 of his 21 years in advancement at SUNY.

CHARLES H. WEBB is Executive Director of the Michigan State University Alumni Association in East Lansing. He is MSU's Officer for Alumni Administration and has been involved in institutional advancement for both public and private institutions for 17 years.

NENA THAMES WHITTEMORE is Vice President for Institutional Advancement at Bryant College in Smithfield, Rhode Island. Previously, she served as Director of Alumni Affairs at Carleton College (1976–1982) and as Senior Development Officer for Major Gifts (1982–1984). As Executive Director of Development and College Relations, she supervised the alumni director at Hollins College from 1984–1987. She has been active in CASE programs, contributing to CASE *Currents* and serving as a faculty leader and speaker at CASE conferences and institutes.

RAY WILLEMAIN, currently Director of Alumni Relations at Northwestern University in Evanston, Illinois, has been with the university since 1957. In 1985–86 he was Chair of the Board of Trustees of the Council for Advancement and Support of Education.

KEITH A. WILLIAMS is Associate Director of the Alumni Association of Michigan State University, a land-grant institution of 43,000. He is responsible for 87 regional alumni clubs within the United States and 15 clubs overseas.

HAROLD M. WILSON, formerly Associate Executive Director of the University of Michigan Alumni Association, is now retired. His 38-year alumni career included service as Managing Editor of the *Michigan Alumnus* magazine and direction of the alumni travel program from its inception in 1962 until his retirement in 1985.

DICK WINTERMOTE retired from the Alumni Association of the University of Kansas in 1983 after 32 years with the Association, 20 as Executive Director and Secretary-Treasurer. He is currently a member of the Executive Board for KU's $150 million CAMPAIGN KANSAS. Dick began KU's successful "Flying Jayhawk" travel program in 1970. He chaired CASE's first Conference on Alumni Travel Programs in 1975, which was the basis for *Passport to Successful Alumni Travel Programs.*

Index